NATIONS OF THE MODERN WORLD

ARGENTINA

H. S. Ferns
Professor of Political Science, University of Birmingham

AUSTRALIA

O. H. K. Spate
Director, Research School of Pacific Studies, Australian National University, Canberra

BELGIUM

Vernon Mallinson
Professor of Comparative Education, University of Reading

BURMA

F. S. V. Donnison
Formerly Chief Secretary to the Government of Burma

CEYLON

S. A. Pakeman
Formerly Professor of Modern History, Ceylon University College; Appointed Member, House of Representatives, Ceylon, 1947–52

CYPRUS

H. D. Purcell
Lecturer in English Literature, the Queen's University, Belfast

DENMARK

W. Glyn Jones
Reader in Danish, University College, London

EAST GERMANY

David Childs
Lecturer in Politics, University of Nottingham

MODERN EGYPT

Tom Little
Managing Director and General Manager of Regional News Services (Middle East), Ltd, London

ENGLAND

John Bowle
Professor of Political Theory, Collège d'Europe, Bruges

FINLAND	W. R. Mead *Professor of Geography, University College, London*
MODERN GREECE	John Campbell *Fellow of St Antony's College, Oxford* Philip Sherrard *Assistant Director, British School of Archaeology, Athens, 1958–62*
MODERN INDIA	Sir Percival Griffiths *President India, Pakistan and Burma Association*
MODERN IRAN	Peter Avery *Lecturer in Persian and Fellow of King's College, Cambridge*
ITALY	Muriel Grindrod *Formerly Editor of* International Affairs *and* The World Today *Assistant Editor* The Annual Register
KENYA	A. Marshall MacPhee *Formerly Managing Editor with the* East African Standard *Group*
LIBYA	John Wright *Formerly of the* Sunday Ghibli, *Tripoli*
MALAYSIA	J. M. Gullick *Formerly of the Malayan Civil Service*
MOROCCO	Mark I. Cohen *Director of Taxation, American Express* Lorna Hahn *Professor of African Studies, American University*
NEW ZEALAND	James W. Rowe *Director of New Zealand Institute of Economic Research* Margaret A. Rowe *Tutor in English at Victoria University, Wellington*

NIGERIA	Sir Rex Niven
	Administrative Service of Nigeria, 1921–54 *Member, President and Speaker of Northern* *House of Assembly, 1947–59*
PAKISTAN	Ian Stephens
	Formerly Editor of The Statesman *Calcutta and Delhi, 1942–51* *Fellow, King's College, Cambridge, 1952–58*
PERU	Sir Robert Marett
	H.M. Ambassador in Lima, 1963–67
SOUTH AFRICA	John Cope
	Formerly Editor-in-Chief of The Forum *and* *South African Correspondent of* The Guardian
SPAIN	George Hills
	Formerly Correspondent and Spanish Programme *Organizer, British Broadcasting Corporation*
SUDAN REPUBLIC	K. D. D. Henderson
	Formerly of the Sudan Political Service and *Governor of Darfur Province, 1949–53*
TURKEY	Geoffrey Lewis
	Senior Lecturer in Islamic Studies, Oxford
WEST GERMANY	Michael Balfour
	Reader in European History, University of East *Anglia*
YUGOSLAVIA	Muriel Heppell and F. B. Singleton

NATIONS OF THE MODERN WORLD

BURMA

BURMA

By

F. S. V. DONNISON

PRAEGER PUBLISHERS

New York · Washington

BOOKS THAT MATTER

Published in the United States of America in 1970
by Praeger Publishers, Inc.,
111 Fourth Avenue, New York, 10003

© 1970, in London, England, by F. S. V. Donnison

Library of Congress Catalog Card Number: 70-76978

Printed in Great Britain

To the Memory of My Wife
whose gift for friendship transcended barriers of race, religion,
or colour, and who, if she had lived to criticize, would have
endowed this book with greater wisdom and charity

Preface

THIS BOOK is for the general reader rather than the expert. But if an expert should look at it he will quickly realize the magnitude of my debt to G. E. Harvey, D. G. E. Hall, John F. Cady, and Hugh Tinker for the period before General Ne Win's military *coup* in 1962. Concerning the *coup*, and the period after the *coup*, little or nothing has been published apart from Frank N. Trager's *Burma – From Kingdom to Republic*. This was written before the effects of the present régime's policies had become as clear as later. And most of my book was written before I had the advantage of seeing Trager's illuminating work. For the period after the *coup*, evidence, as opposed to propaganda, is scanty and hard to come by because of the isolationism of General Ne Win's government. But from publications of his government, from the press in Burma and the United Kingdom, and from a variety of other sources, I have tried to build up a picture that I believe to be true. I write with the somewhat Victorian, and now unfashionable, conviction that law and order are a prerequisite to happiness, since without them there can be no security of person or property, and little freedom of speech or movement. This may lead me to take an unduly gloomy view of Burma's present and future. No one will be better pleased than I if this view can be proved wrong, for I am proud to number Burmese among my best friends, and I wish them and their country well.

I would like to acknowledge much help received but the nature of my sources makes this impossible. I do thank with great warmth the two friends who read my draft and gave me invaluable suggestions.

East Hagbourne, Berkshire   F.S.V.D.
January 1970

Abbreviations

A.F.O.   Anti-Fascist Organization
A.F.P.F.L.   Anti-Fascist Peoples' Freedom League
B.I.A.   Burma Independence Army
B.N.A.   Burma National Army
G.C.B.A.   General Council of Burmese Associations
G.C.S.S.   General Council of Sangha Samaggis
K.   *Kyat*, silver coin that replaced the Indian rupee
K.M.T.   Kuomintang
K.T.A.   Knappen – Tippetts – Abbett
N.U.F.   National United Front
P.B.F.   Patriotic Burmese Forces
P.V.O.   Patriotic Volunteer Organization
S.A.C.   Security and Administration Committee
U.N.   United Nations
U.K.   United Kingdom
U.S.(A.)   United States (of America)
Y.M.B.A.   Young Men's Buddhist Association

Contents

List of Illustrations

(All are inserted between pages 128 *and* 129*)*

1 On the platform of the Shwedagon Pagoda, Rangoon
2 Queen Supayalat's (Thibaw's wife) monastery, Mandalay
3 Rangoon
4 Mandalay Palace shortly after annexation in 1886
5 The outer wall and moat of Mandalay Palace
6 Pagan
7 Chinthes guarding the approach to the pagoda at Mingun
8 Kyankpadaung Pagoda
9 Making umbrellas
10 Monks and acolytes receiving alms
11 Wood-carving
12 The mountains in the Kachin State
13 An old Burmese woman smoking a country cheroot
14 Mandalay Hill
15 Women transplanting paddy
16 Fishing on the Irrawaddy
17 Leg rowers on the Inle Lake in the Shan State
18 Hauling teak out of the Irrawaddy at Mandalay
19 Elephants hauling teak
20 King Mindon Min
21 The arrival of the Burmese delegation at London airport, 1947
22 U Nu
23 General Ne Win
24 An Anyein *Pwè*
25 A group of Burmans travelling to a monastery for an initiation
    ceremony
26 Shwedagon Pagoda, Rangoon
27 Sir Hubert Rance with Aung San

Maps

16

Acknowledgements

ACKNOWLEDGEMENT for kind permission to reproduce illustrations is made to the following, to whom the copyright of the illustrations belongs:

H. S. Bowlby: 4
Keystone Press Agency Ltd: 23
Maung Maung Tin: 1, 3, 6, 7, 8, 9, 10, 11, 12, 13, 14, 16, 18, 24, 26
Sir Hubert Rance: 21, 27
U Khin: 2, 5, 15, 17, 19

Acknowledgement is also due to the following for quotations:

Faber and Faber Ltd: G. E. Harvey, *British Rule in Burma*
The Hutchinson Publishing Group Ltd: D. G. E. Hall, *Burma*
Macmillan and Co. Ltd and St Martin's Press: Thakin Nu, *Burma under the Japanese*
Oxford University Press and the Royal Institute of International Affairs: Hugh Tinker, *The Union of Burma*

Chapter 1

The Country

IN 1960 THE AUTHOR and his wife, on their way to India and Burma by road, reached Zahedan near the eastern border of Persia. They called upon the Indian vice-consul, who happened to be a Sikh with a long family tradition of service to the British Crown. One of the vice-consular staff, a youngish man, also a Sikh, hearing whither these English travellers were bound, approached and said shyly, 'Oh, sir, I was born in Burma, at Paungde, and was at school in Burma. I was at Pyinmana when it was bombed by the Japanese.' The author and his wife said that they also, on their way out from Rangoon, before the city was cut off by the Japanese, had arrived at Pyinmana the morning after the bombing, in February 1942, and had seen the town in flames. 'I walked to India with my family when the Japanese invaded Burma,' continued the young Sikh. 'My father died on the walk, and so did my brother. My mother died as we reached India. My sister and I were the only members of the family left. But,' he added with sudden emphasis, 'I would go back to Burma tomorrow if I could.' Tears filled his eyes. And because of the thought of Burma he asked the travellers where they would be staying in Delhi and warmly pressed them to make use of the house he owned there.

This incident illustrates well the extraordinary fascination that Burma exercises and has always exercised upon those who have made the acquaintance of *Shwe pyi daw*, the Royal and Golden Country. As far back as the sixteenth century European traders visiting Burma wrote of the country in glowing terms. Of these men G. E. Harvey, in his *History of Burma*, writes:

'But the travellers never tire of describing Pegu – the long moat full of crocodiles, the walls, the watchtowers, the gorgeous palace, the great processions with elephants and palanquins and grandees in shining robes, the shrines filled with images of massy gold and gems, the unending hosts of armed men, and the apparition of the great king himself...'[1]

At the end of the nineteenth century an English official who took

[1] G. E. Harvey, *History of Burma*, London, 1925, p. 175.

19

part in the annexation of Upper Burma and the subsequent fighting to pacify the country, writes:

'Months, very many months, I passed with no one to speak to, with no other companions than Burmese. I have been with them in joy and sorrow, I have fought with them and against them, and sat round the camp fire after the day's work and talked of it all. I have had many friends amongst them, friends I shall always honour; and I have seen them killed sometimes in our fights, or dead of fever in the marshes of the frontier. I have known them from the labourer to the Prime Minister, from the little neophyte just accepted into the faith to the head of all the Burmese religion. And I have known their wives and daughters, and have watched many a flirtation in the warm scented evenings; and have seen girls become wives and wives mothers while I have lived amongst them. So that although when the country settled down, and we built homes for ourselves, and returned more to English modes of living, and I felt that I was drifting away from them into the conventionality and ignorance of our official lives, yet I had in my memory much of what I had seen, much of what I had done that I shall never forget. I felt that I had been -- even if it were only for a time – behind the veil, where it is so hard to come.'[1]

It is hoped that some of the qualities that have so attracted so many people to Burma and the Burmese will become clear in the course of this book. Before that, however, it is desirable to set out, by way of preparation and in a more matter-of-fact manner, something of the physical characteristics and of the natural resources of the country with which this book deals.

Burma lies between longitude 92° and longitude 102° east of Greenwich, and between latitude 10° and latitude 29° north. All but about a quarter of the country, in the far north, and that virtually uninhabited, falls within the tropics. The country has two great and powerful neighbours, India to the north-west and China to the north-east. China has always looked acquisitively upon the north of Burma and many Chinese maps have shown this as a part of China. Yet, historically, it is India that has exercised a greater influence upon Burma, through contacts in the fields of trade and religion, and Indians gained entry by infiltration, particularly in the south, under the protection of the British occupation, in far greater numbers than the Chinese. Other, less formidable, neighbours are East Pakistan on the west, Laos on the east, and Thailand to the south-east. There is also a varied coastline, some 1,200 miles in length.

In area Burma is more than three times the size of England, Scotland, and Wales; it is one-quarter as large again as France, and

[1] H. Fielding, *The Soul of a People*, London, 1898, p. 2.

5,300 square miles less in area than the state of Texas. The distance
from the northern to the southern extremities of Burma is equal to
that from Cape Wrath to Mallorca. West to east, at the broadest
point, the width of Burma is the distance from Brest to Stuttgart, or
from London to Dresden.

The main part of Burma consists of a valley, some 600 miles long
and 100 miles broad, surrounded by an inverted horseshoe of mountains, through which flows the River Irrawaddy. In the far north
the curve of the horseshoe is attached to the eastern ranges of the
Himalayas. In the south the Irrawaddy, Pegu, and Sittang rivers
flow out through its open end into the gulf of Martaban and the
Andaman Sea, both of these parts of the Indian Ocean. Beyond the
horseshoe are two outlying areas, politically parts of Burma but
geographically (and also racially, as we shall see later) less clearly so.
The first of these, outside and to the west, is Arakan, a narrow
coastal strip between the mountains and the Bay of Bengal. The
second, below and to the south-east, is Tenasserim, another narrow
coastal strip between the Andaman Sea and the mountains that
divide Burma from Thailand. Both these strips consist of intermittent
narrow coastal plains, with thick tangled forest on the mountain
ranges behind, and very beautiful coastlines, part sand, part rock,
part muddy tidal estuaries. The mountain wall bounding the central
plain of Burma on the west, the Arakan Yomas, is comparatively
narrow. On the east it is much wider, the Shan Hills broadening out
into a plateau, generally some 3,000 feet above sea level. In deep
and narrow gorges through the centre of the plateau flows the
Salween river, rising far to the north even of the Irrawaddy and
reaching the sea in the gulf of Martaban. The whole of Burma,
indeed, is furrowed from north to south by mountain ranges and
great river valleys, narrow and deep in the mountains, wide and
spreading in the plains.

The broad main valley, the central plain of Burma, is divided
longitudinally by a lower range of hills, known in the south as the
Pegu Yomas. In remote, geological times two rivers flowed down
either side of this dividing range, the Chindwin to the west, the
Irrawaddy to the east. Then the Chindwin 'captured' the Irrawaddy,
just below the site of the present town of Mandalay. The Irrawaddy
broke through the dividing range, here not at all elevated, and took
over the channel of its captor the Chindwin. The lower part of the
original Irrawaddy channel survives as the Sittang, an insignificant
river in a broad valley, noted chiefly for the bore that sweeps up its
lower reaches twice a day.

Since most of Burma falls within the tropics, the climate, flora,
and fauna of the plains are accordingly tropical. But the altitude of

the surrounding mountains and of the Shan plateau to the east, results in great parts of the country enjoying a far cooler and more moderate climate. In the far north the boundaries of Burma run into mountains 18,000 feet above sea level, rocky and snow-clad, but remote and seldom seen by inhabitants of the plains.

For six months of the year, from May to October inclusive, the south-west monsoon blows off the great spaces of the Indian Ocean, bringing moisture-laden clouds to Burma. These strike the outer side of the horseshoe of mountains surrounding Burma on the west. They also strike the mountains to the south, between Burma and Thailand, and, since they travel in a north-easterly direction, they enter diagonally into the lower part of the inside of the horseshoe and come up against the mountains to the east of the main valley. They deposit their moisture in these areas against the mountain ranges. The two coastal strips, accordingly, receive an annual rainfall of some 200 inches. Southern Burma, consisting of the delta of the Irrawaddy and the mouths of the Pegu and Sittang rivers, receives 100 to 120 inches. These areas constitute the southern wet zone of Burma. Further north, the central plain, between Thayetmyo in the south and Ye-u in the north, with the present towns of Mandalay and Meiktila and the irrigated rice lands of Kyaukse at its centre, is screened from the monsoon by the Arakan Yomas with the result that the rainfall in this, the dry zone, averages only 25–35 inches a year. Further north is a second wet zone which owes its rain to the interception by the very high mountains to the north and east of Burma of high clouds that pass over the Arakan Yomas. Rainfall in Bhamo and Myitkyina in this area averages 70–80 inches a year, but is heavier in the mountains still further to the north.

It would be reasonable to speak of two seasons in Burma, the wet and the dry. But it is more usual to distinguish three: the cold or cool season from November to February; the hot season from then until early May; and the rains from then until about the end of October. Rain is most infrequent outside the wet season.

In the southern wet zone, politically and administratively known as Lower Burma, mean monthly maximum shade temperatures run from 83° Fahrenheit in July and August, in the rains, to 96° in March and April, the hot weather. Mean monthly minimum temperatures run from 60° in January, the cold weather, to 82° in April. Humidity is high throughout this zone and throughout the year, and the climate is generally steamy and relaxing. In the dry zone of Central Burma, further from the moderating influence of the sea, there are greater extremes of temperature. Mean monthly maximum temperatures run from 91° in June, the rains, to 103° in April, the hot weather, and these averages conceal not infrequent temperatures of 114°. Mean monthly minimum temperatures run from 59° in December, the cold weather, to 77° in May, the climax of the hot weather. Humidity is less and the climate much less enervating. This dry zone, together with the northern wet zone, is politically and administratively known as Upper Burma. On the Shan plateau temperatures are not unlike those of Europe at its best – bright days, sunny but not too hot, cool nights, sufficient rain, occasionally a touch of ground frost, and fresh pine-scented air to fill the lungs of those who are fortunate enough to be able to escape the haze, heat, and staleness of the plains in the hot weather.

The direction of the mountain ranges and of the long rivers will have made it clear that the natural grain of the country runs north and south. This might be expected to cause, and indeed does cause, logistical difficulty for the passage of armies across the grain. But it has never, in fact, prevented invasion of the country, whether by the Chinese from the north-east in earlier times or, in the Second World War, by the Japanese from the south-east, or the British-Indian forces and their allies from the north-west. Nor has it in the past deterred invasions of and by Siam or of Manipur.

Communication with the outer world has never been easy. This, before the British annexation, seemed very far away; there was no need and little desire for contact with it. Standing within the red-brown walls, pink in the evening sun, and within the surrounding watery moat of the old Mandalay palace and fort, the Irrawaddy and the low Sagaing Hills to the west, the blue Shan Hills to the east, it must have been difficult to believe there was an outer world at all. But there was some communication with the exterior, and this was, and still is, primarily by sea, through the port of Rangoon or, more rarely, through Bassein or Moulmein. Before the arrival of Europeans it was mainly Arab traders who reached Burma in this way, though the occasional Indian or Chinese vessel must have put into the ports. From the thirteenth century onwards occasional travellers began to appear from Venice, Portugal, the Netherlands, and England. After its incorporation in the British Indian Empire, British and other European steamship lines and a few Indian vessels began to ply regularly to Burma. The Burmese themselves, masters from a very early age in the handling of small boats in inland waters, were never seafarers. Only since independence has a Burmese government shipping organization, the Five Star Line, come into existence, operating its own small fleet of five cargo vessels, and a good many more vessels on charter from other countries.

But if the most important means of communication with other countries was the sea, there were nevertheless certain ancient overland routes for the carrying of merchandise into and out of Burma.

24 BURMA

Routes to the west to India, and to what is now East Pakistan, were few, poor, and little used or known. From this side the sea gave much easier access. But all these routes were trodden in 1942 by Indian, Anglo-Indian, and European refugees fleeing before the Japanese invasion, and by the exhausted British-Indian forces who were driven out by the invaders. There was a route from the Irra- waddy opposite Prome, over the Taungup Pass to the coast of Arakan, and thence northwards, mostly by boat, through the creeks and islands, to Akyab and then by boat or rough roads to India. There was a more frequented route up the Chindwin river to Kalewa or Sittaung, and thence by land to the Manipur plateau, where Imphal stood 3,000 feet up in the mountains. There were less well- known routes through Homalin to Manipur. There was a route through the Hukawng valley, north-west from Myitkyina, over the Pang Sao Pass to Ledo in Assam. And there were still more remote and dangerous routes further to the north – mere forest paths for the most part, concerning which little or nothing was known. These routes to the west at no time carried any trade, for merchandise could be transported to and from India so much more easily by sea.

To the east matters were different, and there were a number of established trade routes, of immemorial antiquity, linking Burma with China and Siam. The country through which these routes ran was not so difficult as that on the west, and the alternative of trans- porting goods by sea was not practicable since this would have involved a long and difficult journey with a great detour to round the Malayan peninsula. There were routes from Myitkyina, from Bhamo, and from Hsipaw and Lashio, into Yunnan. Along these would travel strings of pack bullocks or ponies, driven by Chinese, following the sound of the twin bells on the leading animals. Here

> ... celestial traders
> Bring their silks and pickled teas.
> 'Tis a glimpse of jogging hampers
> Flapping hats and stolid kine
> With a breathless Chow that scampers
> Up and down the jingling line.[1]

And in the hampers might well be smuggled opium besides the pickled teas. There was a route eastwards from Meiktila, through the southern Shan States, over mountains, across gorges, through opium poppy fields, to Kengtung, and thence to Thailand or, with greater difficulty, to Laos or China. There was a short and not very

[1] J. M. Symns, *Songs of a Desert Optimist*, London, 1924, pp. 11–12.

difficult route from Moulmein into Thailand. And there were forest paths in other places.

Within Burma the most important means of transport has always, even after the building of railways and roads, been water. The main artery of communication is the Irrawaddy river, navigable by shallow-draught vessels for a thousand miles above its mouth, to Bhamo and, in the low-water season, when the force of the stream through the narrow defiles abates, to Myitkyina. The Chindwin, the great tributary of the Irrawaddy, is navigable, though for even shallower draughts, to Homalin or even to Tamanthi, as far north as Myitkyina is on the Irrawaddy. In the rains when the great rivers are swollen, fast, and brown with silt, but the steady monsoon wind blows from the south-west or the south, the high-sterned wooden boats, with bamboo masts and square sails, carry rice from the delta to the dry zone. In the dry season, with the river low between its banks and the cool, fresh wind in the north or north-east, they bring back edible oils, cotton, vegetables, and other local produce. Since 1865, when the Irrawaddy Flotilla Company began its operations, large shallow-draught paddle-steamers have plied on the Irrawaddy – the largest of their kind in the world. Those on the Rangoon–Mandalay run are more than 300 feet long, though they draw a mere 4 feet of water. With two large, roofed barges attached, one on each side, they carry, besides passengers, all kinds of merchandise, rice, dried fish, salt from Lower Burma, tea and oranges from the Shan States, sesamum and ground-nut oil, chillies, tobacco, and many sorts of vegetables from Upper Burma, at one time silk from Mandalay, and lacquer-ware from Pagan. They act as mobile markets, almost as travelling villages. The draught of vessels operating on the Chindwin has to be less still, a mere 2 feet 6 inches, and here stern-wheelers are employed.

The Sittang river is much less busy. It is a smaller river, and navigation in the lower reaches is bedevilled by the formidable bore.

The Salween, the longest but not the largest, and perhaps the most beautiful, of Burma's rivers, is navigable only for a comparatively short distance, less than 100 miles, to Hsa-zeik, the salt moorings or anchorage, beyond which the salt and other boats cannot ascend because of dangerous rapids. Here remote hill-dwellers come down many days' journey on foot to barter forest produce for essential salt.

Many other rivers and tidal creeks are navigable for short distances, and in the coastal strips of Arakan and Tenasserim there is little transport other than country boats or small steam- or motor-launches.

Away from the great water routes transport, before the era of roads and railways, was mainly by bullock-cart, and in the mountain country by pack-bullock, pack-pony, or porters. In the early 1900s the *Sawbwa* (or Chief) of Kengtung, the most easterly and remote of the Shan States, travelled three weeks to annual council meetings at headquarters in Taunggyi, most of the time by elephant.

The construction of railways began in 1877, before the annexation of Upper Burma. The first line linked Rangoon with Prome on the Irrawaddy. This served a fertile strip of country between the Pegu Yomas and the Irrawaddy and its delta, and shortened the time taken over the river journey to Mandalay by almost half. The second line, opened in 1885, the year of the annexation of Upper Burma, ran from Rangoon to Toungoo. It served the Sittang valley and was extended four years later to Mandalay. Ten years later the Sagaing–Myitkyina line was built. Branch lines were added subsequently, three of which followed, broadly speaking, three of the historic trade routes to the east, through the northern Shan States, the southern Shan States, and Moulmein.

With the development of motor transport the need arose for motor-roads. The trunk roads for the most part followed the alignment of the railways, or the course of the Irrawaddy, a wasteful arrangement, dictated, however, by the north and south grain of the country and by the fact that the railways already ran through the most populous and economically significant parts of the country.

Fresh ground was broken in places, however. There were roads along the old trade routes to the east and north-east, beyond the points reached by the railways. One ran from Lashio to Muse and into China and became notorious during the Second World War as the Burma Road, carrying munitions to China. Another ran eastwards from Shwenyaung, through Taunggyi to Kengtung and into Thailand. A third ran from Kyondo near Moulmein to Kawkareik and Thailand. This was the line of the main Japanese advance into Burma during the Second World War. A fourth ran down the Tenasserim peninsula to Mergui. There is quite an extensive road system throughout the Shan plateau, and a road linking the railheads at Lashio and Myitkyina. And there are many local roads throughout Burma, some good, but many offering only imperfect resistance to the weather.

Finally has come air transport. This, as elsewhere, has had two contradictory results. On the one hand it has brought Burma, a distant country, to within no more than a few hours' journey from any other part of the world, and in this sense has destroyed the remoteness behind which Burma once lay. Passport difficulties apart, it is easier for travellers to reach Burma now, or to pass through it, than ever before. On the other hand the very speed and ease of

travel on air routes have, as in the case of motorways, tended to
channel all movement along these main arteries and to isolate more
than ever the country through which these routes pass. It is physically far easier than it ever was to reach Rangoon, and even
Mandalay. But of those travellers who reach Burma it is probable
that a far smaller proportion than in the past ever get outside Rangoon, into the villages and the countryside, or even along the Irrawaddy, to make any real contact with the life of the country. Air
travel has promoted circulation between the cosmopolitan capitals,
but has isolated and starved the extremities of each country which
now often go unknown.

Burma is a rich, or at the least a potentially rich, country, a land
in which there need be no poverty, and certainly no starvation. In
view of the extremely low national income per head of population
normally assumed for Burma, and of the fact that Burma is generally
classified as an underdeveloped country, and in need of aid from
outside, this statement may be held to require justification. The
policy of giving aid is in fact presumably the outcome of recognition
of the potential riches of Burma, and would not be applied if there
were not promising resources to develop. As for the national income
per head of population, in a country where four-fifths of the people
cultivate the soil, in many cases on a subsistence basis, and cultivation on this basis yields enough food for all (with some surplus for
export), and enough housing material, and could be made to yield
enough clothing material for all, the average *cash* income per head
will be low, but ceases to be a very satisfactory indicator of the
country's prosperity. There is, further, the matter of the distribution
of the national income. A high average means little if in fact the
greater part of the income goes to a few people. The average income
for India is half as large again as that for Burma. But no one who
has visited the villages of the two countries will feel that this correctly represents the relative prosperity of the majority of the inhabitants of the two countries.

A visitor to Burma in 1951, who had plenty of criticisms of conditions in the country, wrote:

'And now on the eve of my departure from Burma, I re-
gathered my impressions in an attempt to form some kind of
personal estimate of this fascinating country's prospects . . . I state
here my sincere belief that the average Burmese peasant working
his own land lives a fuller and happier life, and is a more successful human being than the average Western factory hand or office
worker. His work is creative, free of clock-punching and deadly
routine, and allows him an enormous amount of leisure, which he
consumes with expertness and relish. From the leisure aspect only,

it is the difference between filling in coupons, and keeping one's own fighting-cocks; between standing in the four and sixes on Sunday afternoon, and the full-blooded pleasures of a three-day *pwé*.

As for the material basis for Burma's future, it is excellent. The country is wonderfully fertile, and reasonably populated. That is to say, that without much effort enough food can be grown for everyone.'[1]

Indeed, consideration of her natural resources offers plenty of more solid grounds for holding that Burma is a rich country.

The first and greatest of these natural resources is land. A few figures will make this clear. Divide the land surface of the whole globe by the estimated population of the world and it will be found that there are approximately 12·50 acres of land per person. But of this area 2·50 acres are more or less permanently under snow and ice or too cold for cultivation. Another 2·50 acres are too mountainous and rocky, and yet another 2·50 acres are too arid. Unsuitable soils render another 1·25 acres uncultivable. The remaining 3·75 acres are potentially cultivable. But the area that is in fact cultivated is only 1·10 acres per person. This amount of land is sufficient to keep one human being fed at a modest but adequate level.

The United States of America is by any reckoning the richest country in the world. It has 11 acres of land per head of population, a figure strikingly close to the world average. Of this 2·94 acres are under cultivation, and 3·88 under permanent pasture, figures far above the world average.

In 1963 Burma had 7 acres of land per head of population, a figure not so far below the world average, particularly when it is remembered that the area of land that is so cold, so mountainous, or so arid as to be absolutely unsuitable for cultivation must be less than in many other parts of the world. The area actually cultivated is 1·11 acres per person, virtually the world average. Of potentially cultivable land, Burma, with only 1·11 acres cultivated out of 7 acres, almost certainly has more than the United States of America, with a total of 6·82 acres already cultivated or under permanent pasture, out of a total of 11 acres.

But comparison has been with the richest country in the world, and so far Burma does not come out very well. A look at Burma's nearest neighbour, India, will correct the perspective. Land actually cultivated there is only ·83 of an acre, against Burma's 1·11 acres. The total land available per head of population is only 2·2 acres, and of the uncultivated land only an infinitesimal proportion can possibly be considered potentially cultivable. China, Burma's other

[1] Norman Lewis, *Golden Earth*, London, 1952, pp. 268–9.

great neighbour, has only ·58 of an acre actually cultivated, though she has ·82 of an acre under permanent pasture. Her total land resources are 4 acres per head of population, almost twice those of India, but less than half those of Burma. Finally, there is the case of Japan, where land actually cultivated is only ·15 of an acre, with a mere ·04 of an acre under permanent pasture, and where the total available land per head of population is only one acre. There is in Japan no potentially cultivable land that is not cultivated. There is little doubt that Burma has more good land per head of population than most other countries in Asia.

If land is the first of Burma's natural resources, the second is undoubtedly a plentiful and regular supply of water. In Great Britain, indeed over most of northern Europe, rain and a green countryside are taken for granted. Outside Europe there is, over most of the land surface of the world, a permanent problem and continual anxiety over the availability of water. In many parts it is deficient if not altogether lacking. There come into one's mind the Middle East, Australia, and great tracts of India and Africa. Indeed, travelling by air from England to Burma, once the greenness of northern Europe has been left behind, there is little in view, until Burma is reached, but brown sand, dust, or rock, except for the dark green patches of the Nile valley, Mesopotamia, and the Ganges delta. In the wet zones of Burma there is never any failure of rain. In the dry zone the rains can be poor, or late, but they are never entirely lacking. Even the driest parts can expect some 24 inches of rain in the year, though admittedly this is ill-distributed, the whole amount falling in about five months, with the result that much of it goes to waste. But not only is the rainfall of Burma adequate; it has the further great advantage that it falls at regular predictable times, in accordance with the rhythm of the monsoons.

Here, already, are two of the characteristics that endear Burma to the visitor from outside. The country is prosperous and looks green, both in marked contrast to the dusty impermanence and depressing poverty of much of the northern plains of India, and of most of the Middle East. When British forces re-entered the country in 1945, and emerged from the forests dividing Burma from Manipur, their eyes fell with pleasure upon the lush countryside, and the prosperous, tidy villages of the Kabaw valley, with their large, solid, wooden houses, and strong wooden fences. Here was something very different from the squalor and dirt of so many of the places where these men had trained and waited for the day to invade Burma – even though, in fact, deadly malaria lurked in this beautiful valley, beneath the 10,000-foot slopes of Mount Victoria and the Chin Hills. It is hoped that other reasons will appear in the course of this book, but these two gave Burma a good start for many British soldiers of the Second World War.

With this wealth of land, and assured rainfall, it is not surprising that the economy of Burma is overwhelmingly agricultural. The nature of this agricultural wealth and some of the problems with which it is faced will be discussed in greater detail in later chapters.[1] We are at this stage concerned only to notice the main natural resources of the country, not what has been done to use and develop them. With the regular, copious rainfall that much of Burma receives, and with the temperatures of the tropical plains of the country, it is further not surprising that some 70 per cent of Burma's agriculture is concerned with the production of rice. The wet zone of Lower Burma is ideal country for this purpose. In the dry zone of Central Burma rice can only be grown if water is brought to the land. But here irrigation has always played a part, and there are extensive tracts of rice cultivation, particularly in the Kyaukse, Mandalay, Shwebo, and Minbu areas. Elsewhere in the dry zone other crops include sesamum, beans, groundnuts, cotton, tobacco, fruit, and vegetables. In the southern wet zone a certain amount of rubber is grown in addition to rice, the main crop, but conditions are not ideal.

Next to the cultivation of land, the most important of Burma's natural resources is mineral oil. The presence of oil was known to the Burmese from time immemorial, indeed traces appear on the surface. Until the advent of the British it was won from hand-dug wells, some as deep as 300 or 400 feet. Production by modern methods did not really begin until after the annexation of Upper Burma, though unsuccessful attempts were made from 1871 onwards.

Mineral resources, other than petroleum oil, take third place in the natural wealth of the country. These are considerable and varied. They include silver, lead, tin, wolfram, zinc, iron, rubies, jade, and many other minerals in smaller quantities. Their existence has also been known from earliest times, and before the British annexation they were mostly won by Chinese, who appear to have begun their mining operations in the fifteenth and sixteenth centuries. There are doubtfully valuable deposits of low-grade coal.

Finally, Burma is a country of vast forests, and the last of her natural resources that requires mention at this stage is the timber to be found in these. Burma teak is particularly well-known and valuable, but there are many other excellent but less-known hardwoods. Under the Burmese kings export of teak was forbidden. So desirable was teak, however, that a considerable shipbuilding industry grew

[1] See below, pp. 86, 183.

up at Syriam and Rangoon. There is record of many French ships having been built in Rangoon during the eighteenth century.

There can be no doubt that Burma is potentially a rich country, and that in the essentials of life she is already rich. What use has been, or is being made, of her great resources will appear in later chapters of this book.

Chapter 2

The People

THERE HAS BEEN NO complete census of Burma since 1931. In 1941 bare enumeration took place, but the Japanese invaded and overran the country before analysis and classification of the figures could be completed and a detailed report written. All that survived the Japanese occupation was a statement of the total population by administrative districts. Since the war it has not been practicable to take a full census – mainly because administration has not been effective over great parts of the country, but partly also in deference to the principle of first things first. A newly sovereign country with its back to the wall in the struggle to establish its authority has more vital matters to attend to than the counting of heads. What has been done is to carry out a so-called stage census. The first stage was carried out in 1953 when almost complete enumeration was made of urban areas, most of these being under government control. The second stage was carried out in 1954 and was directed towards rural districts. As most of these were not under government control, enumeration could be made only of some 15 per cent of these. The two stages together covered only about 25 per cent of the population. And of those enumerated, only about 20 per cent were sampled for more detailed information about, for example, religion, education, occupation. On the basis of this stage census up-to-date totals have been estimated. For a breakdown of the figures it is necessary to go back to the 1931 census which, subject to certain obvious modifications (for example in the numbers of foreigners in the country), is believed to show reasonably correctly the proportionate numbers of the races making up the population of Burma.

This, in 1966, was estimated to be 25,246,000, an increase of almost exactly 50 per cent since the census of 1941. This total represents about ninety persons to the square mile or 7 acres of land per head of population. The rate of increase is moderate, being probably not much more than one per cent per annum.

Of the indigenous peoples the great majority are of Mongoloid stock. The Burmese proper, who account for some 70 per cent of the population, occupy the lowlands, including both the central valley and the coastal strips of Arakan and Tenasserim. The minority races, the Shans, Karens, Chins, Kachins, and smaller groups, are mostly to be found in the mountains surrounding the Burma plain, including the Shan plateau to the east. All these peoples originated somewhere in the high tablelands of Central Asia and arrived in Burma as the result of population movements southward, driven by pressure from behind, or attracted by the prospect of milder climes and more fertile land. The advance of the Kachin races, the latest comers, was still in progress when the British arrived in Upper Burma in 1885.

There were three main waves or streams in these migrations. The first was that of the Tibeto-Burman races. These included the Burmese, the Arakanese, the Chins, the Kachins, and a considerable number of smaller tribes. This wave probably included also the Pyu who preceded, or were an advance party of, the Burmese, though little is in fact known about them. These peoples entered Burma from the north, through the mountainous country where the Irrawaddy has its sources. The Burmese flowed into the dry zone of Upper Burma and settled there, this becoming and remaining their homeland, notwithstanding later penetration into Lower Burma. Capitals were established by the Pyu at Prome and Halingyi (near Shwebo), and by successive Burmese dynasties at Pagan, Ava, Pegu, Toungoo, Shwebo, Amarapura, and Mandalay. Prome and Pegu departed from the pattern, being outposts pushed forward into the wet zone of Lower Burma; all the rest were in the dry central plain. The Arakanese settled in the coastal strip outside the horseshoe of mountains on the west and adjoining Chittagong. The Chins made their home in the mountains on the north-west, the Kachins established themselves in those of the far north. Minor tribes seldom ventured into the plains and for the most part remained tucked away in the mountains.

The second wave was that of the Mon-Khmer races. The southward course of these peoples lay further to the east, down the valley of the Mekong, and indeed the majority of them followed the course of this river down into the plains and there formed the ancient kingdom of Cambodia. But some branched off westwards and found their way into the lower valley of the Salween, into the coastal strip between this and the Sittang, and so into the delta of the Irrawaddy. Apart from a few insignificant tribes, this wave consisted of the Mons – known to the Burmese as Talaings. Lower Burma became their homeland. Thaton, Pegu, Martaban, and Donwun became at various times the capitals of the Mon kingdom. The Mons have now been largely absorbed by the Burmese and, although slightly darker of skin, are for practical purposes indistinguishable. A certain racial

consciousness survives and, as will be seen later, a nationalist movement has grown up since Burma became independent.

The third and last wave was that of the Tai-Chinese peoples.
These moved into Burma from the north-east, from the high tablelands of south-west China where, in the seventh century A.D., they
had established the kingdom of Nanchao. This wave included the
Shans, who are very closely related to the Thais or Siamese – indeed
Shan and Siam are basically the same word. It also included the
Karens, and numerous small and often picturesque tribes. The Shans
are noticeably fairer-skinned than the Burmese and the Mons. They
occupied the high plateau to the east of Burma, though small groups
penetrated into northern Burma and into Assam. The Karens established themselves on or below the southern spurs of the Shan plateau,
though groups also made their way into the delta of the Irrawaddy.
Remaining for the most part in their mountain fastnesses, the Shans
and Karens have retained their racial identity in a way that the
Mons, living much interspersed with the Burmese, have not. And
inhabiting a country of small valleys, divided by mountain ranges,
a high degree of separatism has persisted with numbers of small
states each, until recently, having its own ruling chief. Of the Shan
States, Hsipaw, Yawnghwe, and Kengtung were the most notable,
each with its own miniature but long history. The Karen States in
the hills were politically and culturally less advanced, but the Karens
of the plains, particularly those in the Irrawaddy delta and the
Thaton and Toungoo districts, many of whom, as will be seen later,
became Christians, attained a high standard of education and,
during the British period, were influential out of proportion to their
numbers.

Of non-indigeneous peoples, Indians, Pakistanis, and Chinese are
the most numerous and the most important. It was during the
British period that Indians and Pakistanis, in virtue of the fact that
both at that time were British-Indian subjects, flooded into the
country until, just before the Second World War, they numbered
over a million out of a population of about 16 million. This immigration and the problems it created will be considered more fully later
in this book.[1] The numbers have been greatly reduced because of
those who fled to India before the Japanese in the Second World
War, and because of Burmese attitudes thereafter. There are now
probably not more than 450,000, and the number may quite possibly
be less. It is difficult to say what is the number of Chinese in the
country. At the time of the last detailed census in 1931 it was almost
200,000. In 1955 it was estimated to be 350,000. There has certainly
been a large increase since then. A fair guess is probably 500,000.

[1] See below, pp. 87, 90, 119, 121, 199, 239.

Europeans, mainly British, numbered about 12,000 in 1941, a total that was made up mainly of two British battalions with their families, of employees of European firms in Rangoon and on the oilfields, and of members of the government services. Eurasians numbered about 20,000, mostly employees of the railways, the posts and telegraph department, and the public works department. The numbers of both these communities have been very greatly reduced since 1941. British troops were, of course, withdrawn at the time of independence. European firms have been expropriated. No Europeans have been retained in the government services. Eurasians are tolerated if they identify themselves with the Burmese in dress, speech, and standards. But even if they align themselves with the Burmese many feel insecure and they are now, since the expulsion of foreign missionaries and closing-down of mission schools, denied the education they seek for their children. Many have, therefore, left the country, and gained admittance for the most part to the United Kingdom and Australia, often in the face of great difficulties, legal and practical.

The great majority, in fact 70 per cent, of the indigenous races of Burma speak Burmese as their mother-tongue. In this context Burmese includes the languages of Arakan, and of Tavoy and Mergui in the Tenasserim coastal strip, which are properly to be considered dialects rather than distinct languages. Most of the Mons, whose language is distinct and no mere dialect, nonetheless speak Burmese as their language of daily use. Burmese is a monosyllabic and agglutinative language, closer to Chinese than to any of the Indian languages, with which, in fact, it has no kinship. A single syllable may have some four completely different meanings according to the tone or stress of its pronunciation. The alphabet came to the Burmese through the Mons, from rock-cut scripts of south India. Being then written on palm-leaves the characters, originally square, acquired a softness and roundness, caused by the change of medium from rock to leaf, so that the Burmese script now presents a mainly circular appearance. The written language tends to be florid and pretentious; the spoken word is pithy, idiomatic, and keen-edged.

The chief languages spoken among the remaining indigenous races are Shan, an even more strongly tonal language than Burmese, Karen, Kachin, or variants of these, and several forms of Chin. There are also a considerable number of Mon speakers. The great majority of these non-Burmese people, probably 70 per cent once more, speak Burmese with facility, as well as their mother-tongue.

The Shans have an alphabet, a written language, and literature of their own, all closely linked to the culture of Thailand. The Karens had no written language until early missionaries devised an alphabet by adaptation from the Burmese. Officials and missionaries have also reduced Chin and Kachin to writing, making use mostly of the Latin alphabet.

The Burmese are of Mongoloid stock and their features are, accordingly, Mongolian, characterized by high cheekbones, broad, but not coarse, noses, and often (though this is perhaps more characteristic of the Karens) square jaws. They have a smooth fine-grained skin, of a light to dark copper colour, quite unlike the smoky black of natives of south India or most of Africa. Any such darkness in the complexion of a Burman generally indicates an admixture of Indian blood. The Burmese have brown eyes, but not almond-shaped as with the Chinese, and black hair, generally straight and well oiled. They are slightly built, but the prosperous tend to put on weight – indeed leanness in middle age is apt to be equated with lack of worldly success. Young women have slightly developed, somewhat boyish figures, but the passage of time often brings a comfortable rotundity. Both men and women have remarkably flexible joints; they sit or squat relaxedly in attitudes that are agonizing to the sturdier, thicker-limbed Europeans, and achieve strikingly graceful movements of the arms, hands, and fingers, especially in their dancing, that are quite beyond the reach of most Westerners unless double-jointed. They are, however, tougher than their slight and flexible build suggests and, if need occurs, or their interest is aroused, are capable of long, sustained effort – to be followed, understandably, by compensating periods of rest and relaxation.

The Burmese national dress for both sexes is a cylindrical skirt reaching to the ankles known as a *longyi*, topped by a short jacket called an *eingyi*. The *longyi* is folded across the front; in the case of men it is knotted, in the case of women tucked in flat, so as to avoid unbecoming bunchiness. For everyday use it is of cotton, generally in bright colours and for men in a check pattern. On more formal occasions it used to be, and when possible still is, of silk, often of shot silk, in bright but delicate shades. But man-made fibres imported from India, the West, or Japan – though there are now foreign exchange difficulties – have increasingly taken the place of the silk that is no longer brought in from China to be woven in Burma. The *eingyi* is single-breasted for men, of plain material in white or sober colours. The women's *eingyi* is double-breasted, often side fastened, usually of transparent light-coloured material, allowing the bodice to show through, and nowadays often short-sleeved. The hair used to be worn long by both sexes, but this is now extremely rare in the case of men, and not universal even in the case of women. On more formal occasions men wear what is sometimes described as a turban but is in fact much less bulky than the headgear generally so named and consists of a silk kerchief of bright colour, tied over a symmetrical basket-work frame, simulating the knot of long hair formerly worn. Women on such occasions used to wear their hair coiled on top in a smooth and tidy cylinder, faintly reminiscent of a small top-hat, but this is a fast-disappearing fashion, partly, perhaps, because it takes much time to arrange. Well-to-do women wear much jewellery which, almost without exception, is preferred as a medium for saving to a bank account or to an investment portfolio, which indeed it would be difficult to acquire in Burma. For more active purposes men gird up their loins by passing the hem of the *longyi* between their legs and tucking this into the waist, so converting the skirt into abbreviated trunks.

Generalization about national character is rash, yet it is impossible to avoid the attempt. For, although the reader is being asked to see the Burman through the eyes of one observer, inevitably biased, and although it would not be difficult to adduce cases contradicting every one of the points made below, yet there is in sum a convergence of characteristics that may fairly be accepted as typical of the Burmese.

Perhaps the most easily recognizable of these characteristics is a happy disposition and a ready gaiety, as bright and vivid as the clothes he wears. He is quick to laugh, and is blessed with an uncomplicated sense of humour, in some ways not unlike that of the Anglo-Saxon peoples, and a notable and irreverent gift for burlesqueing authority and any form of pomposity. He has not been infected by the *Schadenfreude* that afflicts some of his neighbours. He is warm-hearted and affectionate and particularly fond of children. But a streak of heedless brutality must be set against these many happy and attractive qualities. Assaults are frequent, and the fact that most countrymen, and not a few townsmen, in Burma carry a *dah*, a kind of heavy knife or chopper which serves as a domestic and agricultural tool but is also a highly lethal weapon, means that these often result in grievous injuries or death. Passionate murders are frequent. So are trivial murders, sometimes arising from some insult, fancied or real, sometimes the outcome of misunderstanding and argument over a few pence. In robberies or dacoities (gang robberies) the attackers are often ruthlessly and callously ready to kill. And in the next chapter will be mentioned frequent examples in history of cold-blooded massacres of the royal kinsmen in order to safeguard the position of a new king ascending the throne.

Another notable characteristic of the Burmese is a relaxed mental outlook, and a consequent absence of psychological tension; they are remarkably free of the neuroses prevalent in urban and industrialized countries of the West. This may stem in part from their religion.

Buddhism, which will be more fully discussed later in this chapter, is a religion that is accepted without question or hesitation, but that at the same time sits lightly upon many of its devotees. In consequence the Burmese are largely spared both the tortures of religious doubt and self-questioning, and the guilt that springs from failure to match up to the demands of an exacting religion. Partly it stems from an open and healthy attitude in matters of sex and all bodily functions which take their places easily as part of a natural life. There is almost certainly less of sexual complexes and aberrations than in the West. Above all it is probably the result of a sense of humour and of a salutary sense of the ridiculous.

A warm outgoing hospitality is a quality that the Burmese share with most of the other peoples of the Middle and Far East. This is not the hospitality that thrives only on the prospect of a convivial occasion. Rather is it a deep charity, a keen consciousness of the indivisibility of human kind. No traveller arriving in a village unannounced, no sick or old person, will lack a roof or a meal. Partly it is an attitude enjoined by religion; partly it is something in the character of the people; partly, of course, it is easier to give a helping hand to the stranger in trouble in a country of simple and informal habits, of unenclosed houses, of warm temperatures. But Christians of the West need to feel humility in the face of the love and charity of the East generally and, in the present case, of the Buddhists of Burma.

Perhaps, indeed, the climate and natural resources of a country have the last word in the creation of a happy disposition. Where it is not difficult to keep warm, to build a roof over one's head, to grow enough food, there one may expect to find an easy and happy character. In the harsher countries of the North, where these things can be gained only by constant struggle, one must expect a greater dourness – and with this also a greater drive and sense of purpose.

The Burmese are strongly individualistic and by nature averse to regimentation and discipline. Their readiness to mock authority has already been mentioned. Yet against this must be set the present-day prevalence of mass movements, of marching and drilling, of the wearing of uniforms, and of anniversary parades and celebrations. It is difficult to feel that these sit easily upon the Burmese. They are, of course, part of the techniques of propaganda, commonly employed in single-party states.

If the Burmese are happy, they are also happy-go-lucky, and are often said to be lazy and to lack the ability to apply themselves to regular or routine tasks. There is clearly an element of truth here. The Burmese are quite unwilling to work the long, regular, routine hours that, for example, Indian labourers are accustomed to accept.

On the other hand there were, and doubtless still are, government
servants and others, at all levels, ready to work devotedly long hours,
with a great sense of responsibility. And, as has already been said,
Burmans will work without break at high pressure, if necessary
without food, for extremely long periods if they are interested in
what they are doing and are convinced of its necessity and urgency.
But after that they will, not unnaturally, expect rest and recreation
to compensate. Which makes of them valuable helpers in a crisis
but not dependable workers in a routine industrial job. In part this
characteristic is probably a result of the climatic conditions and
agricultural rhythm in which the Burmese villager has to work. The
main crop in Burma is rice, and the cultivation of this involves
intensive and extremely arduous work from the time when the
monsoon rains have softened the ground sufficiently to permit
ploughing and planting until the crop is reaped in the cool weather.
Several leisured months follow in which the ground is too hard for
cultivation and the great heat makes physical exertion laborious.
This is the season for relaxation, for parties, visits, and festivals.
Above all, it would be difficult for anyone who has watched the
Burmese cultivator ploughing, planting, and transplanting, particularly perhaps the last of these which is the task mostly of women,
and has to be done by hand, bent almost double, in tropical rain,
with only inadequate shelter to return to at the end of the day, and
no means of drying wet clothes, to describe the Burmese as lazy. The
truth of the matter is that the Burmese are not materialists. Some,
of course, will steal, rob, or kill for money. With many the prevailing
conversation is of the prices of things. But this is largely convenient
small-talk – the British are not really so passionately interested in
the weather as one might think – and fundamentally money makes
little appeal to the Burmese – unlike the Indian labourer to whom
it is all-important. They are certainly not willing to spend the whole
of their time working for it. This is what Buddhism teaches and
what their natural disposition and environment encourage.

In matters of taste and craftsmanship the Burmese come less well
out of comparison with their neighbours on either side: the Indians
or the Chinese. These matters will be discussed more fully in a later
chapter.[1] But as in so many other countries newly brought into contact with the West and its technological and material advances, this
contact has had a disastrously debasing effect upon indigenous art,
taste, and standards. If bad money drives out good, as we are told,
this law seems to apply equally in matters of taste and craftsmanship. The material and technical successes of the West attract an
admiration that undermines the indigenous canons of taste. And it is

[1] See below, p. 216.

hardly surprising that it is the inferior and meretricious that is absorbed from the West, for there is much of this and little of the good. And in any case the criteria of the West that would help to distinguish the good from the bad are not available to the East, for they are, naturally, rooted in the culture of the West and for the East are merely an arbitrary and meaningless set of rules, not an expression of indigenous and genuine feeling or standards. Furthermore, at the best of times, the Burmese fancy seems always to have been irresistibly attracted by the quaint contrivance, the cunning device, the crafty dodge, rather than by grace, elegance, or refinement of form, and this is a poor foundation upon which to build a sound taste in matters of art or workmanship.

It has often been said, particularly in connection with the First and Second World Wars, and by British military officers, that the Burmese are unmilitary and that it is not possible to train them into satisfactory soldiers. The main accusations are that they do not take kindly to discipline, being, as has already been said, highly individualistic; that they cannot be depended upon in matters of routine; that they are lacking in martial spirit and are quite unmilitary in appearance. But against these accusations must be set a number of considerations.

In the first place, although through much of her history Burma has been a disunited and ineffectual country, torn by internal struggles, there have been periods when, restored to unity and confidence by kings with ability and qualities of leadership, she displayed considerable military prowess and became a scourge to her neighbours. There were many wars with Siam and not infrequently, especially in the late sixteenth century, it was the Burmese who gained the victory. Under Alaungpaya and his successors the military strength of the country reached its peak. In the late eighteenth century war was successfully waged, even against the vast resources of China. At about the same time, and again in 1824, the Burmese were successful in war against Manipur. Indeed it was the last of these incursions into what had by then become a part of the British dominions in India that drew retaliation from the British and led, ultimately, to the loss of Burma's independence. It does not seem that there is any inherent reason why the Burmese should not make good soldiers.

Of the Burmese soldier in the First Burmese War, in 1824–25, Sir Arthur Phayre, than whom few can have known Burma better, wrote:

'Let justice be done to the Burmese soldier, who fought under conditions which rendered victory for him impossible. The peasant is taken from his village home, and brought into the field as a combatant, without having gone through drill or any suitable instruction. He is supposed to know how to load and fire a musket, which he probably does; but up to the end of the war, the musket given him, generally much worn by use and neglect in a damp climate, would have been condemned in every army of Europe. Many in the ranks were armed only with the native sword or spear. The gunpowder, made in the country, would not have been accepted as serviceable in the armies of the princes of India. After the large stores of that material had been lost at Danubyu and Prome, even the rude powder used became scarce; and at Malwun, before the assault, the Kaulen Wungyi, who was second in command to Mengmyatbo, but knew nothing of war even after the Burmese fashion, was seen measuring out the powder in a niggardly way to the soldiers. Cartridges were issued to few, and the soldier had to load as he best could. The artillery branch of the Service was even more inefficient than the infantry. There were a great number of guns in different parts of the country, and these were mounted in the stockades, but they were mostly old ship-guns of diverse calibre, and some of them two hundred or more years old. Round shot was not plentiful; grape or canister there was none. Even at Danubyu, before the death of Bandula, the guns were so ill-served that any one piece was not fired oftener than once in twenty minutes. Generally, the Burmese officers never lead their men except in flight. Yet, with all these disadvantages, the Burmese ill-armed peasant never feared to meet Asiatic troops, though these were well armed and led by European officers. It was only to the European soldier that he succumbed. After the first few months of the war, he found himself overmatched, and no longer fought with hope of success.'[1]

After the Second Burmese War of 1852, during the process of establishing order in the recently annexed province of Pegu, Lord Dalhousie, Viceroy of India, wrote in a private letter to Phayre, Chief Commissioner and writer of the tribute quoted above, of one of the Burmese leaders, whose activities were being put down:

'A man who has 4,000 men under him, who repulses three British attacks, and after a very stout defence is finally routed only by a Brigadier-General, after a month's operations and with severe loss to us, must be regarded as a chief and a soldier – and a good one too.'[2]

In the Third Burmese War there was little or no fighting. But such engagements as took place, and the guerrilla warfare that continued after the formal close of hostilities, showed that the Burmese

[1] A. P. Phayre, *History of Burma*, London, 1883, pp. 258–9.
[2] Quoted by D. G. E. Hall, *Burma*, London, 1950, p. 115.

soldier did not lack courage or martial ardour. It was the total absence of leadership, organization, and training and the miserable quality of his equipment, that gave him no chance against the British and Indian forces. A contemporary and well-informed observer wrote:

'But in the opinion of men who have observed them impartially the Burmese are not to be set down as cowards. They fight with great energy and tenacity on occasions . . . With suitable training they ought to make good fighting men. This is the opinion of British officers who look forward to the time when a Burmese contingent will fight side by side with our native troops.'[1]

But once Burma had become a part of the Indian Empire, circumstances did not in fact give the Burmese much opportunity to show whether they would make good soldiers; and they did not, perhaps did not wish to, make much of such opportunities as did offer. The pacification of Upper Burma after annexation was undertaken by units of the British army and of the Indian army – Indian troops under British officers. Since these forces were engaged in what was virtually a guerrilla war against the Burmese there was naturally no recruitment of Burmans, except for one company of sappers and miners. When the Burma Military Police were raised as a semi-military body to aid the regular forces it was originally intended that they should be recruited half from Indians, half from local men.[2] Some Karens were successfully enlisted, but recruitment of Burmans was quickly abandoned as unsatisfactory. Few recruits came forward and such as did were of poor quality. This was scarcely surprising. Service in a force that was essentially Indian, under British and Indian officers who knew nothing of the Burmese or their language, for the purpose of harrying their own countrymen, can have offered little attraction to a people with great national pride who in any case had little or no desire for a military life. Later, when the more remote hill areas had been brought under British control, there was extensive recruitment of Chins, Kachins, and Karens into the Burma Military Police. Relations between Burmese and these tribesmen were less than cordial, so that the latter were not inhibited by thoughts of being employed on the preservation of internal security, which might involve action against Burmese. With their lower standards of living they found the conditions of military life more attractive than did the Burmese. They were less individualistic and more ready to accept the uniformity of discipline. And they rapidly showed that they could make smart and efficient

[1] Grattan Geary, *Burma after the Conquest*, London, 1888, p. 82.
[2] C. H. T. Crosthwaite, *The Pacification of Burma*, London, 1912, pp. 16, 64.

soldiers, and gained the respect and affection of their British officers. So when in the First World War a number of battalions of Burma Rifles were raised, recruitment was mostly from Karens, Chins, and Kachins. Recruitment of Burmans was once again judged to have been unsuccessful. But the few officers involved in this recruitment who could speak Burmese and understood the Burmese people felt strongly that the new recruits had never been given a fair chance; most of the officers under whom they were placed spoke little or no Burmese, had no understanding of Burmans, and had already given their affection and loyalties to the Chins, Kachins, and Karens of the minority communities. It was also clear that the administrative arrangements for the reception of the Burmese recruits were poor. In these circumstances it was not surprising that they did not give satisfaction.

The truth presumably is that the Burmese are not naturally warlike, but that given a cause which they can understand – which attracts their loyalty, given weapons as good as those against them, and given inspiring leadership, there is no reason at all why they should not become as good soldiers as the many other not naturally martial peoples of the world.

Although Buddhist by religion, and although Buddhism is a very real part of their daily life, the Burmese are a strongly superstitious people. Their religion notwithstanding, there is a widespread belief in the existence of spirits, both good and evil, and many elements of spirit worship have forced their way into Buddhism. The fixing of the date and time for any important event can be undertaken only after consulting the astrologers regarding the favourable moment. The formal declaration of the independence of Burma from British rule had to be made at the propitious but highly inconvenient hour of 4.20 a.m. on 4 January 1948. Children are named according to the date, day, and hour of their birth, which are also believed to determine their characters. Much importance is attached to the horoscopes cast for them. There are lucky and unlucky days, and great attention is paid to omens. Belief in charms dies hard. In particular there are few Burmese who do not believe that invulnerability, and other desirable attributes too, can be conferred by tattooing, by potions, by wearing amulets, or by reciting the appropriate incantations. That rebels or robbers, supposedly immune, are nevertheless seen to be shot dead, merely provokes the reflection, even among comparatively experienced and well-educated persons, that the unfortunates had not on this occasion discovered the effective formula, the appropriate magic.

If it is risky to generalize about national character, it is positively dangerous to do so about intelligence and mental calibre, and what

follows is no detailed statistical study but merely an impressionistic
sketch. The Burman clearly starts with a quick and lively intelligence, and shrewd commonsense in matters of everyday life. The
man (and still more the woman) in the village is full of practical
ability. He, and she, will cultivate the fields, paddle a boat, drive a
bullock cart with deftness and economy of effort. He will build a
house, in rough and ready but competent manner, she will run the
shop or the stall in the market with shrewd business sense. He
quickly grasped the working of the internal combustion engine and
has become a first-class mechanic. He can, with some justice, be
accused of making a new car look old in the shortest possible time.
But on the other hand he will keep it going longer than most others
possibly could. The general level of practical intelligence and rudimentary education compares very favourably with that of neighbouring countries.

At the other end of the intellectual and educational scale, in the
higher levels, such a comparison is far less favourable. Men with a
grasp of broad principles, the ability to think in logical form, and
the authority that flows from these qualities, are few. The best in
Burma have not so far competed with the intellectual giants of India
and China, whether in philosophy, administration, the arts, or the
sciences. And if anyone does stand out above his fellows in Burma,
the probability is that his abilities have been fertilized by an admixture of Chinese blood.

Partly this lack of eminent men is a matter of education. This
will be more fully discussed in a later chapter.[1] At the present stage
a few unsupported observations must suffice. Before the British connection, education was exclusively in the hands of the Buddhist
monks. The bare ability to read, write, and count was widely disseminated; of higher education, except in matters of religion, there
was virtually none. The British, understandably, decided that it was
not possible to build on the foundations of the monastic schools an
educational system that would bring to the Burmese a knowledge of
the modern world. It had already been decided in India that the
educational system must be based on the English language and
culture, not the languages and culture of the Orient. Accordingly
the British in Burma set about creating a system of lay government
schools to provide education which was in fact of a distinctively
British character. This, with its teaching of English history, its now
ludicrous, but even then somewhat embarrassing, attempts to inculcate 'the imperial idea', and its underlying Western philosophy,
never sat easily upon the Burmese. It had no roots in their culture
or their background of experience. Consequently it did little to

[1] See below, p. 204.

develop the innate commonsense or the abilities of the Burmese, or to enlist their interest, but tended rather to become an artificial game, governed by arbitrary rules and conventions requiring to be learnt by rote. Success in this was sought, not for its intrinsic worth, but as the necessary qualification for obtaining a much-coveted government appointment. It is little wonder, in the circumstances, that education so often seemed to achieve nothing but the sterilization of the native good sense of the uneducated villager. The wonder is, rather, that some Burmans nevertheless developed logical and incisive minds. Since the time of British rule education has undoubtedly been given a more distinctively Burmese, and therefore a more realistic and practical, character. But what it has gained in this respect has probably been offset by excessively speedy expansion and by political interference, which have brought about a disastrous fall in the standards achieved. These matters will be more fully discussed in a later chapter.[1]

But misdirected or ineffectual education is not the only reason for the comparative lack of outstanding persons in Burma. The limited background and parochial outlook that result from Burma's isolated position in the world have also played their part. Until the British period there was little contact between Burma and other countries. Burma tended to see herself as the centre of the universe, and her people as superior to all those unfortunates who knew nothing of Burma or of the pure Buddhism that flourished within her borders. Now, once again, after the breaking of the connection with Britain, Burma has withdrawn behind her horseshoe of mountains. Contacts with the exterior are consciously and strongly discouraged – visas for entry of the ordinary traveller from outside are hard to get, foreign journalists are not welcome, and every difficulty is placed in the way of those Burmese who may wish to travel abroad. Employees of the government are forbidden to write to foreigners, and the correspondence of others is liable to be censored and any signs of intimacy to be frowned upon.

If it was only during the period of the British connection that Burma was brought into contact with the knowledge and thought of the outside world, it has to be remembered that this period was extremely short, a passing and brief connection on the scale of history. Upper Burma, the real home of the Burmese people, was annexed only in 1886. The Republic of Burma was proclaimed and the British withdrew in 1948. The full connection lasted only sixty-two years. There must have been not a few Burmans living in 1948 who could remember the time when a Burmese king and court existed in Mandalay. And even while the British connection lasted

[1] See below, p. 204.

the number of those Burmans who visited England and were brought into contact with the thought and ways of the outer world through the West was not large. Partly this was in deference to the idea, then more generally accepted than now, that benefits desired should be paid for by the country seeking them. Partly, perhaps, it was due to realization by the British that the absorption of new ideas is a heady and not always happy matter if proceeded with too fast. So over the whole period of Burma's history there has been little to widen her horizons or break down the parochialism of her outlook.

In matters of the mind as in matters of taste, it is often craft and guile that appeal to the Burmese, the cunning contrivance, the clever trick, rather than lucidity, logic, and cogency. It is tempting to see this as an aspect of the superstitiousness already mentioned. A man who is firmly convinced that some charm, some formula, if he can only get it right, will magically confer invulnerability upon him, will also tend to believe in the ever-present possibility of short cuts, of quack methods, for problems of the mind, and be fascinated by any plan or argument that holds out promise of such quick solutions.

It has often been said that the Burmese are a people without class or class distinctions. It is true that they are mercifully free from the caste system, that extreme form of class which still has such a hold upon India. There is much Hindu influence in Burmese art, and in the Buddhism of Burma, but caste never gained a hold in the country. It is also true, as will be seen later, that in Burma before the British annexation, there was no aristocracy or middle class. On the one hand there stood, at the centre, the king, his officers, and his court. And even officers and court tended to be selected on the random whim of the king; there was little opportunity for the emergence of any hereditary 'establishment'. On the other hand stood the people, dwelling for the most part in villages, and among them there was little or no class stratification. The British, on annexation of the country, removed the king and dispersed, and so very largely destroyed, the royal entourage. But during the British period there emerged an upper class of those in government service. Initial entry to this was largely by educational merit, but those who had entered soon developed a real class consciousness, and marriage and social intercourse was largely confined to their circle. Entry into government service tended more and more to be confined to those born into this élite, for its members were those with appreciation of the advantages of education, and with the means and the knowledge to treasure it for their families. On the departure of the British this aristocracy fell out of favour. Its members were, or had been, the 'haves' whereas the new régime was seeking to woo the 'have-nots'; its members tended also to take a wider view than the régime was prepared to tolerate; and in any case they had been friends with the British from whose tutelage Burma had so recently escaped. Above all, perhaps, their offence was that they overshadowed their new masters in education and ability. If there is any class now, it is the class of the army and of the party member, in a one-party state, a self-constituted élite with a virtual monopoly of salaried employment, and a privileged position in the matter of socialized amenities. But having said all this, it probably remains true that stratification by social class is more nearly absent in Burma than in almost any other country.

In religion the Burmese are almost exclusively Buddhists. So also, among the minority races, are the Shans. Of the million and a half Karens, more than a million are Buddhists. Over 200,000 are Christians, mostly Baptists of the American Baptist Mission, and about 100,000 Animists. The Chins are mostly Animists, though there are some Buddhists and a very few Christians. The Kachins are nine-tenths Animists and the rest Christians. Of the total population of Burma, some 85 per cent are Buddhists. Indeed, the Burmese very largely equate their race with their religion, and the witness in court, when asked for his race, will reply without thought or hesitation, 'Burman-Buddhist'.[1] And to the Burman his religion, although admittedly it sits fairly lightly upon him, is a very real and present factor in his everyday life.

Buddhism will be more fully discussed in a later chapter[2] to include the present with the past.

[1] Except for the English-speaking witness who appeared before the author and replied 'When I am among Buddhists, I am a Buddhist; when I am infested with Christians, I am a Christian.'

[2] See below, p. 216.

Chapter 3

History

IT IS, OF COURSE, presumptuous to try to condense the history of Burma into one short chapter. But some sort of summary must be attempted, which will deal with the story only in broad outline and mention only the outstanding personalities, seeking to avoid burdening the reader with names he cannot pronounce, of people he does not know, or of places he cannot find on the map. Those in search of greater detail are recommended to read the *History of Burma* by G. E. Harvey and *Burma* by D. G. E. Hall (from which two admirable books the present summary has, in the main, been distilled) and the sources listed by these two historians.

Burmese history cannot be said to begin before the reign of Anawrahta in the middle of the eleventh century A.D. From this time on there is a wealth of inscriptions, though of documentary evidence there is little. Apart from the *Yazawingyaw*, and one or two other sixteenth- and seventeenth-century works, the standard Burmese chronicles were written during the eighteenth and nineteenth centuries, and it is very unlikely that the materials upon which they are based date from before the sixteenth century, though these in their turn may be based on inscriptions. However, by comparison and collation of the chronicles and the inscriptions, it has been possible to construct a skeleton of dates and main events and also to put a certain amount of flesh onto these bones.

Before the eleventh century inscriptions are rare, and no documentary evidence survives from this early period except for a very few, generally passing, references by Chinese and Arab writers. There is some archaeological material, upon which, however, more work remains to be done. In this early period Indian and Arab seamen and traders knew the coasts of Burma, established themselves here and there for purposes of trade, and appear to have penetrated occasionally into the plains of Lower and even Central Burma. They brought with them religious and cultural influences that were to exercise a permanent influence upon the inhabitants of the country. In the interior, all three of the main population waves already described[1] made their appearance – the Burmese, the Mons,

[1] See above, pp. 33–4.

48

and the Tai. It is indeed fair to see Burmese history, until the advent of the British, and very possibly again thereafter, as the struggle for dominance and survival between these three racial groups.

The first inhabitants of Burma concerning whom any records survive are the Pyu. They may have been early representatives of the Burmese, but this is not certain. In the seventh and early eighth centuries they had established a capital near Prome on the Irrawaddy at the point where this shakes off the confinement imposed by the foothills of the Arakan and central mountain ranges, and now begins to widen and wander in the sand and silt of the delta. Prome must at the time have been much nearer to the navigable sea than now. In the course of the eighth century the capital seems to have been withdrawn northwards to Halingyi in Upper Burma near the present Shwebo, which was in the mid-eighteenth century to become the cradle of the last Burmese dynasty. The Halingyi site was nearer to the main rice-growing areas of Burma than Prome, until the reclamation of the delta in the nineteenth century. But about A.D. 760 the kingdom of the Pyu was conquered by, and made subject to, the Tai kingdom of Nanchao in Yunnan. In A.D. 832 it was destroyed by tribes in rebellion against Nanchao.

By this time, in Lower Burma, the Mons, who, it will be remembered, entered Burma from the east, had established themselves around the mouths of the Salween and Sittang, with a capital, first at Pegu, and later at Thaton, midway between the rice-growing deltas of these two rivers. It was along this coastline, among the Mons, that Indian and Arab influence had most effect. And it was here that in about the fifth century A.D. Buddhism was introduced to Burma. Mon influence at its height extended northwards from Pegu along the Sittang valley as far as Kyaukse, then the richest rice area of Upper Burma.

The Burmese proper entered Burma from the north sometime during the ninth or tenth century. They seized Kyaukse from the Mons, spread to the other main rice-producing areas of Upper Burma – Minbu, Taungdwingyi, Shwebo, and the Mu River – and established their capital at Pagan, on the east bank of the Irrawaddy in a central position between these oases of cultivation. Traditionally this was in the year 849 and there seems to be no great reason to distrust this date. Originally Animists, it seems that the Burmese in the course of their wanderings about the eastern end of the Himalayas, before entering Burma, came into contact with Buddhism, albeit in a corrupt form, and adopted this as their religion.

The Tai races did not make their appearance in Burma until later, after the beginning of recorded history.

With the accession to the royal throne in Pagan of Anawrahta in

1044, the history of Burma can be said to begin. Anawrahta reigned for thirty-three years, and although it is not necessary to believe the whole of the legend that the chronicles have built up around him, it is very clear that he was a monarch of outstanding qualities and stature. He was the first king to unite under his own control virtually the whole of Burma (other than the Shan State) as we now know it. He achieved this by a series of conquests. To the west, he invaded Arakan and established his overlordship through at least the northern part of this kingdom (whose history will be briefly summarized in a later part of this chapter). To the north his control extended up to the slopes of the great mountains and it is said that he even invaded the Tai kingdom of Nanchao, reaching Talifu, spurred on by the quest for a Buddhist relic. To the east he established his frontier along the foothills of the Shan mountains, and appears to have imposed suzerainty over at least some of the Shan States beyond. But it was in the south that he made his most important conquests, over the Mon kingdom of Thaton, partly, at least, in order to seize the sacred Buddhist scriptures held there. It is said that he not only removed the holy books but deported the whole population of the capital, including king, court, and clergy, to Pagan, and he certainly incorporated the whole kingdom into his dominions. But Anawrahta was not only a man of war. In his desire to glorify Buddhism (and perhaps also himself) he built temples or pagodas in his capital, so initiating an architectural period of 200 years during which Pagan was progressively beautified by incomparably the finest buildings in Burma. He brought from Thaton to Pagan a form of Buddhism which, if not 'pure', was without doubt a great deal less corrupt than that previously current in the northern kingdom. And the Mons, notwithstanding their political subjugation, were to exercise a vigorous and formative cultural influence upon the Burmese. This first unification of Burma must have involved administrative organization and activity on a scale previously unknown. It made possible, and put into currency, the conception of Burma as a united geographical entity. But above all, perhaps, the conquest of Thaton brought the Burmese to the sea and opened a doorway which, although it never encouraged the Burmese to go out, did in the course of time admit persons and influences from the outer world that were to affect Burma decisively.

The dynasty founded by Anawrahta lasted through eleven more reigns, until A.D. 1287. Of his successors it is only necessary to mention three. While Anawrahta had united the lands, Kyanzittha (1084–1112) sought to unify the peoples, of Burma, cultivating particularly the Mons. Externally, he made increasing contact with the outer world; at home he built the Ananda Pagoda, the finest of the Pagan temples, and one of the few still fully used as a place of worship. Alaungsithu, a pious and other-worldly king, built the Thatpyinnyu Pagoda, but neglected the administration of his extensive realm. Htilominlo withdrew entirely into religion and completed the Gawdawpalin Pagoda begun by his father, the last of the three most famous temples of Pagan.

None of Anawrahta's descendants had the authority or administrative ability that their great ancestor had displayed. Indeed there seems to have been a steady decline in vigour and sense of purpose through the whole of this dynasty. The resultant centrifugal tendencies gradually eroded the domination and strength of Pagan. The final collapse was brought about by two attacks from outside and one rebellion from within. By the middle of the thirteenth century the Tartars under Kublai Khan had annexed Yunnan. When the Burmese refused to acknowledge the suzerainty of Kublai Khan they were invaded from the north. Simultaneously the Tais or Shans attacked from the east, three of the Shan chiefs seizing and holding Kyaukse and its rice lands. The internal rising was in the south, where a Mon leader from Pegu, together with Wareru, a Shan adventurer, threw off the rule of Pagan and gained control south of Prome and Toungoo. Under the combination of these blows the dynasty of Anawrahta collapsed and disappeared. For 250 years the fact, and indeed the ideal, of a unified Burma were lost.

The two and a half centuries from 1287 to 1531 were a dark and chaotic period in the history of Burma. The only part that escaped anarchy and the internecine warfare of petty chiefs, which followed the collapse of the kingdom of Pagan, was the country of the Mons, the lower valleys of the Salween and the Sittang. The racial consciousness and national spirit of the Mons had survived both the devastating sack of Thaton by Anawrahta and two and a half centuries of incorporation in the Burmese kingdom of Pagan. And whereas the Tartars and the Shans, when they invaded Burma, were invading a foreign country, to despoil it or merely to establish their suzerainty without much concern to settle down or establish a stable society of their own, the Mons, when they attacked Pagan, were fighting to free their own country from Burmese domination, and to restore and build again something that had been theirs in the past. Their leader Tarabya was a Mon, aided however by Wareru, a Shan adventurer from Siam. These two fell out and Tarabya was murdered by Wareru, who gained the recognition of China and in 1287 founded a stable dynasty that was to last for 250 years. The capital was set up in Martaban at the mouth of the Salween. The new kingdom was subject to constant raids and invasions from Siam

and after a particularly violent incursion in 1363 the capital was
withdrawn from its exposed position to Donwun, west of the Salween, the birthplace of Wareru. A few years later it was moved still
further west to Pegu, in the lower Sittang valley, where there were
better communications and wider areas of rice land. Wareru and
his descendants ruled until 1472. Although seven of these fifteen
kings met their deaths by murder, they were nevertheless able to
ensure to their subjects an orderly, civilized, and peaceful existence
such as Burma had never known before, and was not often to know
again. Razadarit stood out as an able administrator. In 1472 his
daughter, Queen Shinsawbu, handed over to Dammazedi, who was
not in fact of the royal blood. Dammazedi proved the greatest of the
rulers of the Wareru dynasty, if he can legitimately be so described.
He was a man of peace and religion, and during his reign there was
a great revival of Buddhism and of friendly intercourse with the
outer world. It was to the Mon seaports, during this period, that the
first recorded European travellers to Burma came. From now on a
trickle of information concerning the country began to reach the
West.

North of the Mon kingdom of Pegu there was such confusion and
anarchy that it is impossible to give any intelligible detailed account
in a summary as short as the present one. The Tartars withdrew to
China after overthrowing the dynasty of Anawrahta, but the Shan
invaders prevented the re-establishment of the kingdom of Pagan,
fought with each other and with any other chieftains who emerged,
combined, intrigued, and recombined with kaleidoscopic effects
upon the map of Upper Burma. For a while Pinya and Sagaing
became the capitals of separate states. In 1364 these were destroyed
and Ava, controlling the vital rice area of Kyaukse, became the
capital. But there was no stable or unified government and many
Burmese fled from the intolerable conditions southwards to Toungoo,
to which we shall shortly turn our attention. And yet in a curious
way the Shan invaders absorbed a great deal of the Burmese culture
and tradition, which were themselves largely Mon, and these survived, even under the Shans, so that Ava began to assume an
importance in Burmese minds altogether greater than its political
significance at the time. From now on Upper Burma, fundamentally
Burmese, although for long periods at the mercy of the Shans, came
to be thought of and known as the kingdom of Ava, just as Lower
Burma, fundamentally Mon, came to be known as the kingdom of
Pegu.

The only part of Burma north of the kingdom of Pegu that
managed to pull itself out of the surrounding chaos, was Toungoo
mentioned above, well up the Sittang valley and in a kind of no-

man's land between Pegu and Ava. To this village or town, fortified in 1280, many Burmese refugees came from the disturbed and devastated areas further north. Toungoo was fortunate in lying off the main routes connecting Upper and Lower Burma, which mostly followed the Irrawaddy valley, through Prome. It was only the advent of the railway, and of metalled roads, that put Toungoo on the main communications from Rangoon to Mandalay. While armies marched up and down the Irrawaddy valley in the continuing struggle between Pegu and Ava, Toungoo, in its backwater, continued somehow to remain in being and comparatively stable. There was no regular dynasty, but the chief Thinhkaba (1347–58) felt sufficiently established to assume the style of king. In the wars between Ava and Pegu, Toungoo sided now with one, now with the other. Although it never achieved the fame or prestige of its two neighbours, it preserved the nucleus of a Burmese kingdom, while Thais ruled to the south and Shans to the north, and was ready to emerge in the next period of Burmese history.

This began in 1531, though Minkyinyo, who reigned in Toungoo from 1486 until 1531, made possible the expansion that was to follow by seizing and holding Kyaukse, and by this success attracting many Burmese chiefs ripe for revolt against the Shans further north. His son Tabinshweti (1531–50), however, first turned southwards and after several years of campaigning brought the delta, Pegu, Martaban, and Prome under his control. He transferred his capital to Pegu, a move dictated by the greater wealth of Pegu and its surrounding rice lands and by a policy of winning the support of the Mons. He then turned north and occupied Pagan, stopping short, however, of Ava. There followed two campaigns against Siam. These were both disastrous, and demoralization and disintegration set in. Tabinshweti was succeeded by his brother-in-law Bayinnaung (1550–1581), the most remarkable leader produced by Burma. In what Harvey describes as 'the greatest explosion of human energy ever seen in Burma'[1] Bayinnaung first assured himself of a firm base by seizing and holding Toungoo itself. He then attacked and gained control of Pegu, which had been lost to Mon rebels in the time of Tabinshweti's decline. By 1551 he had re-established authority over all the territories of Tabinshweti. In 1555 there followed the conquest of Ava and the north. In 1564 and 1569 he conducted successful campaigns against Siam, which was rendered incapable of causing trouble to the Burmese for a long time to come.

Under the rule of Bayinnaung the kingdom of Pegu flourished greatly. The capital was rebuilt after it had been burnt to the ground by Mon rebels in 1564 while Bayinnaung was conducting

[1] op. cit., p. 174.

his campaign against Siam. A European traveller described Pegu in 1569:

> 'In the new Citie is the Palace of the King and his abiding place with all his Barons and nobles and gentlemen . . . it is a greate citie, very plaine and flat, and foure square, walled round about and with ditches which compass the wall about with Water, in which Ditches are many Crocodiles. It hath no Draw-bridges, yet it hath twenty Gates five for every square in the Walls . . . Within the gate there is a faire large Court, from one side to the other, wherein there are made places for the strongest and stoutest Elephants, he hath foure that be white, a thing so rare, that a man shall hardly finde another King that hath any such, as if this King know of any other that hath white Elephants, he sendeth for them as for a gift. The time that I was there, there were two brought out of a farre Countrie, and that cost me something the sight of them, for that they command the Merchants to goe to see them, and then they must give something to the men that bring them: the Brokers of the Merchants give for everyman half a Ducket, which they call a *Tansa*, which amounteth to a great summe, for the number of Merchants that are in the Citie.'[1]

Bayinnaung was in Burmese eyes a model king, making offerings to pagodas, founding monasteries, feeding monks, and undertaking many other works of religious merit. European travellers and traders, or those who left a record of what they saw, increased in numbers, and there are other accounts by them besides that from which quotation has just been made.

Bayinnaung died in 1581 and by 1599 his kingdom had virtually disintegrated. But Anaukpetlun, a grandson, revived it. Having established his rule in Ava and over a number of the Shan States he gained control of the south, making Pegu once again the capital. He planned to renew the war against Siam but was murdered in 1628. Thalun (1629–48), his brother, was responsible for one event that probably altered decisively the course of Burmese history. In 1635 he transferred his capital from Pegu to Ava, and there, or nearby, it remained until the Burmese kingdom collapsed in 1885. There were good reasons for this move at the time. But, in the words of D. G. E. Hall:

> 'So the idea of a national kingship by union with the Mons was forsaken, a fresh coronation on strictly Burmese lines was held in the new capital, and in Harvey's words, "the Court relapsed into its tribal homeland, Upper Burma". It was a retrograde step, a surrender to traditionalism. Four hundred miles was a long way from the sea in those days. The journey up-stream from Syriam to

[1] Caesar Frederick, quoted by D. G. E. Hall, op. cit., pp. 45–6.

Ava often took as much as two months. Thus, cut off from contact with the outside world, Burmese rulers came truly to believe that their palace was the centre of the universe, that building pagodas, collecting daughters from vassals, and raiding their neighbours for white elephants and slaves was the essence of Kingcraft. It is not without significance that Siam, which, when forced in the next century to evacuate its capital, built one at a seaport rather than further inland, managed to survive as an independent state, while Burma succumbed to foreign conquest. The chief ingredient in the failure of the Burmese Kingdom was supplied not by "Western Imperialism", but by the intransigence and xenophobia which radiated from the Court of Ava.'[1]

Syriam, mentioned above, was the main port of Burma until replaced by the nearby Rangoon in 1756.

King Thalun's successors were ineffectual and stagnation and later disintegration set in. In the mid-seventeenth century Chinese raids disturbed Burma. From the early eighteenth century the small mountain state of Manipur on the north-west began raiding Burmese territory and in 1749 the raiders only just failed to take Ava. In 1740 the Mons in the south proclaimed their independence and set up a king in Pegu again. In 1752 they attacked and destroyed Ava and made captive its king and his family. This was the end of the Toungoo dynasty, and it looked as if the Mons would establish an independent kingdom of their own, as had happened after the downfall of the dynasty of Anawrahta at Pagan in 1287.

But there now emerged another of the great military leaders of Burmese history, comparable in his dynamism to Bayinnaung. This was Alaungpaya (1752–60), the *Myothugyi* or headman of Shwebo, some 50 miles north of Ava, but on the other side of the Irrawaddy. His short reign covered eight years of incessant fighting. The first three were spent overcoming the Mons and driving them back to Lower Burma. The small town of Dagon, across the river from Syriam, was, with premature optimism, renamed Rangoon, 'end of strife', to mark his success. But Syriam and Pegu were still holding out, when Alaungpaya had to return north to deal with his enemies there. He first devastated Manipur and then invaded the Shan States, most of which made their submission. By 1756 he was back to capture Syriam. In 1757 he destroyed Pegu. By the cold season of 1758–59 he was back in Manipur, but a few months later returned to Rangoon to deal with Mon disaffection. The troubles here drew him on to Siam which he invaded at the end of 1759. But in May 1760 he was mortally wounded by the explosion of one of his own cannon while besieging Ayuthia. Alaungpaya made no contribution

[1] ibid., p. 66.

to religion, culture, or administration. But his outburst of warlike energy reunited Burma, established what was to be the last dynasty of Burmese kings, inculcated respect among his neighbours, and restored the morale of the Burmese, indeed, filled them with a not altogether justified sense of invincibility, that was ultimately to prove their undoing.

Of his successors, Hsinbyushin (1763–76) and Bodawpaya (1782–1819), both sons of Alaungpaya, carried on his aggressive and expansionist policy. Hsinbyushin moved his capital to Ava, nearer to Kyaukse. He invaded Siam and captured and destroyed Ayuthia. In 1766 he had to turn north to deal with Chinese aggression. In four successive years he completely defeated Chinese attempts to invade Burma. His forces then invaded Manipur and placed a nominee of the Burmese on the throne. After this he resumed the war against Siam, but with inconclusive results.

Bodawpaya's reign began with a particularly gruesome example of the traditional massacre of the kinsmen. All possible rivals with their followers, servants, and children were slaughtered. His predecessor's queens and lesser ladies were burnt alive holding their babes in their arms. A little later, plotters against the new king, a prince, who had escaped the first killings, and one of Hsinbyushin's commanders, and their families and servants, were massacred. Shortly after, another aspirant to the throne and his 200 armed followers who had attempted to murder the king, were all done to death. Once Bodawpaya had established his authority, however, he displayed a different aspect. He overhauled the administration. He initiated a revenue survey. He then invaded Arakan, whose earlier history can for the purposes of this highly condensed summary be dismissed in a few sentences. The earliest known inhabitants were of Indian race, probably akin to the Bengalees. The Burmese arrived during the tenth century and established a remarkably stable kingdom that, despite occasional Mughal, Burmese, and Mon interference, had retained its independence until this time. The Arakanese were basically Burmese by race, though with considerable Indian admixture over the centuries, and were Buddhist by religion. After Arakan had been brought at least nominally under the control of the Burmese, the struggle against Siam was renewed, with varying fortunes and no conclusive results.

Towards the end of his reign he invaded Assam, but by now was showing increasing signs of religious mania. Although hectoring and aggressive to all other neighbours, he respected, and fostered good relations with, the Chinese. His invasion of Arakan sowed the seeds of the ultimate downfall of his dynasty, for Arakanese who had fled across the border into British India there conspired to recapture their country, so provoking the Burmese to raid into British territory in pursuit. It was these infractions of the frontier that ultimately led to intervention by the British. At the time of Bodawpaya's death the map of Burma was virtually identical with that of the present day, except only that the Chin Hills and the far north-east were not included, although much of Assam was.

Bagyidaw (1819–37) succeeded Bodawpaya. But before tracing the events of his reign and the fate of his successors we need to turn back and see how the British came on the scene, for events now threw the British and the Burmese into a close and significant relationship for almost 150 years, a relationship which had a decisive effect in the fashioning of Burma of the present day.

The first recorded, if somewhat passing, glimpse of Burma through European eyes is that left by Marco Polo, the famous Venetian traveller, who in 1282–84, at the time of the Tartar invasions which brought Anawrahta's dynasty down, was serving Kublai Khan, the Tartar Emperor of China. But the first European certainly known to have set foot in Burma was Nicolo di Conti, a merchant and also a Venetian, in 1435. For 200 years, until 1635, most of the Europeans who came to Burma were Portuguese, and were divided, broadly speaking, into merchants, missionaries, and adventurers. These were backed, if at all, by the Portuguese Crown, or more immediately by Goa, and enjoyed the blessing of the Pope. There were also Venetians, the first recorded Englishman, Ralph Fitch, and later the Dutch. But by far the most numerous at this time were the Portuguese, and among these the most significant were the adventurers. It was the possession of firearms, the knowledge of how to use these, and, perhaps one should add, their complete lack of scruples, that gave them their power. Their two main centres were at Dianga near Chittagong and Arakan, and at Syriam. At Dianga the Portuguese were plain pirates and slave traders. Making common cause with the Arakanese, also pirates and slave raiders, they terrorized and despoiled eastern Bengal. At Syriam, De Brito, although nominally in the service of Arakan, set up a trade monopoly of his own, and attempted, with the help of the Mons, ever anxious to throw off the Burmese yoke, to create also a kingdom for himself. But in 1613 the Burmese besieged and took Syriam and De Brito suffered the penalty, being impaled and dying after two days of agony.

In 1635 a new phase began in relations with Europeans, which lasted until the end of the eighteenth century. This was dominated by the activities of the Dutch, the British, and the French East India Companies, on the whole better organized, better controlled, and a little more regular in their operations than their Portuguese forerunners. Dutch trading-posts, then known as factories, were intermittently in existence in Arakan, Syriam, and inland at Ava, from 1635 until 1679. English factories were established at Syriam and elsewhere from 1647 until about 1657, and again from 1709 to 1743. Indeed, from 1720 to 1743, the British set up a shipyard and kept a permanent Resident in Syriam, in order to build their ships of teak, export of which the Burmese would not allow. The French likewise established a shipyard in 1729 which continued in use until 1742. Private merchants of various nationalities also operated in Syriam and elsewhere during this period. And in Mergui there was Samuel White, one of a number of private traders poaching on the East India Company's preserves. But throughout this period it was broadly speaking the Chartered Companies that represented the Europeans and conducted their relations with the Burmese. They sought to trade in and with Burma, but had little success, mainly because the Burmese did not want to trade, or, if they did, wished understandably to establish their own monopolies, and therefore imposed vexatious restrictions or indulged in obstruction and non-co-operation. It was not possible during this period to establish any official relations between the Burmese government and the British East India Company.

These began only in 1795, and initiated a new, third, phase in contacts between Burma and the Western world. In that year Captain Michael Symes was sent by the Governor-General on a mission to Ava. As a result of this mission Captain Hiram Cox was posted as British Resident in Rangoon from 1796 to 1798. The British were at this time seeking three concessions: a commercial treaty that would permit trade, especially in teak; a settlement of the situation which had followed the Burmese annexation of Arakan and led to a succession of frontier incidents; and, above all, the exclusion of the French (with whom England was then at war) from the Burmese ports and shipbuilding facilities. The need to keep the French out, originally paramount, soon ceased to be of importance, since French power in the East was waning. In respect of the remaining two concessions the British encountered little but hostility and deliberately imposed humiliation. That the Burmese should not wish to trade was not unreasonable, and in any case this was very much their own affair. In the matter of frontier incidents their case was less good. Burmese imperiousness was at its height, following the defeat of the Siamese, the repulse of the Chinese, the conquest of Arakan, and the overrunning of Manipur, Assam, and neighbouring countries. Within the somewhat circumscribed Burmese horizon there was nobody left to humble. For the next twenty-five years the British continued to experience frontier irritations, which spread from Arakan to Assam where a Burmese invasion drove refugees across the frontier into India, producing a situation similar to that on the boundaries of Arakan and Chittagong. From British territory these refugees plotted subversion and would invade Burmese territory. The Burmese, rightly or wrongly, suspected that the British encouraged and connived at these activities. In driving out rebel refugees the Burmese would violate Indian territory. It became more and more certain that war must ultimately come, for the Burmese were aggressive and high-handed, contemptuous of Indians, and had no conception at all of the fundamental strength of the British in India.

When Bagyidaw came to the throne in 1819 he appointed the ambitious and warlike General Bandula Governor of Assam. It was clear that aggression was in the air. The succession of frontier incidents reached its climax early in 1824 when the Burmese massed troops in Arakan for an invasion of Chittagong. They had in their ignorance chosen a bad moment. The government of India's commitments over the Maratha War were at an end, it was now in a position to retaliate. In May 1824 the fleet landed the main British force at Rangoon which fell without opposition. Subsidiary operations were undertaken in Assam, Arakan, and Tenasserim. Strategically sound, these operations were nevertheless an administrative disaster, and it took the British, notwithstanding their greatly superior military resources, nearly two years to defeat their opponents, a fact that went a long way to confirm the Burmese in their total misapprehension of the real power of Britain. Ultimately, however, the British-Indian forces prevailed, and by the Treaty of Yandabo on 24 February 1826, the Burmese were made to cede Assam, Arakan, and Tenasserim and to undertake not to interfere in Manipur, Cachar, and Jaintia.

The essential Burma, the geographical unity within the surrounding horseshoe of mountains, retained its independence. But its power, which in any case was only comparative, was broken. Under the peace treaty the Burmese were required to accept a British Resident. But in the words of D. G. E. Hall the British representatives had 'to encounter all the arts of subterfuge, evasion and studied rudeness, with which earlier envoys had had to contend'.[1] Major Henry Burney, the second Resident, nevertheless succeeded remarkably in gaining the confidence of King Bagyidaw and many difficulties were consequently resolved. But Bagyidaw, generous and kind when sane, became liable to recurring insanity and in 1837 was deposed by his younger brother Tharrawaddy Min, a hot-headed and arrogant chauvinist, impossible to deal with, so that in 1840 the British Residency was withdrawn. Tharrawaddy Min also developed

[1] op. cit, p. 107.

symptoms of insanity and died in 1846, being succeeded by his son
Pagan Min. The new king indulged in a massacre of the kinsmen.
But this was not the end of slaughter and it is said that in the first
two years of his reign there were 6,000 executions. Frontier irritations and arbitrary and oppressive treatment of traders continued.
The arrest of two British sea captains on false charges of murder,
which had been preferred in order to extort money, brought matters
to a head. The Sikh War was over, the conclusion of this released
military resources, and Lord Dalhousie, the Governor-General,
decided that the Burmese must be taught a lesson. He did not want
war, but was quite prepared for it if necessary. Commodore Lambert
was sent in H.M.S. *Fox*, accompanied by two East India Company
ships, to demand compensation. A refusal by the Governor of Pegu
Province to receive a deputation to discuss a claim for damages led
to a blockade of Rangoon and reprisals against Burmese shipping.
When Burmese shore batteries opened fire they were answered
with a broadside from the British ships, and the destruction of all
Burmese war boats, after which the British mission withdrew. An
ultimatum and demand for compensation were presented but the
Burmese vouchsafed no reply. The war began in April 1852 and
British forces occupied Rangoon, Martaban, and later Bassein. This
demonstration did not, as had been hoped, bring the Burmese
government to terms. An advance then began on Prome where the
Burmese were defeated after token resistance. Administrative
arrangements for these operations, unlike those for the First War,
were exemplary. Dalhousie had no intention of annexing Upper
Burma, but on 20 December 1852 he proclaimed the annexation of
the old kingdom of Pegu, so linking together Arakan and Tenasserim
which had been annexed after the First War, the whole becoming
British Burma, a new province of British India. Peace talks followed,
but in no way could the Burmese king be persuaded to enter into a
treaty surrendering Burmese territory. So the British retained Pegu,
but the Burmese did not recognize their possession, an obviously
dangerous position. Defeat by the British led to the deposition of
Pagan Min and the accession of Mindon Min in 1853. After several
years of disturbances on both sides of the limit of the British advance,
and across it, friendly relations were established by the good sense
and goodwill of Phayre, the British Commissioner of Pegu, and
King Mindon Min, a wise patriot and the best of Alaungpaya's
successors. Although the Burmese would enter into no treaty, *de
facto* recognition of the 'frontier' gradually emerged and was
accepted.

In 1862 a commercial treaty was concluded with Mindon Min
and under this the British Residency was reopened at the capital

which had now been moved to Mandalay. During the next twenty years world events and politics for the first time sucked Burma into their orbit. England, France, and the United States of America were all anxious to expand their spheres of influence and trade in the Far East. The great unknown and potentially exploitable area of this was China. The opening of the Suez Canal, and also of the first transcontinental railway across America, brought the interested parties effectively nearer to the goal, and sharpened their rivalry. In Mandalay competition developed over commercial and other concessions between the British and the French. The former were established to the south in the province of British Burma. The latter were in Indo-China to the east. King Mindon maintained friendly relations with the British, but wisely sought to balance British influence by negotiating treaties with the French and Italians as well (his envoy, the *Kinwunmingyi*, visited both France and Italy on his mission to Europe in 1872). When Mindon died in 1878, he was succeeded by Thibaw, a younger son born of a lesser queen. Thibaw was inexperienced, unattractive, and completely under the influence of his immature, ignorant, but totally selfish and ruthless wife. A massacre of the kinsmen took place, horrifying not only because of its scale but because it was enacted before a world that had grown much smaller and could not but feel the slaughter as a close and contemporary event rather than as a remote page in medieval history. Thibaw and his court, resentful of loud British disapproval and of the curb imposed by the British presence in Lower Burma, sought to pick a quarrel. Frontier incidents and other irritations multiplied, and relations with the British deteriorated. In 1879 the British Residency was withdrawn for fear that its members might be massacred, with a further worsening of relations. In 1885 the Burmese government, drawing strength, as it believed, from French support, took action against the Bombay Burmah Trading Corporation, a British firm that had been given a contract to extract timber from forests in Upper Burma. The Burmese government accused the Corporation of felling and removing more than twice the number of logs they had paid royalty for, of bribing Burmese officials, and of not paying their Burmese employees. It is probable that some of these charges were justified – it is certain that without bribery the operations of the Corporation would have come to a swift stop. But it was not out of concern for breaches of the laws or rules that the case was brought. It was a pretext which should enable the Burmese government to withdraw the concession from the Bombay Burmah Trading Corporation so that it might give a contract to a French syndicate. Unfortunately the British-Indian government was also looking for a pretext for taking action against Burma. It had by now discovered, or believed it had discovered, that the French were secretly negotiating a treaty with the Burmese that would give them not only ordinary trading rights but also concessions of military value, and that the French had promised to supply arms to the Burmese government. The British demanded that the case be re-opened. The Burmese government refused. The British delivered an ultimatum expiring on 10 November. No support was forthcoming from the French who were now pulling in their horns as a result of difficulties in Indo-China, China, and Madagascar. The British invaded Burma on 14 November. There was virtually no resistance, Mandalay was occupied a fortnight later, and King Thibaw surrendered. Burma's medieval isolation was at an end.

Chapter 4

Burma at the Annexation

KING THIBAW HAD SURRENDERED, but the British were reluctant to annex Upper Burma, though previous experience of the Burmese as neighbours made them resolved to exercise some control. The policy of re-establishing a Burmese government under British-Indian protection appeared to offer many advantages and had many advocates. The existence of an effective buffer state between the British in India and Lower Burma, the French in Indo-China, and the Chinese in the north-east, would have been very convenient. But the policy was abandoned as impracticable because there was in Burma at the time no person of sufficient authority, and no organization sufficiently coherent, to establish control and overcome the disorders bequeathed by the weakness of the monarchy under Thibaw, disorders greatly exacerbated by the sporadic, irregular fighting that followed the swift conclusion of the formal war of annexation. A buffer needs to be tough and resilient if it is to perform its function. Instead, on 1 January 1886 the British government in India, not without misgivings, annexed Upper Burma, so terminating the rule of the dynasty of Alaungpaya and the existence of the court of Ava. It was decided to incorporate Upper Burma into British India as a part of a new province of Burma and to establish direct administration on the British-Indian pattern – a task that was to prove a great deal more difficult than some, but by no means all, had expected. With this decision, for better or worse, the Burmese emerged from their medieval backwater into the mainstream of world events. Before carrying the history of Burma forward through the British period, it is desirable to attempt to summarize what sort of country it was that the British took over.

Two reasons make it worth trying to do this in some detail. In the first place, it will only be of interest to describe in the later chapters of this book Burma of the present day, if it can be shown how and why this contemporary society has developed out of the largely medieval community that was Burma less than a hundred years ago. In the second place, we may find that the Burma of today is, after all, not so different from that of the mid-nineteenth century.

The government – an oriental monarchy such as was found

63

throughout India before the advent of the British, and in many other parts of Asia also – consisted of the king, his Ministers, and the attendant court. The king's power was in theory absolute. The court, the Ministers, the judges, the provincial governors, all held office at the pleasure of the king – or, more often perhaps, at the pleasure of the king's favourites, of either sex. These themselves, however, could hope to retain their position only so long as they, by the use of charm, force of personality, flattery, servility, intrigue, or bribery, succeeded in safeguarding their own influence over the king from erosion by rivals. A mid-nineteenth-century observer described Burma as the most complete of oriental despotisms. Yet, in practice, there were extensive limitations, albeit of greatly varying effectiveness, upon what the king could do. First and foremost, custom and traditional etiquette carried great weight. Indeed, Hall believes that little or nothing had changed in the court ceremonies from the eleventh to the nineteenth centuries and that the nature of those in force at the court of Pagan may safely be deduced from the nature of those at the court of Ava. These forces must have been strongly conservative in their effect, have circumscribed the king's power of independent action, and have lent great support to the courtiers and Ministers around him in their natural desire to prevent any course of action that might disturb the existing order and their position in it.

Another powerful restraint upon the waywardness of the king was the Buddhist religion. Its tenets were, and still are, so widely and unquestioningly accepted as to create an atmosphere of opinion, accepted and recognized by king and people alike, that also effectively restricted the king's power of choice in many directions. This remains true notwithstanding the blatant disregard of the prohibition against taking life displayed in massacres for political or personal ends, on the accession of a new king, or at other times. Buddhism strongly and genuinely colours the outlook of all in Burma. In addition to the teachings of religion, the bare fact of the existence of the monastic order also frequently influenced the monarch. The king might be the head of the state in secular matters and the chief benefactor and defender of the religion, but he none the less, in spiritual matters, humbled himself before the monks, a mere man in the presence of superior beings. The influence exercised upon the king by the monks was great and for the most part good, although there were, not unnaturally, also cases of rulers falling victims to the personality of charlatans.

Furthermore, public opinion at large was apt to be far more effective, admittedly not in matters of detail, but in the last resort, in the final verdict whether the government was tolerable or not, than is suggested by the use of the word 'despotism'. The king's government was seldom strong enough to be effective, and if it wished to maintain its hold upon the country, and upon its revenues, it had to take some account of the feelings of the people and of the dangers of revolt by rivals seeking to make capital out of discontent.

Under King Mindon, in the eyes of Burmans the best of his line, government had been comparatively good, and humane. Conditions for the people of Burma at large had been far from unpleasant. Under King Thibaw they could hardly have been worse. Sir Charles Crosthwaite, a trained and observant administrator who became Chief Commissioner of Burma in 1887, writes:

'Thebaw was weak and incompetent . . . The rapacity and greed of the Court, where the Queen Supayalat was the ruling spirit, set the example to the whole hierarchy of officials. The result was a state of extreme disorder throughout the whole kingdom. The demands made on the people for money became excessive and intolerable. Men left their villages and took to the jungle. Bands of armed brigands, some of considerable strength under native leaders, sprang up everywhere. Formed in the first instance as a protest and defence against extortion, they soon began to live on the country and to terrorize the peasantry. After a time, brigands and Ministers, finding themselves working for a common object, formed an unholy alliance for loot. The leaders of the bands came to an understanding with the more powerful officials, who in turn leant upon them for support.'[1]

Even Fielding Hall, most sympathetic of writers to the Burmese, admits 'It would be difficult, I think, to imagine anything worse than the government of Upper Burma in its later days. I mean by "government" the King and his counsellors and the greater officials of the Empire.'[2]

The unpleasantness and insecurity of life in Burma under the king and court was reflected in the startling growth of population in those parts of the country that had passed under British control. The population of Arakan and Tenasserim rose from 170,000 in 1826 when they were annexed to 555,000 in 1855, thus trebling itself in a mere thirty years. The population of Pegu doubled itself in the shorter space of ten years, rising from 632,000 in 1852 to 1,351,000 in 1862. In both cases three-quarters of the increase was ascribed to immigration from independent Burma.[3] This was encouraged by the British in various ways because labour was needed to expand rice cultivation in Lower Burma. But this immigration is a fact that

---

[1] C. H. T. Crosthwaite, *The Pacification of Burma*, London, 1912, pp. 6–7.
[2] H. Fielding, *The Soul of a People*, London, 1898, p. 87.
[3] F. Burton Leach, *The Future of Burma*, Rangoon, 1937, pp. 26–7.

needs to be remembered when reading present-day Burmese accounts of the oppression and exploitation of which the British are now said to have been guilty in Burma. It does not seem to have appeared quite in this light at the time.

The king's Executive Council, the *Hlutdaw*, consisted of four or five Ministers appointed by the king and holding office at his pleasure. There was no allocation of portfolios, the Ministers, or *Wungyis*, being collectively responsible for all the business of the state. The Ministers were assisted by Assistant Ministers or *Wundauks*. The Council normally sat in public. Its decisions were recorded by *Sayedawgyis* (Royal Clerks) and promulgated by *Thandawzins* (Heralds). The Council, besides dealing with executive matters, was the ultimate Court of Appeal from the judges, whether in the civil or the criminal courts.

The king also had his personal staff and private secretaries known as *Atwinwuns*. These were, by protocol, of inferior rank to the Ministers, but their position within the palace, and frequent intimate contact with the king, gave them influence altogether out of proportion to their official standing.

There were two courts at the capital. In the *Yondaw* the *Myowuns* (or Governors of the city) dealt with important criminal cases. In the *Tayayon*, the civil court, the two *Tayathugyis* were appointed by the king and held office at his pleasure. Of the courts away from the capital we shall have more to say later.

There were, of course, countless other less important officials. Except that King Mindon attempted, but without much success because of lack of funds, to introduce a system of remuneration by salary, all these officials from the highest to the lowest, were remunerated by the allocation to them of the revenues of a district, which in apt Burmese parlance they 'ate'. Less important officials were remunerated by the allocation of land on the royal domain. These sources of income were augmented by such tolls, fees, commissions, or bribes as custom or the standing of the officials made it possible for them to collect. Gouger, who was at the court of Ava a little before the great days of Mindon, remarked that '. . . bribery is the mainspring by which all manner of business is moved throughout the country'.[1] Conditions may have improved a little in the time of King Mindon but it would be naïve to expect them to have been materially different in the time of his depraved successor King Thibaw. Indeed 'All these ministers and governors were corrupt; there was corruption to the core,' writes Fielding Hall.[2]

[1] H. Gouger, *Personal Narrative of Two Years' Imprisonment in Burmah*, London, 1860, p. 50.
[2] H. Fielding, op. cit., p. 88.

Outside the capital there was even greater variety and lack of uniformity. The country was divided into districts or provinces, some of which were almost sub-kingdoms, some territorially insignificant. The Provincial or District Governor, known as the *Myowun*, was appointed by the king, probably because he had been the most lavish or successful in his bribes, and like the Ministers at the centre, held office during the king's pleasure, which often meant until someone out-bribed him. His three chief assistants, probably also appointed by the king, were his deputy (the *Yewun*), the collector of taxes (the *Akunwun*), and the collector of customs (the *Akaukwun*). The *Myowun* and his three assistants together constituted the District or Provincial Council. As agents of the central government or of the king, the *Myowuns* enjoyed considerable power and authority. But as they were generally 'foreigners', if only in the sense of coming from other parts of Burma, and were liable to transfer, they had little local following, and could always be reported to the palace by local personages whom they had offended. In this way considerable restraint was imposed upon their otherwise extensive powers.

Below the provincial level, officials were local men and the roots of the administration ran down into the villages. Each village had its head or *Gaung*. Villages were grouped into circles or *Taiks* under a *Taikthugyi* or Circle Headman. Circles were grouped into townships under a *Myothugyi* or Township Headman. And the townships were under the immediate control of the Provincial Governors. But this tidy administrative pyramid was complicated by the fact that the jurisdictions of some headmen were occupational, not territorial – there might, for example, be headmen of salt-boilers, of charcoal-burners, of boatmen, or of fishermen. Some headmen's charges might be a combination of the territorial and the occupational. There was little uniformity. The *Gaungs* in the villages were appointed by the *Taikthugyi*, and were little more than village policemen whose duties extended to all administrative matters, but whose independent authority was not great. The *Taikthugyi* and the *Myothugyi* above him (but sometimes the *Taikthugyi* was not subordinate to the *Myothugyi*, the two designations then becoming alternative titles for officials of somewhat similar rank) were men of substance and local standing, and succession to these offices tended to be hereditary, at least in a family, if not always from father to son. These headmen enjoyed considerable authority, in the collection of revenue, in the administration of justice, and in the executive control of their charges. Furthermore, there was a feudal character about their functions and powers, for the *Myothugyis* were also commanders of the regiments formed of those men who lived in villages, and held land in the *Myothugyis'* charges, on condition of rendering military or other service whenever required. In regard to the regiment which he commanded, the *Myothugyi* exercised special powers and responsibilities for the maintenance of discipline and the settlement of disputes.

The *Myothugyi* has been described as 'the backbone of the social administration in Upper Burma'[1] and there seems little doubt that at the level of the village and the *Myo*, Burma enjoyed a reasonably stable, continuous administration, firmly based on custom, religion, and personal authority. If government at the centre was bad, government in the villages was a very great deal better.

But even against a vicious government the people enjoyed certain safeguards. The central government, in a country of great distances and poor communications, with no police force or regular army, and with a feudal 'territorial' army probably more loyal to its immediate commander, the *Myothugyi*, than to the king, was generally ineffective and frequently unable to enforce excessively oppressive measures. As for the provincial governments, in a thinly populated country with much cultivable land unused, if conditions in one place became intolerable it was an easy matter to move elsewhere.

Sir Charles Crosthwaite writes:

'In a country which is under-populated and contains vast areas of land fit for cultivation unoccupied and free to all, migration is a great check on oppression. Life is simple in Burma. The climate for the most of the year makes a roof unnecessary; flitting is easy. Everyman is his own carpenter. He has put together his house of bamboo and planks cut by his own hands. He knows how to take it down. He has not to send for contractors or furniture vans. There are the carts and the plough cattle in his sheds. He has talked things over with his wife, who is a capable and a sensible woman.

One morning they get up, and instead of going to his fields or his fishing or whatever it may be, he takes his tools, and before sunset, his wife helping, the house is down and, with the simple household goods, is in the cart. The children find a place in it, or if they are old enough they run along with the mother. If the local magistrate is so blind to his own interests as to oppress his people, there is another wiser man a few score leagues away who is ready to welcome them. For what is the good of land without men to live on it? Is not the King's revenue assessed at so much to the house? But suppose the worst comes to the worst and the man in power is a fiend, and neither property nor life nor honour is safe from him, even then there is the great forest, in which life, though

[1] D. G. E. Hall, op. cit., p. 134.

hard, is a real pleasure to a man; and, given a good leader, the oppressed may soon change places with his oppressor.

We are too ready to imagine that life under such a King as Mindon or even as Thibaw must be unbearable. We fancy them armed with all the organization of the Inland Revenue Department and supported by a force like our constabulary. Fortunately they were not . . .'[1]

If we turn to the economy of Burma, the most striking fact is that there was virtually no external trade. Partly this resulted from the geographical isolation of the country. Partly it sprang from deliberate policy of the Burmese kings who placed severe restrictions both on the export of the country's resources, and on the activities of foreign traders – experience with some of the early European adventurers, such as De Brito, had justifiably left deep suspicion of their activities. Such a policy was made practicable by the variety of climate and the large reserves of unused cultivable land enjoyed by Burma which together created complete self-sufficiency in all the country's, fairly simple, requirements, especially in the matter of food. Furthermore, at the time of the annexation of Upper Burma, there were few commodities produced by the country which interested the outer world – excepting only teak which had for long been favoured for shipbuilding. The absence of external trade meant also that there was in Burma no trading class, or at least no such class of any wealth and influence, and consequently none of that knowledge of the ways of the outer world that comes with the existence of such a class.

Internally, Burma was almost entirely agricultural, a country of villages and a nation of villagers. There were few cities – it is probably fair to say there were none, for even the capital was much more an overgrown village than a town. It was true at the time of the annexation, and is probably still true now, that the Burmese have never learnt to live in cities. In the matter of food, Burma produced ample supplies of rice, millet, fruit, vegetables, vegetable oils, fish, and salt. In the matter of clothing she grew her own cotton, imported raw silk, and wove these in the villages. As for housing, bamboo, timber, and thatching materials grew in every forest, of which there were vast areas easily accessible. Timber for ploughs, carts, and boats was obtainable from the same sources. Pottery, tools, weapons were made in the country. There was specialization to the extent that cotton, oil-seeds, and some rice were grown in Upper Burma, while fish, salt, and virtually limitless quantities of rice were supplied by Lower Burma. The country's internal trade was built on the exchange of these commodities up and down the great and

[1] Crosthwaite, op. cit., pp. 5–6.

picturesque trade route of the Irrawaddy. Apart from this interchange, each village was largely self-sufficient.

There were few large towns and certainly no industries other than
village crafts such as weaving, pottery, and iron-working.

Money scarcely entered into this economy. Taxes were paid in
kind or by the rendering of service. Other transactions were largely
conducted by barter. Indeed there was very little minted money in
circulation. If barter was not possible payment tended to be through
the medium of silver bullion. This was valued by Assayers or *Pwèzas*.
The value both of the commodity to be bought, and of the 'money'
with which payment was to be made, could be established only by a
process of bargaining for each.

In this economic system the laws of supply and demand doubtless
exercised some influence upon what a man received in payment for
his work. But custom and the general opinion of what was a fair
payment played a far larger part than the blind and impersonal
economic forces which, with the arrival of the British, were to flow
into Burma from the turbulent oceans of the Western capitalist
system.

The social structure of Burma will have emerged, in part at least,
from the preceding description of her government and economy. At
the centre were the king and his family, surrounded by his court and
Ministers, all dependent upon the king for the continuance of their
position and livelihood, many of them toadies of the worst description. But however bad the monarchy and the court were administratively, they nevertheless provided a focus for feelings of loyalty
and national pride, and maintained standards, or at the least
aspirations, in the fields of taste and culture. Above all they provided
a symbol of Burmese nationhood.

At the circumference were the villages, where probably 90 per
cent of the people lived. Here, in contrast to the corrupt and
decadent centre, were vigorous local communities. The mainspring
of these was provided by the headmen or *Thugyis*, men of substance
and standing, eligible generally for their office on hereditary qualifications, but actually chosen in many cases with some regard for
popular preference. In the villages there would be few rich men,
and no great landowners. Most of the villagers would be cultivating
what was in effect their own land – though the tenures on which
the land was held might impose certain duties and responsibilities –
and the result was a sturdy, independent peasantry. There would be
a shop or two and a few petty traders, though most buying and
selling would be conducted in the market, held perhaps daily, perhaps once in five days. Lastly, there would be a monastery, in larger
villages perhaps several, with a monk or monks, and in the monas-

tery a school for the children of the village. Indeed, school and
monastery are the same word in Burmese. In these communities
rights, duties, social relations, were governed very largely by habit
and custom. The villages were largely self-sufficient communities,
not only economically, but also in dealing with local problems, in
preserving order, and in settling disputes. There was probably little
contact with the centre except when the required proportion of the
revenues collected was remitted to headquarters, or if, in an emergency, the local militia was called out, under its commander, the
Thugyi. Between the court and the villages there was no aristocracy
and very little in the way of a middle class.

This simple system worked well. Fielding Hall, who lived and
worked in Upper Burma for a short while before the annexation, as
an employee of the Bombay-Burmah Trading Corporation, and then
served as a government officer after the annexation, writes:
'Each village was to a very great extent a self-governing community composed of men free in every way . . .

So each village managed its own affairs, untroubled by squire
or priest, very little troubled by the state. That within their little
means they did it well, no one can doubt. They taxed themselves
without friction, they built their own monastery schools by voluntary effort, they maintained a very high, a very simple, code of
morals, entirely of their own initiative.'[1]
A less committed observer, Sir Charles Crosthwaite, writes:
'The really stable part of the administration on which everything
rested was the village . . .

The headman of each village, assisted by a committee . . . settled
the sum [of taxes] due from each householder, and this was as a
rule honestly and fairly done . . .

As to the administration of justice between man and man and
the security of life and property, there was no doubt little refinement of law and not always impartiality in the judges. The
majority of civil cases in a society like Burma, where there are
few rich men and no great landowners, must be trivial, and in
Burma disputes were settled by arbitration or by the village headmen, who could rarely set at nought the opinion of their fellow-
villagers.'[2]
The religion, the arts, and the crafts of the Burma of 1885 are
discussed in a later chapter,[3] for it has seemed more intelligible to
deal with these in one rather than two places and to include the past
together with the present.

[1] op. cit., pp. 96, 100.
[2] op. cit., pp. 4, 5.
[3] See below, p. 216.

Education, apart from a very few Burmese lay schools and foreign mission schools, was confined to that given by the monks. On the other hand, this education, for what it amounted to, was very widespread, for it was a matter not only of educational but of social and religious routine for all boys to attend the monastic schools and to spend some time in the monastic order. For girls, education was less universal though it still compared well with that in many neighbouring countries. As a result, the bare ability to read, write, and count was probably more general in Burma than in neighbouring countries. In this limited sense Burma could, not unfairly, claim to be a literate country. Apart from these rudiments, however, monastic teaching consisted almost entirely of the learning and repetition, parrotwise, of the Buddhist scriptures, consisting for the most part of the mythological cosmogony and moral principles of the Buddhist religion. There was, indeed, nothing else that most of the monks were fitted to teach, although there was also some study of astrology, alchemy, and medicine. And of what they taught the monks can themselves have understood little. Good standards of decency and conduct were inculcated, and very generally observed, village opinion reinforcing the teaching of the monks. But of what was happening elsewhere in the world, or of any other subjects, little or nothing was known or taught. This was to pose a problem for the British when they arrived and assumed responsibility for Upper Burma. There will be fuller references to education again in a later chapter.[1]

In the world at large, the chief characteristic of Burma was isolation, political as well as economic. The physical features of the country and the absence of communications with the outer world were the direct cause of this, and also, through their influence upon the character of the Burmese people, an indirect cause. Relations with China to the north-east were compounded of respect and fear; the intelligence, industry, and determination of the Chinese were well appreciated; so was the size and ultimate power of their country. But, in fact, Burma, though she had often been invaded, had never been subjugated by the Chinese. As for India to the north-west, the Burmese have never felt anything but contempt for her people, largely because of their joyless poverty and lower standard of living. As to the British government of that country, they consistently failed to appreciate its fundamental strength, since there was little outward warlike display, and since the hidden resources of sea-power were altogether incomprehensible to them. As for other neighbours, Siam was an old sparring-partner, respected and understood; but in the latest encounters between these two, Burma had prevailed. It was therefore not surprising that the Burmese enjoyed an altogether exaggerated idea of their own power and importance in the world of nations.

Internally, that part of Burma inhabited by the Burmese proper was fairly effectively unified, not by any administrative achievement, or even by the authority of the king, but by a common language, culture, religion, and pride of race – though it should be added that recent events have shown that fusion of the Mons with the Burmese was not so complete as the Burmese claimed and most outside observers judged it to be. But, as we have seen earlier, a great part of what was politically claimed to be Burma was not inhabited by Burmese, and we need to note the relations of the Burmese king with these territories.

There were, first, the Shans. These were governed by their own chiefs known as *Sawbwas, Myosas,* or *Ngwegunhmus,* some thirty in number. These were nominally subject to the king, but in fact very largely independent so long as they paid their fixed tribute to him – tribute which in the case of Kengtung, the most remote state, consisted of large and small gold flowers, large and small silver flowers, gold ornaments for pony trappings, silver ornaments for pony trappings, and other items of less value and aesthetic or antiquarian interest. Over a few of the nearer states the Burmese exercised somewhat more positive control.

Of the Karens, some had settled within Burmese-controlled territory, but three small states in the mountains south of the Shan States, Kantarawadi, Bawlake, and Kyebogyi, claimed independence. This was recognized by the British but not conceded by the Burmese, whose attitude was not fundamentally modified despite an agreement entered into with the British in 1875 to recognize the independence of these Karen states.

Chins and Kachins were warlike peoples living in the northern mountains and organized on a tribal basis, over whom the Burmese rarely, if ever, established any effective control.

It is difficult to say what was the attitude of the Burmese towards the monarchy. It is hard to believe that there can have been much loyalty to the last king, Thibaw, for he was about as heartless a tyrant as can be imagined. Figures have been given earlier for the numbers of Burmese subjects who had fled across the boundary into the British portions of Burma from the time of their annexation. But for Thibaw's predecessor, Mindon, it is clear that there was considerable respect, affection, and a positive loyalty. And notwithstanding the Burmese saying that 'fire, water, foes, robbers, rulers – these are the five great evils', and notwithstanding a general healthy scepticism regarding the merits of any government (or perhaps just because of the latter) there can be no doubt that, given the choice, the Burmese, like anyone else, would have preferred a government of their own, however bad, to one imposed by a foreign people. If the strength of this feeling had not been appreciated by the British before the annexation, it soon became clear during the strenuous years that followed, while the new administration was being established.

Chapter 5

The British Administrative System

THE DECISION IN 1886 not to re-establish or continue the Burmese monarchy meant that, for better or worse, the whole of Burma became a part of the Indian administrative system.[1] Already this had happened to Arakan and Tenasserim when they were annexed after the First Burmese War in 1824. Both were at first placed under the direct control of the Governor-General. But Arakan was soon incorporated into the adjoining Presidency of Bengal, at first as a part of the Chittagong Division, later as a separate division with a commissioner of its own. Tenasserim became a division with a commissioner, at first under the control of the Governor of Prince of Wales Island, at Penang. Later it was placed under the direct control of the Governor-General, but later still, in 1834, it was placed under Bengal in judicial and revenue matters, though remaining under the Governor-General in other respects. After the second Burmese War of 1852, the Burmese provinces of Pegu and Martaban were annexed. A commissioner was placed in charge of the Pegu Division, under the direct control of the Governor-General. Martaban was added to the charge of the Commissioner, Tenasserim. The whole of what later came to be known as Lower Burma had become a part of British India, under three commissioners. Each of these held a slightly different administrative position; the Commissioner of Arakan was under the full control of the local government of Bengal, the Commissioner of Pegu was under the full control of the central government of India, and the Commissioner of Tenasserim was in a middle position, under both these governments for different purposes.

In 1862 these anomalies were removed and those parts of Burma which had been annexed to the Indian Empire were constituted into a separate province of British Burma, independent of Bengal but under the government of India. The Commissioners of Arakan, Pegu, and Tenasserim were subordinated to a Chief Commissioner responsible direct to the Governor-General. The annexation of the kingdom of Burma, after the Third Burmese War of 1885, more

[1] A more detailed study of what this was and how it was applied to Burma can be found in the author's *Public Administration in Burma*, published in 1953 by the Royal Institute of International Affairs.

than doubled the Chief Commissioner's area of responsibility. The
newly added territory was divided into four commissioners' divisions.
The whole of Burma had now been brought within the British-
Indian system.

In 1886 the Burmese government surrendered, its country was
annexed, and the monarchy was abolished. With few exceptions the
Burmese administrative officers, and the headmen under them,
accepted the new masters, not only without opposition – this is not
surprising for, indeed, they had not the resources with which to
oppose – but, so far as can be judged, not unwillingly. Similarly, the
majority of the people accepted the new situation not unwillingly –
to the Burmese all governments are evil and the new government
might even prove better than that of Thibaw; indeed it could hardly
be worse. But throughout the newly annexed territory there were
numerous armed gangs at large, robbing, raiding, resisting the
annexation forces, partly because they were foreign, partly because
they were seeking to put down disorder in which the gangs had a
vested interest, most frequently, perhaps, fighting each other. For
some five years after both the Second and the Third Burmese Wars,
but especially after the latter, there followed a period of what, by
the British, was euphemistically described as 'pacification'. The
Burmese now, also euphemistically, describe the members of these
gangs as 'undaunted patriots'.[1]

Harvey is probably much nearer the truth when he writes: 'But
the brigands who had swarmed under Thibaw's misrule were now
joined by his disbanded soldiery and by the more spirited peasantry
who could not abide the thought of foreign rule.'[2] Pacification meant
the hunting-down of these gangs by small parties of, mainly, Indian
troops with a British officer in command and, wherever possible, a
British civil officer attached whose task it was to establish contact
with township or circle headmen and other prominent persons, and
to bring into being some sort of rudimentary administration, using
whenever possible the existing headmen and administrative officers.
Much of this work was humanely done. But in such conditions of
anarchy and disorder, a government seeking to establish its authority
is easily driven to brutalities that would not be committed or
tolerated in more settled times – as the Burmese government itself
has found since gaining independence of the British. And there are
inevitably in armies and police forces persons harsher and more
cruel than the rest. In the first few months there were executions
without trials, indiscriminate and brutal, and not a few shocking

---

[1] *Burma's Fight for Freedom*, p. 27.
[2] G. E. Harvey, *British Rule in Burma 1824–1942*, London, 1946, pp.
22–3.

incidents. These were progressively stopped as the British civil officers arrived and established control. The country was not peaceful during the process of pacification. But by degrees the new government established itself, partly by creating fear, partly by competent firmness, most of all, perhaps, by the personal qualities and influence of its officers. There followed a period during which order was better maintained than at any other time in the history of Burma, before or after. It became possible to travel freely and with little danger throughout the country. The government was incomparably more authoritative and effective than any other that Burma has ever known. (Indeed it is probably necessary that a foreign government should be so, if it is to survive, lacking the reserves of popular support deriving from tradition, history, and patriotism that an indigenous government can draw upon, however incompetent or evil it may be.) This new government succeeded in attracting a very high degree of loyalty from its Burmese officers and subordinate officials, and was not at all unwillingly accepted by the people of the country. But, of course, it was foreign, despite the fact that the great majority of government servants were Burmese. For all higher appointments in the government were held by British officers and all real power in Burma was concentrated in them. It is true that these officers were themselves controlled from above, but this was from India or, in the last resort, from London, and this remote control was even more foreign, and in addition lacked personal contact with the people of Burma and their problems.

The description that follows of the British-Indian system, as it was applied to Burma, is to some extent a composite picture; for all its features did not necessarily co-exist at any given moment. It seeks to convey a broadly correct representation of the system at its hey-day – say in 1909. A picture more meticulously accurate for any precise moment would be wearisome and indeed of less value to the reader, in the present context.

Originally, and in essence, the system was direct administration built round the hierarchy of the Chief Commissioner, the commissioners, and the deputy commissioners, each responsible within their charges – the province, the divisions, and the districts – for all aspects of government. This bare framework was soon expanded and modified, but its essential principle of centralized responsibility survived. The author has written elsewhere:

'In the East there is a tradition of personal authority which enables the ordinary citizen to make his not-very-complicated contacts with one local head and representative of the government. Not only is this convenient to him, but any other arrangement is illogical and unrealistic to the mind of one who looks upon the law, not as an abstract conception governing both himself and the government of the country, but merely as one of the weapons which the government may employ against himself. For the executive head of the district and representative of the government to disclaim responsibility for, or authority to interfere in, a considerable portion of the official business of his district appeared to the Burman as disingenuous, or at the best as a device of the government to make things more difficult for him, and to make it possible for the government to avoid action by playing off one functionary against another. Furthermore, in a society where peace and orderly administration depended so much upon the authority and respect enjoyed by the government (which in most parts meant the Deputy Commissioner of the district) it was preferable to concentrate rather than to disperse authority and to arm the representative of government in a district with as much power and as many sources of influence as possible.'[1]

The Chief Commissioner was from an early stage assisted by an Inspector-General of Police, a Chief Engineer, and the heads of other specialist departments, such as the medical, education, forest, and customs departments, though ultimate responsibility for the work of these departments remained on him. He remained directly and personally responsible, however, for judicial and revenue matters and for all other unassigned functions of government. To assist him in the discharge of his duties over the whole field of government he was provided with a secretariat containing a small but increasing number of officers. All officers so far mentioned were British; most of the clerical staff were Indian – an aspect of the administration that will be more fully discussed later.[2]

In 1872, ten years after the constitution of the province of British Burma, a judicial commissioner was appointed to relieve the Chief Commissioner of his judicial functions. The Judicial Commissioner was exempted from control by the Chief Commissioner, a first small step towards application of the principle of the separation of the judicial and executive functions of government which led ultimately to the establishment of a High Court in Rangoon whose judges were appointed by His Majesty, not by the Governor-General, and were irremovable. In 1890 a judicial commissioner was appointed for the newly annexed Upper Burma. In 1888 a financial commissioner had been appointed to relieve the Chief Commissioner of his revenue functions. Unlike the Judicial Commissioner the Financial Commissioner remained under the general control of the Chief Commissioner.

[1] F. S. V. Donnison, *Public Administration in Burma*, London, 1953, p. 41.
[2] See below, p. 90.

In 1897 the Chief Commissioner was elevated to the rank of Lieutenant-Governor. Specialist departments multiplied; the Secretariat expanded. The significant development resulting from this elevation was that the Lieutenant-Governor was furnished with a Legislative Council. For the first time since the application of the British administrative system to Burma it was possible to enact legislation for Burma in Burma. Admittedly, the Council consisted of four officials and five nominated non-officials, there were no elected members at all, and its powers were strictly circumscribed. In 1909 and 1915 the size of the Council was increased, but the only two elected members were chosen by the Burma Chamber of Commerce, the representative organization of British business in Burma, and by the Rangoon Trades Association, the organization of the European retail trade. There was no self-government whatever for the people of Burma. But the elective principle had been allowed to creep in.

Under the Chief Commissioner (later the Lieutenant-Governor) came the commissioners of divisions, of whom after the annexation of Upper Burma there were at first seven, later eight, each controlling some five deputy commissioners in charge of districts. In theory commissioners at first exercised all functions of government in their charges. In practice, the commissioners' divisions never acquired the individuality which distinguished the deputy commissioners' districts. Partly this was because most districts had a long local history and character of their own, whereas divisions originated in little more than administrative convenience. Partly it was that the courts were organized, police forces were recruited, and justice was administered on the basis of the districts, not the divisions. From 1905 onwards commissioners were progressively relieved of their judicial functions. Ultimately their chief concern came to be with the collection of the revenue, the administration of the land, and with local government. And even in regard to these remaining functions they tended to become appellate and inspecting authorities interposed between the headquarters government and the districts, rather than executive officers.

The backbone of the administration in the field was provided by the deputy commissioners in charge of districts, of which there were about forty. The deputy commissioner in his own charge was the agent of government, in all aspects. Specialist departments were represented at his level as required – police, public works, medical, education, forests. For the work of the specialists the deputy commissioner retained a general responsibility, particularly as it might affect his basic responsibility for preserving order and administering the law, although in technical matters the specialists were subordinated to their own specialist officers at headquarters in Rangoon. For law and order, for the assessment and collection of the revenue, and for the control of the village headmen who had by now replaced the circle and township headmen of the Burmese system, the deputy commissioner remained directly and personally responsible. The substitution of village headmen and of village tracts for the circle or township headmen and their larger charges sprang from applying to Burma experience of Indian conditions where the basic social and political unit was the village or group of hamlets within sight or hail of each other. It had two objects: to maintain and strengthen the village tract; and to use this unit in the restoration of order by enforcing the joint responsibility of the village community for crimes committed within the tract. The change was unfortunate because it sacrificed what were possibly the most vital indigenous social and political units to the insatiable desire of all governments to make uniform that which was not so.

A typical district would compare with a large English county in area. Its population would be much less, numbering 300,000 to 500,000. It would be divided into some 300 village tracts, each with a village headman in charge. The village headman would be responsible for collecting taxes, organizing the defence of his village against robbers or predatory gangs, trying petty criminal cases, calling in the police in more serious crime, keeping records of births and deaths and of vaccinations performed, reporting serious diseases of humans or cattle, keeping the township officer, the subdivisional officer, and the deputy commissioner informed of conditions in his charge, and, in brief, seeing to the general administration of his village. Village tracts would be grouped into, say, six townships with a township officer in charge of each. Townships would be grouped into two or three subdivisions with subdivisional officers in charge, responsible directly to the deputy commissioner. Again, subdivisional officers and township officers were responsible, under the control of the deputy commissioner, for all functions of government within their charges -- the maintenance of order, the administration of justice, the assessment and collection of the revenue, the inspection and control of the work of village headmen. The deputy commissioner and some of the heads of specialist departments at his headquarters would be British. One of the subdivisional officers might be British. Other officers would be Burmese with a sprinkling of Anglo-Burmans and Indians. Office staffs -- the deputy commissioner's own office would number about fifty -- would be predominantly Burmese but with a disproportionate number of Indians, particularly in departments dealing with accounts. Centralization of responsibility in the deputy commissioner was the key to the system, so that the governed could see their governor, and go to him with any grievance. Whatever might happen in his district was in some degree the concern of the deputy commissioner, either directly, or indirectly through his specialist officers.

Village headmen were local men of standing and substance, part-time officers remunerated by commission on taxes collected by them. The township officers and all other officers of the general administration above them, right up to the Lieutenant-Governor himself, were whole-time, salaried, civil servants, liable to transfer anywhere within the province in accordance with the 'exigencies of the service.' Some 130 of these officers were members of the Indian Civil Service, since Burma was at this time a province of India. They were recruited in the United Kingdom, by open competitive examination, and were at this time all Europeans. United Kingdom qualifications and standards of pay applied to them. They were members of an all-India service, theoretically but not normally liable to transfer outside the province of their choice, though from time to time an officer might be required for service with the central government of India. These officers filled all the more important posts in the general administration, serving at headquarters, in the Secretariat, or in the field as commissioners, and deputy commissioners, as judges, and in a variety of junior posts. In the early stages, until there had been time to build up the establishment of the Indian Civil Service, a proportion of these officers was recruited by secondment of British military officers to civil duty, a proportion which decreased as civilians became available. In addition to this all-India service, there was a provincial service whose members were recruited in Burma, on local qualifications and standards of pay, for service in Burma only. This service was divided into two grades, the Burma civil service, which in the main filled posts of subdivisional officers, and the subordinate civil service which in the main filled posts of township officers. The strength of the Burma civil service was about 180; that of the subordinate civil service about 400. The greater number of the members of these two services were Burmese (or of other indigenous race), but there was a sprinkling of Indians, Anglo-Indians, and Anglo-Burmans especially in the Burma civil service. The specialist departments were in general staffed in a similar two-tier fashion, by an all-India service recruited in the United Kingdom, and a provincial service recruited within Burma from persons domiciled in the country.

The Shan States constituted an exception to the system of direct administration established elsewhere in Burma. As we have seen earlier[1] the chiefs of these states, some thirty in number, were, at the

[1] See above, p. 73.

time of the abolition of the monarchy in Mandalay, technically subject to the Burmese kings but in fact very largely independent so
long as they paid their tribute. After annexation the British government of Burma held itself to have inherited this constitutional position – though it required some spirited, if miniature, military
expeditions to enforce it. Once it had been established that the chiefs
were subject to the government of British Burma, they were confirmed in their offices and allowed to continue to govern their states
subject to the payment of tribute, and provided that their administration attained certain modest standards of competence and
decency. In constitutional theory, there was a difference between
their status and that of the Indian princes, since these were not
subjects of the Indian government and their relations with that
government were regulated by treaties. In administrative practice,
however, the position of the Shan chiefs was not so dissimilar. Chiefs,
or groups of chiefs, were required to accept a representative of the
government of Burma whose business it was to observe and, in case
of egregious maladministration, to bring pressure upon the chief
concerned to mend his ways. Administration was indirect also in the
hill areas inhabited by Chins, Kachins, Nagas, and others of non-
Burmese race. There were also three small Karenni states which,
though in most respects far more primitive than the Shan States, had
been jointly recognized by the British government in Lower Burma
and, albeit reluctantly and without conviction, by the Burmese
government, as being independent. These, after the annexation of
Upper Burma, entered into treaty relations with the British government of Burma, these treaties according them status constitutionally
not unlike that of the Indian princes.

In the field of local government forty-four towns had been constituted municipalities by 1909, with municipal committees most of
whose members were elected, though a proportion was nominated
by the provincial government. Sixteen town funds had been constituted and were administered by local officers of the provincial
government with the help of advisory committees. The functions of
these various local authorities included the provision of education up
to a certain level, the making of a contribution towards medical
services, the provision of markets and slaughterhouses, the construction and maintenance of minor roads, the licensing of pawnshops,
sometimes the provision of a water supply, and the sanitation of the
towns. Their revenues were mostly derived from taxes on house
property, market-stall rents, and fees for the issue of various licences,
e.g. for vehicles. Where there were no municipal authorities, responsibility for providing these services remained on the officers of the
provincial government. At the village level local government con-

tinued much as it ever had. The authority of the village headman was recognized and confirmed to require villagers to aid in clearing and maintaining paths, in looking after wells, and in providing burial grounds; and he was made responsible for reporting cases of disease. In fact life in the villages went on much as in the past, with an occasional tidying-up for the visits of European or other officers passing through on tours of inspection.

The overwhelming majority of the members of this administration set up by the British from India, was Burmese. But the system was made to work by the centralization of responsibility and power in the framework provided by the Chief Commissioner–commissioner–deputy commissioner hierarchy. These officers were at this stage all British. And they were ultimately and exclusively responsible to the government of India, to the British government, and to parliament in London. The co-operation, service, and advice of the Burmese were sought, with remarkable success, but they were given little or no part in the formulation of policy. It was a highly centralized and paternalistic system, not at all unlike that imposed by the Burmese kings – except that it was vastly more effective (and to that extent more burdensome) and of course, that it was imposed by foreigners. It could not altogether free itself from the taint of corruption, but it set, and on the whole maintained, higher standards.

In 1917 the end of this brief period of virtually undiluted bureaucracy was heralded by the announcement in parliament by the Secretary of State for India that

'the policy of His Majesty's Government, with which the Government of India are in complete accord, is that of the increasing association of Indians [and Burma was, of course, a part of India and Burmans Indians for the purpose of this statement] in every branch of the administration, and the gradual development of self-governing institutions, with a view to the progressive realization of responsible government in India as an integral part of the British Empire'.

From this time on the British were committed to the ultimate, but perhaps distant, goal of sharing power and responsibility. The subsequent march of events will be told in the next chapter, treating of the growth of nationalism as a political force. But before doing this we should see what sort of a thing it was that the British had created in Burma, its merits and demerits, and the way in which it influenced the life of Burma.

A prime function of any government is the administration of justice. In criminal matters the law administered was the law of British India which was itself a codification based on British law. This did not, *ipso facto*, make the law inappropriate to Burmese conditions for there was no great disagreement between Britons and Burmans as to what acts should be punished – killing, wounding, robbing, stealing, cheating were criminal acts to both. But differences tended to develop as to how these offences should be punished, the Burman feeling that offences against the person were more serious than offences against property, the Briton being inclined to take the opposite view. And to Buddhists capital punishment, even for murder and after fair trial, was abhorrent – an attitude that foreigners had difficulty in reconciling with the ruthless massacres, so frequent in Burmese history, of totally innocent persons, merely because it was their misfortune to be of the royal kin.

In civil matters the intention of the British was to administer the law of the country. But this immediately brought them up against great difficulties. The first was to discover what that law was; the second (which stultified attempts at discovery) was that British and Burmese conceptions of law were fundamentally different. To take the second of these difficulties first, the British conception of law was of rules which, whether customary or statutory, were readily ascertainable, clear cut, and mandatory in application. The Burmese thought of law rather as broad general principles expressed, sometimes only suggested, in the traditional laws of Manu, and in the decisions of kings, and to be applied only to the extent that they commended themselves as reasonable in all the circumstances. When British jurists sought in the Burmese books for a code of law, they were looking for something that was not there. When they questioned Burmans, it seemed that the latter did not know their own law. And when the British tried to codify what they found they inevitably distorted it by giving it a rigidity and authority that had never been intended.

With this difference of attitude as to what the law was, went a not unconnected difference of outlook as to the procedure for its enforcement, in both civil and criminal matters. According to British thinking the function of a judge is to apply the established and ascertainable law to the facts of the case before him. To the Burmese his function is rather to reach a compromise that can be considered reasonable within the elastic framework of the law, and that will be accepted by the parties to the case. Indeed the whole conception of the law is of something to be negotiated, rather than of something to be imposed by the authority of the court. The function of the court is that of an arbitrator or conciliator rather than that of a judge. The British felt themselves to be engaged in a crusade to introduce the conception of absolute justice, the impartial rule of law. For the Burmese, although some of the law introduced was intelligible, much remained an artificial system imposed from above, without roots in Burmese attitudes, destructive of established social and economic customs. The system came to be treated as a game to be played to win, according to rules that made little real sense to the Burmese, but which, if mastered, held the possibility of gain, and which in any case had to be reckoned with, as the British insisted upon administering them. Since the system involved the administration of a set of rules, rather than the negotiation of a compromise, it inflated the importance of those who had learnt the rules – the lawyers. The artificiality of the system, together with the vested interest of the lawyers, led to a lamentable growth of litigiousness. This cynical utilization of a set of rules for selfish, if not improper, ends was the result of enforcing a system without indigenous roots. We shall see precisely the same thing happening when another set of alien rules was later introduced, those of Western parliamentary democracy.

We need to look for a moment at the revenue system established by the British. Throughout the Far East, in Burma as well as in India, from time immemorial, the most important, or one of the most important, of the sources of government revenue has been a share in the produce of the land. Under the British this continued as the main tax. Others were a capitation tax in Lower Burma, an equivalent tax first introduced by King Mindon, on property in Upper Burma, royalties on timber and minerals, excise duties on opium and alcohol, stamp duties, and customs duties. Later a tax on income was imposed which gradually increased until it yielded almost half as much as the land revenue. But initially and for some time afterwards, land revenue was the most important of these taxes. This was not in principle a new tax. But whereas the Burmese government had taken it in kind, or in the form of service to the Crown, at rates that were largely customary, the British required payment in hard cash. Holdings were demarcated and surveyed. A record of rights and interests was compiled. Acre rates of tax were fixed which varied according to crop, soil, and distance from markets. The resultant tax was payable by the occupier of the land in cash. This system distributed the burden of taxation with considerable accuracy and fairness for rice-growing land but with far less accuracy for other crops, despite the meticulous methods of assessment employed. On the whole, however, accuracy and justice and a great increase in the revenue were gained without placing oppressive burdens on any portion of the community. On the other hand, since the greater effectiveness of the new government made the evasion of tax-payment more difficult, its demands were apt to feel more burdensome than those of the Burmese government. And the destruction of the old-established, indigenous, social fabric based on well-known customary duties and payment in kind, was a loss that it is not possible to measure against pecuniary gains. The other taxes were all of kinds to which the Burmese were not unaccustomed, though again all were probably felt to be more burdensome, because more effectively collected. The only exception was the income tax when this came to be levied. This was a new and unfamiliar levy. But its collection was very largely confined to government servants, and the foreign firms and their employees. The number of Burmese who paid this tax was small.

The Burmese gained the exactitude and integrity of the tax system. But they had to pay for what many must have felt to be inappropriate perfectionism. Here particularly, perhaps, was there justification for the remark of the Retrenchment Committee in 1938 that a Ford country cannot afford a Rolls-Royce administration – though this remark was more particularly directed against the employment of Europeans by the government, which had, of course, to be on European scales of pay.

The economy of Burma, before annexation by the British, was, as we have seen earlier,[1] a predominantly agricultural subsistence economy. There were virtually no exports or imports, and Burma grew enough rice and other essential foodstuffs for her own needs and no more, isolated from the rest of the world inside her political frontiers, which largely coincided with the physical barriers to intercourse. The inclusion of Burma within the British Empire meant the pulling-down of the political frontiers, so far as British subjects were concerned. This facilitated access to Burma by sea, which outflanked the physical barriers that existed on land. In regard to the economy of Burma, these changes meant throwing open the door to the entry of Indians, of British trading or industrial firms, and of *laissez-faire* economic principles, so giving unrestricted play to the power of capital and the forces of supply and demand. Not surprisingly, the effect on the economy of Burma was revolutionary and in some ways disastrous.

But these new factors came into operation only gradually. It was the opening of the Suez Canal in 1869, shortening and cheapening the journey between Britain and Burma, that really set them moving. There was in the delta of the Irrawaddy a vast area of swamp and jungle that was potentially good rice land. So long as there was no market for exports of rice there was no incentive to undertake the arduous task of bringing this land under cultivation. With the opening of the Suez Canal and the establishment soon after by British firms of regular sea communication between Burma, India, and Europe a market for rice began to open up first in India, later in

[1] See above, pp. 69–70.

Europe. A market also opened in Burma for British manufactures. The possibility of profits from the cultivation of rice in excess of the subsistence level was realized, and a rush began from all over Burma, to stake out claims in the delta, to clear the jungle and reclaim the swamps. This was arduous and slow work and years might pass before there were any profits. It was seldom the original pioneer who enjoyed them. There was need for finance and there was need for labour. Indians flooded in to supply both, Chettyars, money-lenders, from Madras, and coolie-labour from Madras and other parts of India. Meanwhile British trading firms established them-selves in Rangoon to handle exports, and the imports which these bought. The new trade expanded phenomenally. The value of exports rose from Rs.30 million at the time of the opening of the Canal to Rs.159 million about 1900, Rs.389 million in 1913–14, and Rs.659 million in 1926–27. Allowance for changes in the value of money does not materially affect this trend. Most of the imports were of consumer goods – food, clothing, and household com-modities. About a third consisted of capital goods for industrial production.

This fantastic boom twisted the subsistence economy of Burma into something quite different, an economy almost entirely dependent on exports, and on the export of one crop at that. It brought profits to the trading firms, mainly British, which handled the exports and imports. It brought profits to the Indian moneylenders who financed so much of the reclamation and cultivation of the land. It brought profits, too, to the Burmese cultivator and a rise in his standard of living. But the lion's share, not unnaturally in the climate of *laissez-faire*, went to the trading firms and the Chettyars whose capital alone had made the expansion possible. And the benefits to the Burmese cultivator brought with them also marked disadvantages. It was some years, however, before these were perceived, and in the meanwhile it seemed to all that an era of unexampled prosperity had dawned for Burma.

But gradually the disadvantages showed themselves. The Chettyars were moneylenders, not agriculturists. The more they could lend, so long as it did not exceed the full selling value of the land offered as security, the better for their business. The cultivators, unaccustomed to money, unversed in the economics of borrowing, whose operations in the past had been largely limited by the quantity of rice required for their own needs and their customary quasi-feudal obligations of payment in kind, were dazzled by the offers of comparatively un-limited credit, and took all they could get. What was not immedi-ately required for the cost of cultivation tended to be spent on consumer goods. It was often several years before newly reclaimed

land showed any profit. There might be crop failure, sickness, loss of
cattle. The cultivator fell irretrievably into debt and the Chettyar
was forced to foreclose. The land would be sold to a fresh cultivator,
but the probability was that he would be a man of less experience
and substance. The process was likely to be repeated. Then a change
occurred in the pattern. Gradually the buyers of land, when the
Chettyars foreclosed, tended to be non-agriculturists, merchants,
traders, particularly those concerned in the rice trade and wishing to
establish control of some land, anyone wishing to make an investment, for example retired government employees. Or the Chettyars
would retain the land themselves. In either case holdings would be
let out to yearly tenants, who offered the highest rents. These would
not have the capital or the security of tenure that would enable
them to make long-term improvements, or even to cultivate in the
most efficient manner. There was inevitably a rapid turnover of
tenants as inexperienced or irresponsible optimists outbid sitting
tenants. By the 1930s the agricultural indebtedness of Burma was
estimated at £40 million, and almost half the land in Lower Burma
was owned by absentee landlords – in the chief rice-producing areas
the proportion might be as much as three-quarters. What had
started as a boom in the economy ended as an insoluble problem of
land tenure and agricultural indebtedness.

With this growth of exports came a complementary, though not
equal, development of imports. The value of these rose from Rs.25
million at the time of the opening of the Suez Canal, to Rs.100
million about 1900, Rs.254 million in 1913–14, and Rs.386 million
in 1926–27. Over this period the proportion of capital goods in these
imports grew from 19 per cent to 30 per cent. The bulk of the
imports, however, consisted of consumer goods. These undoubtedly
represented a rise in the standard of living of the Burmese people.
But here also there were serious drawbacks. Imports of food, some
of which could have been grown in Burma, represented, or allowed,
the transfer of agricultural manpower from crops required for internal consumption to the more profitable growing of rice for export,
so increasing the rising and dangerous dependence of the economy
on a single crop. Many other imports, for example of textiles,
earthenware, umbrellas, were of goods that could have been produced in Burma. Because they were cheaper, because their machine-
made finish appealed to unsophisticated buyers, they drove the
indigenous products out of the market, and their manufacturers out
of business. Native skills and taste were progressively lost or de-
bauched. And dependence upon the import of goods that could
have been produced in Burma tended still further to increase the
dependence of the economy on a single crop, for broadly speaking

they could be paid for only by the export of rice. This dependence had its obvious dangers – the risk of crop failures, the possibility of a collapse in the rice market, above all the placing of the economy at the mercy of foreign capital which alone had made the growth and continuance of the export trade possible.

The sudden exposure of the Burmese cultivator to money, credit, and the uncontrolled working of the forces of supply and demand, took away, or tempted him into casting away, the restraints imposed by social and economic custom, and by the strict limitations of subsistence requirements. This, as we have seen, put the cultivator into debt. It also went a long way towards destroying the largely feudal social structure within the modest and familiar limits of which he had lived, with success. This had effects that were not confined to the economic sphere.

This excess of exports over imports suggests, at first sight, a healthy balance of external trade. But most, if not all, of this surplus was removed out of Burma by remittances to India of the savings of Indian labourers and of the profits of the moneylenders, and by remittances to the United Kingdom of interest on loans and of profits of British firms. Opposite views can be held as to the utilization of this surplus. Furnivall writes that the annual export surplus 'is often attributed to invisible imports representing payments for services rendered, but to some extent the imports are invisible because they do not exist, and the surplus includes profits for which no services are rendered'.[1] Furnivall took the view that Burma gained little or nothing out of the surplus. Harvey, on the other hand, wrote that the 'removal of profits is not necessarily a drain on a country when they come from newly-created wealth, created by the foreigner who unearths the talent hidden in the ground'.[2] The use of the word 'necessarily' concedes that it could not have been regarded as satisfactory if the country received no share of the surplus. A Burmese economist, Maung Shein, writing in the 1950s, concludes that '. . . the real income of Burma rose because of the expansion of output, but the rise would have been even greater if the gains from the favourable turn in the terms of trade had not been absorbed by the large external "drains" '.[3]

Obviously the view to be taken of what in such circumstances constitutes an equitable division of the surplus of a favourable balance of trade, can differ greatly according to the comparative weight to be allowed to the contributions made by the provision of

[1] J. S. Furnivall, *Colonial Policy and Practice*, Cambridge, 1948, p. 187.
[2] G. E. Harvey, *British Rule in Burma 1824–1942*, p. 59.
[3] Maung Shein, *Burma's Transport and Foreign Trade*, Rangoon, 1964, p. 145.

capital, of managerial and technical skills, of labour, of enterprise, and by the accident of occupation, or of subsequent annexation. On the basis of what ought to be, most readers will feel, in the present era of aid to underdeveloped countries (even if the aiding countries have been blackmailed into this new generosity by fear that competing countries may jump in and outbid them), that Burma received less than her fair share of her surplus – in fact that Burma was exploited, though less by intent than by the blind and undiscriminating forces of capital. On the basis of the doctrines of self-help and *laissez-faire* and the uncontrolled play of economic forces, doctrines unfashionable now, but very widely and respectably held at the time of the economic expansion of Burma, it could fairly be claimed that the country was an outstanding example of commercial progress with benefits to all – even if these were not very lavish for the Burmese.

We have seen how, in the economic field, one of the results of the inclusion of Burma within the British Empire was an influx of Indian moneylenders and Indian agricultural and other labour. A large number of Indian traders and petty shopkeepers also flooded the country, so that much of the retail trade fell into Indian hands.[1] But it was not only in the economic field that this Indian penetration took place. The troops employed in the Burmese Wars had been largely Indian. Still more was this true of the troops employed in the 'pacification' of Upper Burma after the Third War. And since it was from India that Burma was annexed it was generally the case that the British officers who entered Burma knew and understood Indians and their language, whereas they knew nothing of the Burmese. Almost as important was the fact that Indians had grown accustomed to working for Europeans and knew what was expected of their employees. In any case the administrative system that was introduced to Burma on annexation was the Indian system. Indians understood and could work this; to the Burmese it was as strange and unintelligible as the mixed territorial and occupational jurisdictions and the different conception of law found in Burma were to the invaders. And lastly the Indians had a long start of the Burmese in knowledge and use of the English language. It was hardly to be wondered at, therefore, that in recruitment for all posts that did not particularly require local knowledge, the easiest course was only too frequently taken of employing Indians rather than Burmese. As a result, in many of the public services in Burma there was a preponderance of Indians, greatly out of proportion to their racial strength in the country. Particularly was this true of the Accounts Department, the railways, the Building and Roads Branch of the

[1] 'Indians' in the present context include 'Pakistanis'.

Public Works Department, the Medical Department (other than nurses, the majority of whom were Karen or Burmese), the Posts and Telegraphs Department, and the clerical services of the headquarters Secretariat. In such departments Indians had established a virtual monopoly, which was made by them to apply also to further entrants. Burmans who managed to secure a post in such a department were apt to find themselves manoeuvred out again. And when the government desired to recruit more Burmese it was defeated by the superior ability of Indians for passing examinations, their capacity for hard work, and their nimbler intellectual qualities. Indian predominance amongst menial workers, such as messengers and watchmen, was due mainly to the lower standard of living of the poorer Indians, which enabled them to live and remit money to their families left behind in India on a pay that the Burmese found quite inadequate; it was due also to the greater readiness of Indians to perform exacting routine work with regularity. At its highest, just before the Second World War, the population of Indians (Hindus and Muslims) in Burma numbered about one million, out of a total population of 16 million. This minority had seized a share, and exercised an influence, in the affairs of Burma, altogether disproportionate to its numerical strength. And its numerical strength had been built up, despite Burmese aversion, under the protection of the British, as a result of the removal of frontier barriers between India and Burma. A dangerously explosive situation had been created, with results that we shall see in a later chapter.[1]

But behind these various aspects, good and bad, of the British administration one broad tendency made its appearance. In both Lower and Upper Burma it was natural enough that annexation should be followed by some years of disorder. Then, after an arduous period of pacification, an unprecedented state of order and quiet was established. But in both Lower and Upper Burma, about twenty-five years after annexation, a serious growth in violent crime began, especially robbery, dacoity (a more serious form of robbery committed by gangs), and murder. The police forces were increased, vigorous action was taken by executive officers, committees investigated, the government legislated, but nothing that the administration did could hold back this mounting wave of crime. There was at the time a tendency to consider this a peculiarly Burmese problem, largely caused by the hot-tempered character of the people. More recent experience elsewhere, even in the United Kingdom, chasteningly suggests that the matter is not to be explained away so easily. The Burmese are quick and violent-tempered. But there were other forces at work also.

[1] See below, pp. 119, 121.

It is probably significant that the increase in crime came just about a generation after the annexation of the territory concerned. There had been time for a section of the community to grow up that did not remember the violence and misery of Thibaw's lurid reign, and therefore did not appreciate the compensations of calm and security that the British had brought. Older persons may not have liked the British régime, but they did realize that it had conferred some advantages. There had been time also for a generation to grow up that did not remember the sharpness, indeed the brutality, of the early years of British pacification, and therefore no longer feared the authority of the British as their elders did. And whether these people realized it or not, it was clearly inconceivable that the British should return to the draconian measures previously employed. If these were permissible, or at least understandable, when a new government was battling to establish its authority, they were quite unacceptable when authority had been established and there were police and courts and procedures under the law for the apprehension, trial, and conviction of criminals – when, in short, civilized conditions of life had been brought into existence.

It is probable that, as in other countries, sheer boredom was a factor in the increase of violent crime. Partly this resulted from the destruction of Burmese nationhood that followed the annexation. Aspects of this were the abolition of the monarchy after the Third Burmese War, and the absorption of Burma into the remote and impersonal administrative machinery of India. The Burmese were deprived of self-respect and left without any symbol of national purpose – the symbol is valuable even if the purpose is non-existent. Partly it resulted from the facelessness, orderliness, and predictability of the British régime. The Burmese are great gamblers and uncertainty is the spice of life to many of them. Dacoity and robbery developed almost as forms of national sport. Football, introduced by the British, became immensely popular, but could not yield quite the thrills of a successful dacoity.

Mainly, however, it was the breakdown of the Burmese social and economic system that was responsible for the growth of crime. The result of this was to weaken many of the moral and social forces that until then had governed the behaviour of the community. Partly this resulted from the destruction of the monarchy. Partly it resulted from the weakening of the influence of the monks. Above all it was due to the unrestricted play of economic forces that followed the incorporation of Burma in British India, which has been described earlier in this chapter.

Chapter 6

Britons and Burmans

THROUGH ALL ASPECTS OF the establishment of British administration in Burma, the more significant of which have been touched
upon in the preceding chapter, ran the personal relations that grew
up between the two races. It is difficult to generalize, for any assessment is inevitably subjective, and the facts to be taken into account
are so completely heterogeneous. The same will not be true of the
British business and trading community, of the British military
community, and of the British in the civil administration. Nor will
the same thing be true of the Burman villager, of the educated
Burman, and of the Buddhist monk. Nor, again, will the same thing
be true of Rangoon and of up-country districts. Nevertheless an
impression must be attempted.

In general there was little social contact, notwithstanding Maung
Htin Aung's statement that, ' . . . no social barrier was created between the ruler and the ruled'.[1] There was little opportunity for contact, because social customs, interests, education, language, were so
completely different. Sport – racing, football, and, to a lesser degree,
tennis – offered a meeting-ground. What other opportunity did offer
was often not welcome to either side. Neither felt really at ease in
the presence of the other. The British were an 'expatriate' community – though the term was not yet in current use. Some enjoyed,
and took an interest in, their surroundings. More lived only for the
day when they could take leave or retire to England. Meanwhile,
instead of making a life out of what they found around them, they
preferred to attempt to create for themselves an imitation of 'home',
or what they thought and wanted 'home' to be. Language was a
real obstacle. Burmese is a difficult tongue. Most Europeans gained
the sort of smattering that would enable them to go shopping or talk
to their servants. Some gained greater proficiency – indeed government employees were required to do so, but their competence was
often confined to the technicalities of their work. A very few made
a serious study of the language. Virtually none could speak like a
Burman. Few or none could establish any real contact of minds
through the vernacular. On the other hand, the great majority of

[1] Maung Htin Aung, *A History of Burma*, New York, 1967, p. 268.

Burmans spoke no English. Most Burmese government officers, a few clerks, and others of similar standing, did speak English extremely well, especially when it is remembered that all but an infinitesimal number had never been to England or heard English generally spoken around them. A few others had some slight understanding of English. The rest, the village headmen and officials, the police, the dwellers in villages, knew, and were expected to know, no English at all. The universal teaching of English now given was then impracticable, and to have required all Burmans to learn the language, would have been felt by the British to be an unwarrantable interference with the Burmese way of life.

If social contact was difficult, it also contained dangers. Sixty years ago, an Englishman who loved the Burmese described them, and his words remained true throughout the British period:

'A Burman will never come and see you for your *beaux yeux*, nor even for your wit. It follows, therefore, that if he comes to you, it is for a purpose. He has something to gain. And as the only side on which you touch the Burman at all is official, it must be some official gain. He wants to speak to you about a case maybe, or to gain an official favour. He comes to you privately instead of in office, because he wants to get at you. I do not mean that he wishes to bribe you; attempts at bribery to Englishmen are very rare; but he wants to influence you in some unrecognized way, some way that you cannot allow; perhaps it is to tell you scandal about his opponent, or to flatter you into complaisance. There is not ever, there could not be, any other reason for a man or woman coming to visit you except they wished some gain.

Yet sometimes the object may be very carefully hidden.

There was once the head of a district, very energetic, very zealous, very anxious to be friends with all the people. He liked them, and they liked him. He wanted to see more of them, to increase the intimacy and the friendliness. He asked them to come and chat to him after office hours. Occasionally one or two came.

Presently the "two" dropped off, and the "one" remained. He was a merchant in the town, a man of good standing, of considerable wealth for a villager, a sportsman who knew a pony and a man of influence.

Yet he had no official position, was not a municipal councillor, a board elder, or honorary magistrate, or anything else connected with government. He never asked for any land grants, he petitioned for no exceptions, he had no relations in troubles.

He talked mostly of racing ponies, and for long periods he would sit in the verandah and chew betel and be happy. If any

Burman ever visited a European out of sheer friendliness, without any ulterior motive, it seemed to be this merchant, and the official was much pleased. He took it as a compliment to himself.

Well, after some months of this there was a row one night in the town. This merchant, while crossing a monastery compound, was set upon and nearly killed. There was great excitement. An inquiry followed, and soon facts came out. Alas, for this pure and simple friendship! This merchant had an object. He was ambitious. But his ambition lay not towards honours or money, it lay towards religious sway. He wanted to be the leader of a religious section of the town, to obtain a certain monastery for his monks, and displace those who disagreed with him. To this end had been his visits. He came and sat in the official's verandah and smoked and talked "horse", and when he went away he said, "You all see me, I have been half an hour with the Deputy Commissioner. I told him all about you and the monastery. He says I am quite right. Tomorrow, out you all go; my men come in. If you won't, the police will take you to the gaol".[1]

Much of British social life went on in clubs, where tennis, bridge, and billiards were played, whisky was drunk, and gossip and a certain amount of quiet business took place. These clubs were un-compromisingly British in habits and atmosphere, once again seeking to create an illusion of 'home'. Clubs were a British, not a Burmese, institution, and most Burmans had no desire to join, feeling ill at ease in them. As for the British, after a day's work, often heavy, often in arduous conditions, always requiring allowance to be made, not for bad work – often work was good – but for the fact that the people they were dealing with were of another race and of totally different outlook, their one idea was to throw aside this preoccupa-tion and to be allowed to act and speak without the inhibition of having to mind racial p's and q's. The clubs, therefore, if they did not exclude, did not actively seek to include, Burmans, and this tended to harden into exclusion. When the numbers of educated Burmans increased, when they perceived that a social bar had grown up, and when they realized how often decisions in important official matters were virtually taken between colleagues over a whisky and soda at the club, they felt excluded, and the demand for admission to the clubs took shape, although in truth club life was not congenial to them. In small stations, where Europeans were few, Burmese were welcomed as members. But in these places there were not many educated Burmese. In the bigger towns, where there were more Europeans, and where there were also more educated Bur-mans, there was not the same advantage to be gained from admitting

[1] H. Fielding Hall, *A People at School*, London, 1906, pp. 165-7.

Burmese members, and exclusion tended to continue. This naturally rankled and became the cause of much ill-feeling.

British women on the whole exercised a divisive influence, though there were notable exceptions. In the early stages of occupation, when the country was considered too unsettled and too unhealthy for European women, many men lived with Burmese women in what might be a marriage under Burmese law but no marriage under British law. These unions enjoyed varying intimacy and varying fortunes, but, happy or not, they did establish a certain contact between the races, which had its advantages as well as its disadvantages. When conditions became more settled, more Englishwomen came to Burma. By their presence and by making homes they drew men away from these earlier contacts. And for many reasons they tended to keep Burmans at arm's length. Few spoke Burmese; they were encouraged by the government to do so but not, as were their husbands, required to learn. They did not have the opportunities, enjoyed by the men, of working with Burmans and so getting to know and like them. There was a far greater social reluctance to meet Burmans, springing from – what? Distrust of the unknown? Consciousness of colour? Fear that in some way advantage would be taken of them? An instinctive feeling that they would in some way be tainted by meeting Burmese women with whom Englishmen had been 'living in sin'? Knowledge that here was a shadowy, unknown world where you might suddenly find yourself meeting the sons or daughters of your husband or of your friends? A little, perhaps, of many or all of these considerations. But certainly there was a feeling that it would be safer, and more *comme-il-faut*, to confine social contacts to British circles.

Amongst many Europeans there was certainly a feeling of racial superiority. It is not clear whence this derived. Immediately, it must have been imported from India. But it had not always been present there. In the eighteenth century, and even in the early nineteenth century, it was absent, or certainly less marked. It seems to have grown as Indians lost their own sovereign rulers and became 'subjects' of the British. Once deprived of political independence it seems that Indians were no longer acceptable to the British as quite life-sized men. A Burman has written: 'Yet it is a fact that the British do not have regard for peoples whom they rule over as much as they do to those who rule themselves.'[1] What, indeed, was the justification for being in Burma as a ruling race, if one did not feel superior? In its later manifestations the feeling of racial superiority was also a reaction from fear. After the mutiny, the confidence of the British was never fully restored. An underlying, if often un-

[1] *Burma's Fight for Freedom*, p. 11.

recognized, fear reinforced the tendency to hold the Indian away and down. This racial consciousness was probably least strong among the most and the least educated of the British – many members of the superior civil services, and many British private soldiers, each in their own very different way, succeeded in treating Indians on their merits, not as impersonal and slightly inferior beings. It was a disease that attacked those between the two extremes of the educational spectrum with greater force. British women were particularly prone to it – their fears possibly sharpened by subconscious sexual apprehensions. It is also clear, as has already been suggested in connection with clubs, that feelings of racial superiority flourished more readily where the European community was large and more self-sufficient. In Rangoon, where the number of Europeans, and the number of European clubs, made possible a self-contained society, the Burmese were held very much at arm's length. Up-country, in the small towns that were the headquarters of administrative districts, such segregation of the communities was impracticable if there was to be any social life at all. In such places, British and Burmese tended to come much closer to each other. Those Britons were fortunate who began their careers in Burma out of Rangoon.

However, the picture is not all as black as this. Real personal contacts between British and Burmese were not numerous. But contact, if established, was a positive, active, factor in the situation, whereas absence of contact was merely negative. Where real friendships arose they exerted an influence, left a mark, out of all proportion to their numbers. The names of Stewart, Dunn, Swithinbank, Furnivall, Searle, of the civil service, Luce, of the university, were long remembered. If they have now been forgotten, the influence of these men nevertheless continues. The very difficulty of reaching across the racial barrier made these friendships the more precious and valuable. Their influence, and the memory of them, must be a prime cause of that warm affection between Burmese and British that is still not far below the surface, notwithstanding the many setbacks it has suffered from the thoughtless contempt shown by many other Britons, and the continuing propaganda of the present régime in Burma against the so-called imperialists, colonialists, or capitalists. As has already been said, it was easier for British men than women to make friends, for they met Burmans over their work and in this way social and racial barriers were softened or obliterated. It was easier for government servants than for employees of the firms, for their work was concerned with people, rather than things. And government servants found it easier to get on terms with the village headmen and their villagers than with the more educated Burmese. Many were successful in establishing an easy sort of squire–tenant relationship, with the people they met in the villages. In these cases, topics of conversation were limited – crops, the weather, crime – but this in many ways made things easier; and, in any event, it was in these topics that the government servant was interested for the purposes of the administration of his district. With young educated Burmese it was much more difficult to make contact. Topics were less limited, but this at once put a greater strain on the Briton's Burmese vocabulary. On the other hand, the command of English enjoyed by this stratum of Burmese society was far more extensive. But here a different difficulty arose. The imposition of an alien system of education, a system largely without roots in the country and its culture, meant that the mental concepts which had been inculcated in educated Burmans were often artificial playthings to be handled according to artificial and meaningless rules. Not surprisingly those who played with them made mistakes. The effect upon those Burmans who partook in this game tended to be to drain away their native good sense, their realism, their ability to think for themselves. The uneducated, unimproved, villager, in contrast, operating with concepts that, albeit limited, were natural to him and rooted in his life, was full of shrewd, earthy commonsense. The Briton respected this, but tended to become very impatient of what to him seemed so often the half-baked nonsense talked by the supposedly educated. Above all, however, the more educated Burman was, naturally, unwilling to drop into the superior–inferior, teacher–taught, relationship that came easily enough to the uneducated villager. Many Britons did not desire, or want to impose, such a relationship. But some did. And the Burman did not know where he stood, and was liable to resent something that nobody might be asking of him.

For many Britons their chief contact with Burmans was through their servants. It is fashionable to decry the paternalism of this relationship. And indeed it could be abused. But it could yield very warm and genuine contacts. The present writer cannot forgo the opportunity to pay tribute to service and loyalty from his servants far in excess of what was paid for. The writer was in Rangoon at the end of 1941 and the beginning of 1942, when the invading Japanese were bombing the city. It was no uncommon occurrence for Europeans to wake to find that all their servants had decamped overnight. The writer's servants were absolutely steadfast. When the bombing became more persistent it was agreed that the cook should have a few days' leave to take all the families out of Rangoon to a place of safety. 'That's that, you won't see him again,' said the writer to his wife who, however, expressed complete confidence that the cook would return. And he did. Not only so, but when it became necessary to recall him before his leave of absence expired, he made his way back, by bus and otherwise, far sooner than the train could have brought him. Dereliction of duty for his own safety was not conceivable. The bond forged with these servants was largely the creation of the writer's wife. But it could not have grown if there had not been a deep loyalty and sense of duty on the other side. There was here something of great and permanent value, and the writer wishes to record his humble gratitude.

It has often been charged that, although British administration in India and Burma might be good, it was impersonal. The charge is usually allowed to be established by default. But is it in fact true? There is little doubt that British administration was more competent and authoritative than anything that went before, or has come after. But was it so impersonal? It is true that its key members were foreign and lacked social and other contact with the people of the country, and that in consequence their administrative decisions might sometimes be unrealistic. In part this remoteness and absence of contact was deliberate in order to secure impartiality in the administration. If 'impersonal' means that the members of the administration could keep themselves uninfluenced by the often subtle and indirect intrigues and pressures that were continually being brought to bear on them, then this was not an attribute to be ashamed of, though it might have to be paid for in other ways. But there is another side to all this. Under the British administration it was laid down to be an important part of the duties of officers to tour their charges, even to remote and little known parts. Not all officers were equally assiduous in discharging this aspect of their duties, but most did tour freely, if only because they liked to get away from their office desks, for a taste of human reality, and to take gun, field glasses, or camera with them into wild places. Burmese officers did not, and do not, do this to the same extent. When the writer asked a Burmese friend whether the officers of the present government in Burma ever penetrated to the more remote parts of their charges, the reply came swiftly 'No government officers in Burma have ever visited such parts, other than the British'. British officers knew the headmen, the leading personalities, the villages, particularly the remote villages, of their charges, better than government officers before or since have ever done. And these officers were probably known, at least by sight, and if only for their peculiarities and eccentricities, over far wider areas than their Burmese counterparts. At the present time, indeed, it is quite unsafe for the latter to travel in large parts of their charges. In this sense, the British administration can fairly claim to have been far more personal than anything before or since. A measure of the interest and sense of personal commitment felt by British officers for the country in which they served is the number of books and

articles written by them, many of great erudition and still unique in
their field. These range from gazetteers containing much detailed
information on Lower Burma, Upper Burma, and the Shan States,
and many of the administrative districts of the country, to an out-
standingly good book on the birds of Burma, to monographs on
silver work, glass mosaics, and ivory carving, and to a wealth of
articles on varied subjects in the Journal of the Burma Research
Society. It is scarcely too much to say that it was the British who
taught the Burmese to appreciate their past, as Curzon taught the
people of India. And it was a British official who took the leading
part in forming the Burma Research Society. In addition, work on
the Burmese dictionary, now being compiled at the School of
Oriental and African Studies in London, owed its inception to three
British administrative officers. If these men were sometimes impersonal when they were acting as judges or heads of the administration, this does not seem to have prevented them from taking a keen
personal interest in what went on around them, or in making lasting
friendships with Burmese.

Chapter 7

The Growth of Nationalism

To speak of the growth of nationalism is perhaps misleading, for nationalism is no new thing in Burma if by this is meant consciousness of nationhood and of a religion and a language virtually co-extensive with the nation; a love of the country and of the way of life of its people; pride of race; and a sturdy conviction that Burmans know their own business better than can any foreigner. Indeed it would be a drab, downtrodden people that did not nurse or respond to such feelings, and an unsympathetic one that did not recognize and respect them. What this chapter will be concerned with is the emergence and growth of nationalism as a political force that hastened, and to some extent may have caused, the relinquishment of power by the British to the Burmese.

That this force ultimately dictated the timing of the transfer of power is beyond dispute. That it was the cause of the political process that culminated in the transfer is less clear. For after annexation by the British, Burma became a part of the Indian Empire, and liberalization of Burma's institutions was more in the nature of a by-product of the pressure generated by Indian nationalism and of the British policy evolved to meet this pressure. And this policy itself, although partly the result of nationalist pressure, had its roots, ultimately, as also did much of Indian nationalist thinking itself, in the nineteenth-century liberal movement in England. It was this that inspired the passing of the Indian Councils Act of 1861 under which, for the first time, non-official representatives were to be included in the various legislative bodies of India, hitherto exclusively official. It was this that influenced Lord Ripon as Viceroy to press forward, against widespread opposition, with a policy of reforming, introducing, and progressively increasing, institutions of local self-government throughout India. And while the sponsors of these two major reforms did not contemplate their ultimate development to the point of full democratic self-government, or of complete independence, and would indeed have denied that this was their objective, yet they had set their feet on a road from which, whether it is seen as winding uphill all the way to heaven, or as plunging down Avernus to chaos, there is in practice no turning back.

It was against the background of these two reforms in India that Upper Burma was annexed and incorporated into the Indian Empire in 1886. A start, but a largely unsuccessful start, had already been made in Lower Burma with the introduction of local self-government 'as an instrument of political and popular education'. This policy was in due course extended to Upper Burma. But for the first five years after the annexation, the period of the 'pacification' of Upper Burma, there was little time to attend to political or constitutional experiments. The whole of Upper Burma was in disorder and all the resources of the government had to be employed in the assertion of its authority and the establishment of order. If much of the disorder was ascribable to gangs of robbers and to other criminals taking advantage of the disintegration of the previously existing social order so as to commit crime, it is nevertheless clear that the opposition to the new régime did represent a strong eruption of nationalist feeling. This was gradually repressed, by force, and assumed a more recessive character as the more orderly elements in the country came to accept not only the fact but the power of the new régime, as well as the many advantages it did without doubt bring to the ordinary citizen, anxious only to cultivate his fields and go about his business in reasonable security. In this chapter we shall trace the gradual re-emergence of nationalist feeling, after the possibly misleading political calm of the immediate post-pacification period, and its influence on the history of Burma.

In 1897, with the consolidation of authority, the establishment of order, and the expansion of the economy the Chief Commissioner was elevated to the rank of Lieutenant-Governor.[1] This carried with it the creation of a Legislative Council. It is true that none of the members of this were elected – there were four official members and five unofficial members, all nominated by the Lieutenant-Governor. There was no element of self-government and the powers of the Council were in any case circumscribed. But what was important was the recognition by the British of the principle that it was desirable to associate the people of the country with its government.

In 1905 Japan astonished the world and delighted the Orient by inflicting a resounding military defeat upon Russia. In the words of H. A. L. Fisher, '. . . it is inferred that the Orient has no further reason to abase itself before the West'.[2] In the following year in Burma a Buddhist monk, the *Ledi Sayadaw*, began preaching and writing in a religious revivalist campaign which generated much interest and enthusiasm among the better and the less educated Burmans. In the same year, 1906, there was founded the Young

[1] See above, p. 79.
[2] H. A. L. Fisher, *A History of Europe*, London, 1957, p. 1024.

Men's Buddhist Association. It was in some respects inspired, as its name suggests, by the Young Men's Christian Association which was active in Rangoon. To a general interest in religion, morals, and education, there was added a strong urge to preserve and revive interest in all that was distinctively Burmese in these and other fields, particularly history and literature. In 1908 the President of the Rangoon Y.M.B.A. was U May Oung, a young lawyer who had studied for the Bar in England. In August of that year he gave a lecture to the Rangoon College Buddhist Association on 'The Modern Burman' and was reported as opening his talk with the following words:

'By the expression "The Modern Burman" he did not mean the native of Burma in general at the present day – it would require a whole volume to treat of him – but by modern Burman he meant the Burman who had received the not unmixed blessing of a Western education. He intended to speak of themselves, the large majority of those assembled together in that hall. For it was on them and those like them – on their training, acquirements, exertions, – that the future of their race would in no small measure depend. On all sides they saw the ceaseless, ebb-less tide of foreign civilization and learning, steadily creeping over the land, and it seemed to him that unless they prepared themselves to meet it, to overcome it, and to apply it to their own needs, their national character, their institutions, their very existence as a distinct nationality would be swept away, submerged, irretrievably lost.'[1]

Here was the nationalist ideal enunciated by a Western-educated leader for Western-educated Burmans – and very moderately enunciated, for, unfortunately, it was not only the civilization and learning of the West that was flowing over the country but many of its less desirable concomitants. In the event, however, as we shall see, it was not the more highly, the Western-educated, Burmans who carried their country to independence but a more home-grown and far less educated product.

In the following year, 1909, the background to the growth of nationalism was slightly, but only very slightly, changed by the introduction of the Morley–Minto reforms in India. The Burma Legislative Council was enlarged from nine to seventeen, was given somewhat wider functions, and its composition was altered to include two elected members. But since these were elected by the Burma Chamber of Commerce, the representative organization of European business in Burma, and by the Rangoon Trades Association, the organization of the European retail trade, this did nothing whatever

[1] *Journal of the Burma Research Society*, XXXIII, Part I, April 1950, p. 2.

to give the people of the country any share in legislation. But the importance of the change was that the elective principle had been allowed to creep in. Nevertheless Lord Morley was still able to say: 'If it could be said that this chapter of reforms led directly or indirectly to the establishment of a parliamentary system in India, I for one would have nothing at all to do with it.'[1] But, of course, British attitudes had moved forward, along a road from which, as has been said above, there was in practice no turning back.

In 1910, on the initiative of Mr J. S. Furnivall, a member of the Indian Civil Service serving in Burma, there was founded the still-existing Burma Research Society, its objects being '. . . the study and encouragement of Art, Science, History and Literature in relation to Burma, and the promotion of intercourse between members of different communities, with a common interest in such objects'. The society was to grow into a fruitful meeting-ground for scholars and experts, British and Burmese, and to do a great deal to foster understanding of the national culture and character. It succeeded for a great part of its history in keeping out of politics. The same year saw vigorous growth in the Y.M.B.A. movement, fifteen branches being established. There was in this no meeting of British and Burmans, the movement remaining exclusively Burmese. It now reached far outside the original circle of Western-educated Burmans, indeed these came to play only a subordinate part in the movement. And the movement very soon developed political activities. These were initially directed at embarrassing and, if possible, humiliating Europeans, often in trivial matters, but all with the purpose of building up the status of Burmans and of proving that '. . . the Orient has no further reason to abase itself before the West'. So began the somewhat ludicrous 'footwearing' controversy, ludicrous as to the cause of battle but none the less a genuine conflict of national wills.

The Burmese show respect for their surroundings, whether religious buildings or a private house, by doffing shoes and going barefoot. This is uncongenial to Western habits and dress, and the European instead removes his hat. Europeans visiting Burma before the annexation were required to conform to Burmese custom. After the annexation it became accepted that they need not. Few can have withheld the appropriate European signs of respect when entering houses, but difficulty was created by visits to pagodas when the glare of the tropical sun made many Europeans genuinely unwilling to remove their hats for fear of sun-stroke. But disrespect was seldom intended and this came to be well understood and accepted. However, there was here, in the omission to doff shoes, something that could give genuine offence to Burmans, that could plausibly be

[1] Quoted *Cambridge History of India*, Vol. VI, Cambridge, 1932, p. 567.

represented as disrespect to Buddhism, and that could easily be inflated and utilized to embarrass the European and in some small degree to humiliate the government. 'No Footwearing' notices appeared at pagodas. Since the underlying motive was, without question, to humiliate and discredit the government and its representatives in the eyes of the people, and since the government depended for its day-to-day authority on prestige, rather than upon votes, its officers understandably felt unable to comply with these notices. Henceforth they either did not visit pagodas displaying the notice, or ran the risk of unpleasantness if they did. In retrospect one may feel that this was an issue that could have been avoided by according respect in the Burmese fashion at an early enough stage – though in that case some other pretext would have been found for challenging the government. As events developed this was a clear victory for the Burmese. The only lesson to be drawn from this, in some respects trivial, chain of events is how easy it is to embarrass any government, but particularly a government which is unwilling or unable to apply the full logic of force. In 1910, also, a young Burmese monk, U Ottama, demonstrated the interest which Japan had aroused, by going on a visit to that country. He was to become a bitter opponent of the British government in Burma, and one of the most fanatical of the *Naingnganye Sayadaws* (or political monks) who were to play a prominent part in the politics of nationalism.

The First World War followed in 1914. This had little direct impact on Burma. India, however, played an important part, both by the contribution of her army, and by her function as a base for supplies. A very critical political situation developed as a result of nationalist agitation using the military importance of India as a lever to gain its demands. To meet this agitation, and if possible to retain the co-operation of the Indian people, the British government made promises of further political advancement. In August 1917 the Secretary of State for India, the Rt. Hon. E. S. Montagu, announced that

'the policy of His Majesty's Government, with which the Government of India are in complete accord, is that of the increasing association of Indians in every branch of the administration, and the gradual development of self-governing institutions, with a view to the progressive realization of responsible government in India as an integral part of the British Empire'.[1]

India, which of course included Burma, was by this announcement firmly set on the road to self-government. However, the Montagu–Chelmsford Committee, set up to apply this policy, took the view

[1] *Hansard*, Commons, 20 August 1917, col. 1695.

that 'Burma is only by accident part of the responsibility of the Governor-General of India. The Burmese are as distinct from the Indians in race and language as they are from the British'; that 'Burma is not India'; and that the people of Burma are of 'another race in another stage of political development, and its problems are altogether different'. The report accordingly, whilst holding out prospects of emancipation, excluded Burma from its recommendations for constitutional reforms – although its authors did not doubt but that an analogous constitution should be provided for Burma. Until this time there had been little interest in politics on the part of the Burmese. The proposals in the report for constitutional reforms, still more the withholding of the reforms from Burma, perhaps most of all the government of Burma's published proposals for an 'analogous' constitution which, in fact, conceded less responsibility than was proposed for India, not surprisingly quickly aroused political interest and activity. Here was encouragement to the nationalists and a goal offered beyond anything that had yet been formulated by the movement. Here also was the prospect of a new career in politics, and the possibility of power, whether for the benefit of party or person. And the spark to ignite all this combustible material was there too, in the suspicion, aroused by the withholding of the reforms from Burma, that her people would be denied concessions accorded to India, that this was yet another case of the British seeking to divide and rule. The Y.M.B.A. emerged as the political nerve-centre of nationalism – there was indeed no other organization in the country which could take on the functions of a political party. Two delegations were sent to London, in July 1919 and in May 1920, the Y.M.B.A. taking the leading part in both cases, to press, and ultimately to press successfully, that Burma should receive no less favourable treatment than India. The second delegation actually pressed for separation from India. Nationalism had emerged as a political force, organized and articulate, though it was as yet largely confined to the Y.M.B.A., its branches, and a few kindred but lesser bodies.

In the course of the next four years political nationalism was to reach out from the coterie of Western-educated intellectuals to the people at large and so, most unexpectedly to those in authority at the time, to become a real popular movement. It was not a 'grass roots' movement in the sense of being something pushed up from below. Indeed it seems to have been extensively encouraged from outside by the Indian Congress for its own ends. The Burmese delegation to London in 1920 would have been happy to settle for the grant to Burma of constitutional reforms no less liberal than those offered to India. It was only after the return of the delegation to

Burma that nationalist objectives were stepped up and demands put forward for Home Rule or complete self-government on the model of the British dominions. Partly this was the technique, by no means confined to oriental bazaars, of asking initially for more than was expected ultimately to be conceded. But partly it stemmed from interchange of ideas with Indian politicians, a desire not to lag behind India and not to let Indians down, and the hope that support for the Indian Congress now might pay dividends later in the shape of help by the Congress for Burma. After the tragedy of Amritsar in 1919, Indian political opinion, in any case more advanced and sophisticated than opinion in Burma, rejected the reforms proposed and decided to stand out for more liberal concessions, these demands to be supported by a policy of boycott and non-co-operation with any lesser reforms. Burma followed suit and was shortly also to employ the weapons of boycott and non-co-operation. But nationalism soon became a 'grass roots' movement in the sense that the emerging political leaders evolved and presented to the people (as any politician must seek to present) a cause or causes that appealed to them and swept them into support.

First, students were drawn in. Rangoon University was established in 1920 on the foundations of two existing colleges and other institutions. Accepting the view of the time that the function of a university was to train an élite, and resolved to establish academic standards that would merit recognition beyond the bounds of Burma, the government planned to stiffen entrance requirements, to make the new university residential (which would involve keeping down numbers), and to protect the university from political interference. Protection from political interference, an admirable objective in itself, was to be secured by choosing the governing body predominantly from representatives of educational interests. As the educational hierarchy was then constituted, this meant the virtual exclusion of Burmans from any control over the university. Some provision was made for ascertaining Burmese views, but out of a body of forty-eight, some five to nine only were likely to be Burmans, and only three of these were elected by the Legislative Council. On 1 August 1920 the Y.M.B.A. convened a mass meeting which protested against all these proposals, and against alleged failure to consult Burmese opinion. When the university opened in December the protesters prevailed upon the students to strike. There was at first little enthusiasm for what was obviously a political boycott, but appeals to patriotism and some intimidation succeeded in bringing out virtually the whole body of students. This cynical exploitation of students for political purposes set a pattern of school and university strikes and disorders that was to culminate in the tragic events of more than forty years later when the troops of the present revolutionary government opened fire on the students of Rangoon University, killing seventeen and wounding thirty-nine. Unrest was extended to the Anglo-vernacular schools, when those who had instigated the boycott of the university set up 'national' schools and sought to attract pupils, partly by representing it as a patriotic duty to boycott government schools, but also, oddly, by offering earlier teaching of English.

Next, support was enlisted from the monks. Members of the order were numbered among the instigators of the university boycott. Many, probably most, of its members were men of religion who eschewed politics. But many political agitators, to say nothing of lawless men on the run, had found shelter within the order. And the new breed of 'political monks' had arrived, who felt that patriotism was not incompatible with their religious vows. Any attempt by the government to extract them from their shelter at once provoked the cry of religion in danger. These elements required little wooing; they were prepared to follow any trouble-making lead or themselves to take the initiative. And it was not long before the preaching in the villages of nationalism and of the duty to oppose the government was taken over by them. In 1922 a political association was formed within the order known as the General Council of Sangha Samaggis (or G.C.S.S.) – a counterpart to the General Council of Burmese Associations (or G.C.B.A.), into which in 1921 the Y.M.B.A. had converted itself, as the association for laymen. And it was a 'political monk' who injected into the nationalist movement a bitter fervour previously lacking. U Ottama, who had visited Japan in 1910, was a fanatical politician in monk's robes. Having learnt Congress methods in India he aligned himself with the G.C.B.A. in 1921, preaching opposition to the constitutional reforms, demanding Home Rule, raising the cry of religion in danger, and inciting the people viciously to violence. The government was forced to prosecute and imprison him with the inevitable result that he became a martyr. On release from prison he renewed his agitation, and was imprisoned again for three years. On release in 1927 he at once took part in a campaign to prevent payment of taxes and had to be reimprisoned, this time not to be released. He became mentally unbalanced and died in 1939.

Thirdly, the nationalist movement was extended into the villages by the efforts of the G.C.B.A. and the preaching of the monks. There was in the villages no understanding of the political issues involved. At the most lucid, Home Rule might be thought to mean the restoration of the Burmese monarchy – which, in fact, no one advocated. But equally there was little understanding of such benefits as the government did confer – admittedly these were slender in the more remote parts. To many villagers officers of the government were known only as tax-collectors. It has never been difficult to raise opposition against the revenue men. In many villages there was already a natural division of the people, as a result of local power politics, into pro-headman and anti-headman parties. Here was an opposition ready-made and quick to respond to the inflammatory speeches that now began to be poured out all over the country. Through 1921 and 1922 the activities of the G.C.B.A. led to the formation in many villages of political organizations to oppose the government and undermine the authority of its local representative, the village headman. These organizations were known as *Wunthanu Athins*. (*Athin* meant a society and had been a term applied in pre-annexation Burma to regimental royal-service units. *Wunthanu* meant 'preserving one's own race'.)

Notwithstanding this opposition, the Montagu–Chelmsford reforms modified by the Whyte Committee for the conditions of Burma, were put into effect at the beginning of 1923. They made provision, first, for the creation of a Legislative Council of 103 members, of whom eighty were popularly elected. They then provided for the devolution of authority by the central government of India to the government of Burma in respect of certain functions of government, to be known as 'provincial subjects'. The remaining functions were termed 'central subjects', and continued to be dealt with by the government of India. This was free from any popular control, although in practice heed was paid as far as possible to the views expressed in the Indian legislature which was largely a popularly elected body. But as Burma was represented in this legislature, which had a total membership of 145, by only five members of whom one was an official nominee and one was elected by the European community in Burma, it is clear that popular opinion in Burma could have little influence in regard to central subjects. In any case Burma lay far away from India and her problems were very different.

It was in the field of the provincial subjects that a measure of popular control was conceded. These subjects were in their turn divided into 'reserved subjects' and 'transferred subjects'. In regard to the former the Governor acted in consultation with an Executive Council of official members, subject to the general control of the central government. In regard to the latter he was required to act on the advice of Ministers elected by the Legislative Council 'unless he sees sufficient cause to dissent from their opinion, in which case he may require action to be taken otherwise than in accordance with that advice'. But in practice it was a rare and difficult thing for the

Governor to act in this way: it would have provoked a political crisis and would have amounted to a confession of failure in the experiment to which the British government was committed since, in the words of the preamble to the Act of 1919, 'the time and manner of each advance can be determined only by Parliament' which '. . . must be guided by the co-operation received from those on whom new opportunities of service will be conferred, and by the extent to which it is found that confidence can be reposed in their sense of responsibility'. Cautious and hesitant though these words may have been, the spirit in which they were applied was altogether different, and the grant of self-government in regard to the transferred subjects, though not complete, was very real. In the words of one who helped as an official in the working of the experiment, 'The reader may think the system was only a façade. But nobody who was there and witnessed the change, especially if he were on the inside of the machine, is likely to forget it. The year 1923 was the parting of the ways.'[1] It should be added, however, that popular control and discretion were limited by the fact that the reserved subjects had first call on the available revenue. This proved a very frustrating limitation. The reforms further required the admission of Burmans to the all-India services. In the case of the Indian civil service recruitment of Britons and Burmans was to be in equal numbers.

An inevitable but somewhat unsettling air of impermanence was thrown over the whole of this period because the constitution was declared to be but the first step in a process of constitutional advancement and because the provisions of Section 41 of the Act required that after ten years a statutory commission should be appointed to consider what further instalments of self-government might then be introduced.

The important transferred subjects of government were education, public health, agriculture, forests, excise, public works, and local self-governing institutions. The main subjects reserved were finance and revenue, the maintenance of law and order, and the administration of justice and the police.

But almost half the area of Burma, and about one-third of the population, were excluded altogether from the scope of the reforms, and continued to be governed much as they had been in the past. These were the indirectly administered areas inhabited by the Shans, Chins, Kachins, and other minority races of Burma – but not the Karens or Mons who, though numerous, were more mingled with the Burmese, and did not form such homogeneous racial blocs, or inhabit areas that could so easily be demarcated. These people were excluded from the reforms, partly because they were less advanced

[1] Harvey, *British Rule in Burma 1824–1942*, p. 78.

politically than the Burmese, but mainly because there was no demand for reforms. On the contrary, opinion in the minority areas tended to be opposed to reforms. The people were not Burmese and viewed the Burmese with fear and distrust, which sprang from unhappy memories of friction and racial conflict in the past. The minorities saw clearly that in any reformed democratic Burma, where power would depend on the counting of heads, they would be at the mercy of the permanent Burmese majority. Furthermore the minorities had been governed indirectly, through their own chiefs. The chiefs were the only channels for the expression of their peoples' views and they saw that any democratic form of government, besides putting power into the hands of the Burmese, must inevitably undermine the aristocratic basis of their own position. Neither chiefs nor people wanted reforms. Both were actively loyal to the British. Without the latter they would be exposed to the danger of being overwhelmed or absorbed by the greater numbers, wealth, and ability of the Burmese. Because of their loyalty to the British they were apt to get a fuller and more sympathetic hearing from the government. Accordingly these hill areas were excluded from the scope of the new constitution, and from the jurisdiction of the High Court.

As the time for elections under the new constitution approached a split developed among the nationalists, never very firmly united, and two political parties emerged. The moderates, who came to be known as 'The 21 Party', and had the support of most of the intelligentsia, decided to co-operate in the matter of the new constitution at least to the extent of contesting the elections to the Legislative Council. The more extreme nationalists under the leadership of the G.C.B.A. and assisted by the G.C.S.S. decided to boycott the elections and the constitution entirely, and set about organizing non-co-operation and deliberate flaunting of the authority of the government. That less than 7 per cent of the electorate voted was naturally claimed a success for the extremist non-co-operators. But it was probably due at least as much to a wide lack of understanding and interest regarding the democratic processes that the British were seeking to introduce. In 1924 and 1925 non-co-operation led to a vigorous campaign to prevent the payment of taxes, and later to incitement to rebel against the government—in 1927–28 there was an abortive rising in Shwebo, followed by a good deal of large-scale dacoity. False allegations and rumours were spread in order to engender violence. It was widely believed in the villages that U Ottama had contracted an alliance with the King of France, that 10,000 foreign soldiers with four aeroplanes were to come to help the Burmese against the British, and that Home Rule would mean

the abolition of all taxes.[1] In 1925 the fragmentation to which all
Burmese political parties seem peculiarly prone, attacked the
G.C.B.A. which split again into less and more extreme wings. The
more extreme wing was fanatically opposed to co-operation of any
sort with the government or the constitution. It was supported by
the politically minded monks and soon fell under the domination of
the General Council of Sangha Samaggis. The less extreme wing felt
able to discuss and consider the question of co-operation, but in the
end also decided against it. This continued under the control of the
G.C.B.A. By 1929, however, the G.C.B.A. had again split into at
least four groups following their respective leaders.

This rapid growth of a popular political movement took everyone
by surprise. An official report read: 'For years past it might be said
that there were practically no politics in Burma. The year 1920–21
saw a rapid development of political activities among the people
which few, if any, of those most conversant with the psychology of
the Burmese people ever predicted or could have predicted.'[2] With
the advantage of hindsight this seems to suggest a considerable
failure to understand the Burmese psychology. If so, it sprang from
the fact, mentioned in the previous chapter, that while the British
had succeeded in establishing sympathetic, if limited, relations with
the people of the villages, they had largely failed to do so with more
educated people. But there were not many of these yet, and there
did indeed seem to be little or no spontaneous interest in politics.
Three factors brought about this sudden growth of a political movement. There was in the first place without doubt not so much an
active opposition to, but rather an underlying non-acceptance of,
foreign rule. Then the promulgation of the Montagu–Chelmsford
proposals for liberalization of the constitution gave at the same time
an opportunity and a direction for political activity where previously
there had been none, and also opened up the prospect of a career in
politics. Lastly, there was pressing instigation from politicians in India.

With the emergence of conscious political movements it becomes
convenient to follow the subsequent development of nationalism at
two levels. The one is the more articulate political level, which, if it
sometimes appears unbelievably trivial and less than rational, can at
least be rationalized. The other is the instinctive, unreasoning level,
where was generated the potentially dangerous pressure that under-
lay the frequently trivial political happenings, and that ultimately,
reinforced by the effects of the Japanese invasion, swept away the
cautious restraints the British sought to impose upon political
advance in Burma.

[1] Report of Indian Statutory Commission, 1930, Vol. XI, p. 27.
[2] Report of the Administration of Burma, 1920–21.

When the prospect of a liberalization of the constitution under the Montagu–Chelmsford reforms first stimulated activity at the conscious, political level, the one important question of principle thrown up, which dominated all political thought and action, was whether or not to participate in the new machinery of government. The declared long-term objective of both co-operators and non-co-operators was the extraction of further concessions that would lead to Home Rule and freedom from foreign domination. The point of difference was whether these could best be gained by co-operation and pressure within the liberalized constitution or by boycotting the new government, agitating, and making demands from without. This point continued to divide politicians after the introduction of the reforms. It is, disappointingly, fair to say that no other question of principle emerged, during the politics of this constitution. The plain fact was that, in trying to introduce a liberalized constitution, the British were giving to the Burmese something they did not want and did not know how to use. All that they did want was that the British should get out and leave them to mind their own affairs.

It was a part of the Montagu–Chelmsford reforms that their working would be reviewed after ten years with the intention of embarking upon further reforms if experience showed this to be practicable. As the time for the review approached – it began in 1929 – the question whether or not to participate in the first instalment of reforms ceased to matter. The one topic that arose to take its place was whether or not Burma should be separated from India. Controversy over this question became very involved.

The germ of the proposal to separate was contained in the Montagu–Chelmsford report where it was said that 'Burma is not India' and that the people of Burma are of 'another race in another stage of political development, and its problems are altogether different', and where Burma was excluded from the recommendations of the report and reserved for separate consideration. When the Burma government made proposals for an analogous constitution for Burma it made no recommendation for separation, but accepted that this would ultimately come about. In the first session of the Legislative Council under the 1923 constitution a resolution was passed favouring separation. There was no doubt that this correctly represented the views held by most of the country. The feelings of the Burmese for Indians in the mass were compounded of contempt, dislike, and a fear of being undercut by them because of their lower standard of living. Official circles, and more informed Burmese opinion, felt that the Indian connection was working to the disadvantage of Burma in several ways. The government of India took a considerable slice of the revenues of Burma, and a growing slice since the taxes that were allocated to central revenues, income tax and customs duties for example, were the elastic sources of revenue, whereas the provincial taxes, mainly land revenue, were incapable of much expansion. The benefits afforded to Burma in return were not impressive. When twenty years later the Japanese invaded the country, India, responsible for defence, was unable to prevent invasion. Then the central government of India was far away, and often gave scant consideration to the views and interests of Burma. Accordingly, as the time drew near for review of the working of the constitution, the government of Burma prepared recommendations which favoured the separation of Burma from India.

At once Burmese opinion took fright. It was remembered that all political advance had come to Burma as a part of India. It was feared that if Burma were to be separated from India she would drop out of the stream of constitutional progress. The very fact that the British government of Burma was pressing for separation roused the suspicions of the Burmese, political circles attributing this to an intention to withhold further constitutional advances. Official pronouncements by the British government that separation of Burma from India would in no wise prejudice her constitutional progress did nothing to allay these suspicions. Indian interests would be adversely affected by separation, and Indian money came to the support of the anti-separationists. A general election held in 1932 was fought on the separation issue and the result was an almost solid, if very surprising, vote *against* separation. First thoughts and speeches on assembly of the new house did not bring much light. But gradually it became clear that while Burmese opinion, as had been expected, favoured separation in principle, it wished, as a matter of tactics, to defer this until after Burma had derived the maximum political advantage from continued, albeit terminable, association with India. The British government was not prepared to give to Burma the option she desired of contracting out of the Indian government when she thought this might suit her convenience and decided that in view of the pledges given that separation would not prejudice political progress, the wishes and the welfare of the Burmese people would be best met by immediate separation. Separation was 'forced' upon Burma and accepted with a sigh of relief. There was no audible criticism, and the issue passed straight out of politics.

On 1 April 1937 Burma was separated from India and a new constitution came into force conferring a very real measure of self-government. The constitution was given body in the Government of Burma Act, 1935, and spirit in the Instrument of Instructions from

His Majesty to the Governor. It was no longer designed for a provincial government, subordinate to a central government in India: the new Burma was a fully individual government with a self-contained constitution. All functions of government that had under the previous constitution remained with the central government were now transferred to the government of Burma. Except in regard to functions which he was required to discharge 'in his discretion' or in respect of which he was required to 'exercise his individual judgment' (technical expressions which will be explained below), the Governor was required by the Instrument of Instructions to act on the advice of Ministers who commanded a majority in the legislature; and when acting on their advice he was removed from any control and superintendence by the Secretary of State and, therefore, by the British parliament. In respect of these functions of government real self-government was conferred upon Burma.

The legislature was expanded from a Legislative Council of 103, of whom eighty were elected, to a bi-cameral legislature consisting of a Senate of thirty-six members, half elected by proportional representation by the members of the other chamber and half nominated by the Governor 'in his discretion', and of a House of Representatives of 132 elected members, ninety-one from general constituencies and the remainder from communal, university, commercial, and labour constituencies. The Burmese always held 72 per cent of the seats in the House of Representatives, and the Ministries were almost exclusively Burmese.

The franchise was wide, perhaps dangerously wide, all males over eighteen who paid taxes, complied with certain property qualifications, or were military pensioners, being included, and all females over twenty-one, if able to pass an easy literacy test. Buddhist monks were accordingly not entitled to the vote – and would not have exercised it if they had been. The hill areas inhabited by the minorities remained outside the scope of the new constitution, for the same reasons that had led to their exclusion from the reforms of 1923. They were now known as the scheduled areas.

To return to the two technical expressions employed above, when the Governor was required to exercise his functions 'in his discretion' his Ministers were not entitled to place advice before him and he was required to act without their advice, provision being made for the appointment of official counsellors to advise him in regard to these functions. When the Governor was required to 'exercise his individual judgment' his Ministers were entitled to lay advice before him which normally he was required to accept, but the Governor was in specified circumstances, set out below, entitled, in fact required, to discard this. When discharging functions 'in his discretion' or in the 'exercise of his individual judgment' the Governor remained under the ultimate control of the Secretary of State and through him of the British parliament.

The more important subjects with which the Governor was required to deal 'in his discretion' were foreign affairs, defence, monetary policy, currency, coinage, and the administration of the scheduled areas. He was required to 'exercise his individual judgment', generally speaking, not in respect of specific functions of government, but in respect of any acts which touched certain special responsibilities laid upon him. These were broadly speaking the preservation of peace and tranquillity, the safeguarding of the financial stability and credit of the government, the prevention of discrimination against minorities, public servants, or British subjects, or against United Kingdom or Indian goods, and the securing that the discharge of his discretionary functions was not prejudiced. In the Instrument of Instructions the Governor was warned to be 'studious so to exercise his powers as not to enable his Ministers to rely upon his special responsibilities in order to relieve themselves of responsibilities which are properly their own'. Moreover, he was required to encourage the practice of joint consultation between himself, his official counsellors, and his Ministers, even in matters such as defence which were reserved to his 'discretion' or 'individual judgment'.

Indeed it cannot be too strongly emphasized that, whatever the written constitution may often seem to say, the Burmese parliament now had complete control, at least in internal affairs. Even the Governor's reserve powers were greater in theory than they proved to be in practice. It must again be added, however, that the prior claims upon the budget of the 'discretionary' and 'individual judgment' functions seriously curtailed the popularly elected ministry's room for manoeuvre.

After the introduction of this new constitution, there were, in the event, less than five years to go before Japan plunged the Far East into war and in so doing for the second time exercised a decisive influence upon the growth of Burmese nationalism. The separation issue was settled, and there was now no boycott of the constitution by the main parties. It might have been hoped that this would allow questions of policy and principle to take the centre of the stage. But such hopes would have been disappointed. For little or nothing of the kind developed from the friction between the several groups represented in the house. These were united in demanding further political advance but strongly divided as to the speed and methods advocated for this. But now that a real measure of power had been transferred, and that it had become clear that the future would see further transfers, what really divided and was the principal concern of those parties large enough to enjoy some prospect of power, was the resolve to make certain that it would be to themselves and not to their rivals that authority passed when the British ultimately relinquished control. An unedifying struggle for power developed. The obvious tactics were to outbid all opponents in demands for political advancement (and hence for the reduction or elimination of British influence) since such a policy made the greatest immediate popular appeal and was therefore the surest way to retain power within the existing rules, and also (to the extent that it succeeded in eliminating the British) to gain greater power under the rules as they might come to be altered. A disturbing development was that the two main contenders were not content to confine their campaigns to political, still less to constitutional, action, but began building up private armies for the exercise of political terrorism and for the seizure of power when the British left. Both developed clear Nazi or Fascist tendencies.

Initially there were three main contenders: Dr Ba Maw, leader of the *Sinyètha* Party; U Ba Pe, leader of the United G.C.B.A. Party; and U Saw, leader of the *Myochit* or Nationalist Party. Dr Ba Maw and U Saw prepared to seize power by force and were ready to cast themselves for the part of dictator. The former created the *Dahma Tat*, the latter the *Galon Tat*, both *Tats* (or armies) partaking of the character of the contemporary Black Shirts in Britain. Dr Ba Maw held office first but was overthrown by a coalition of the G.C.B.A. and *Myochit* parties under U Pu. After various convulsions within this coalition, U Saw ousted U Pu, in September 1940, and had become premier when the Japanese struck at Pearl Harbor in December 1941 and in due course invaded Burma. In February 1940, the House of Representatives had passed a resolution condemning the Germans, but seeking to make political capital out of this gesture by making Burmese support of the Allies conditional on the promise of early dominion status for Burma. In October 1941 U Saw visited London in an attempt to extract from the British government a promise of dominion status after the war. Disappointed in the reply he received, he set off for the United States and Burma, probably intending to visit Japan on the way. As he reached Hawaii war broke out and he was forced to turn back eastwards. The British had discovered that U Saw was offering help to the Japanese if they invaded Burma. Accordingly he was arrested in Egypt as he was making his way back to Burma, and kept in detention in Africa for the rest of the war. U Tin Tut, the senior Burmese member of the Indian Civil Service in Burma, who had accompanied U Saw as adviser, was also arrested but subsequently exonerated of complicity in the treasonable negotiations with Japan and released.

In this somewhat depressing pre-war scene one other development must be noticed. We have seen how in the early twenties nationalist feeling grew, was encouraged, if necessary implanted, and exploited for political ends, among students. From this there developed in the University of Rangoon through the 1930s an active interest in politics, particularly the politics of nationalism. One of the most forceful, not to say truculent, of the students in this movement was named Aung San. In 1936 an older student, Thakin Nu, and Aung San took part in offering deliberate provocation to the university authorities, Aung San's share being the publication of a distasteful libel concerning the Burmese bursar of University College. When these two ringleaders were expelled, students were brought out on strike in the cause of freedom. The University Council appointed a committee, with political representation, which recommended that most of the demands, including the reinstatement of both leaders, should be conceded. In 1938 Aung San became President of the Students' Union, and on leaving the university became General Secretary of the *Thakin* or 'Master' Party. This was a nationalist revolutionary group that had first come to notice in 1931, and in the general election of 1936 had managed to win three seats in the House of Representatives. It was recruited mostly from ex-university students, was communistic in outlook, using the hammer and sickle as its emblem, and was in touch with left-wing extremists in India, if, indeed, it did not owe its existence to them. It had the purblind integrity of many fanatics. It was hostile to all that could be considered foreign; was opposed, as a matter of tactics, to any political party that was willing to attempt to work the existing constitution; and critical, on idealistic grounds, and with much justification, of the leaders of these parties as being corrupt and venal. It would accept nothing less than complete independence for Burma and was perfectly prepared to use violence to attain this end. Aung San, after spending seventeen days in prison for promoting strikes and disturbances, visited India in 1940 as leader of the *Thakin* delegation to the Indian National Congress and met Gandhi and Nehru. When in 1940–41 the government of Burma was at length driven to proscribe this numerically insignificant group because of its hostility to the established government and to the Allied cause, some thirty of its members, including Aung San, escaped to Hainan where they were intercepted, received, and given military training by the Japanese.

We must turn back to trace the growth of nationalist feeling at the inarticulate level. Here something much more important was happening than the controversies over council-entry and separation, or the squabbles for political power.

In May 1930, in Rangoon, there was an outburst of racial violence, unexpected and unprecedented within the British period, when Burmese mobs attacked Indian labourers for two days throughout the town. Official reports placed the casualties at a hundred killed and about a thousand injured, but they were probably higher, possibly much higher. These riots were not political in any conscious sense. Against a background of economic deterioration causing increased resentment against Indian moneylenders and a heightening of competition between Indian and Burmese labour, they were sparked off by embittered feelings which not surprisingly were generated when Indian dock-workers struck for higher wages. Burmans were employed to break the strike, and then were discharged when this had been achieved. But if the riots were not political, they revealed suddenly the pressure of resentment against the presence of foreigners that had been building up amongst the Burmese.

At the very end of the same year, 1930, a rebellion broke out in Tharrawaddy. The leader, Saya San, gathered several thousand supporters around him in the hills and forests on the east of the district, and the rising spread to twelve out of forty districts. Saya San was captured, but not until August 1931, and the rising was not finally put down until March 1932. The troops employed for the purpose amounted to about one division and were mostly Indian. Casualties on the government side, including troops, police, headmen, and civilians, were about 70 killed (two of these were British) and 88 wounded. 'Several score' of Indians lost their lives.[1] On the rebel side known casualties amounted to 3,000. Some 9,000 surrendered or were taken prisoner. About 350 were convicted. Of these 78 were hanged. The others received heavy prison sentences. No death penalties were inflicted upon any persons who were not either active leaders of the rebellion or guilty of murder under the ordinary criminal law.

The view now officially disseminated in Burma is that
'The epic struggle of the Burmese peasantry against imperialist might in the early 1930s was not, as fabricated by some official records at the time, a classic effort of adventurism on the part of an unenlightened rabble incited by a visionary eager to seize power and crown himself a new king. It was essentially a desperate resort to armed force by a long-suffering people, as the only

[1] J. F. Cady, *History of Modern Burma*, New York, 1958, p. 317, fn. 91, based on H. of C. Debates, Vol. 262, 9 May 1932, pp. 1817–18, and H. of C. Sessional Papers, Vol. XIX for 1931–32 (Cmd. 3991), pp. 135–7.

available means to overthrow an imperialist régime which was pauperizing and bullying them to a point of endangering their survival.'[1]

The 'fabricated' official records say of the rebellion that 'Its object was the overthrow of Government and the enthronement of a jungle King, for in its prime origin it had little to do with either modern politics or economic stress . . . [It was] an outburst of medieval superstition of a recurrent and recognizable type.'[2]

The rebellion had little or nothing to do with the emerging nationalist movement, and nothing with the political issues of the time. Its leaders certainly did not comprehend these. It was not instigated by any of the political parties, though one section of the G.C.B.A. seems to have been to some extent involved. There was no real political support for it – though naturally there was considerable sympathy for the rebels, and there was some political capital sought to be made out of the rising. But if the rebellion was not instigated by the political parties it was certainly encouraged by the inflammatory anti-government talk of the politicians, and facilitated by the debilitating effect upon the administration of the constitutional reforms introduced. The rebellion was not predominantly due to economic causes – the slump in the rice market did not actually come until after it had broken out, and long after it had begun to be planned – though there was undoubtedly a background of agrarian discontent, and it may be that the wind had begun to blow before the approaching economic storm. It was just such a rising as had happened again and again in Burmese history, with the simple object of overthrowing the government and usurping the throne. Many had failed but some had succeeded and had led to the founding of new dynasties. In this, as in earlier risings, leaders and led acted in naïve ignorance and gross superstition. Harvey writes of the rebellion:[3]

'It was spread by an ex-monk who claimed magical powers. By tattooed charms, pills, oils, needles buried under the skin, he made men invulnerable, invisible, their bodies would rise and fly through the air, they could cause a hostile army to drop its weapons by merely sounding their enchanted gongs, and if they pointed their fingers at an aeroplane it would crash on the spot. They advanced on to our machine-guns believing these things, and they continued to believe even after they were wounded.'

If this picture is less than fair, because incomplete, it nonetheless conveys an important aspect of the atmosphere of the rising. What

[1] *Forward*, March 1965.
[2] Report on the Administration of Burma, 1930–31.
[3] *British Rule in Burma 1824–1942*, p. 73.

the rebellion did bring out was that the objection of the Burmese to being ruled by foreigners, and their resentment at the presence of foreigners, had not really grown less since the time of the pacification. It also made clear the ignorance and credulousness of the people, the ease with which they could be roused by demagogues or agitators, and the resultant danger to the maintenance of order.

In January 1931, even as the rebellion was spreading, rioting broke out again in Rangoon, this time against the Chinese. Attacks spread up-country from the capital, and a number of Chinese and Indians lost their lives.

For some years after the suppression of Saya San's rebellion in 1932 quieter conditions were restored. In this the beginnings of economic recovery in 1934–35 helped. But there was nevertheless a feeling abroad of uneasiness and strain. The next explosion came in 1938 with rioting and attacks upon Muslim Indians, which broke out in Rangoon and then swiftly spread all over the country. The official figures for casualties caused by Burmans to Indians (mostly Muslims) were 192 killed and 878 injured. The number of persons injured by the police in restoring order was 171, of whom 155 were Burmans. The destruction of shops and houses, and the looting of property, were extensive. The riots were deliberately caused by 'a piece of unscrupulous political opportunism'[1] which played upon and inflamed religious and nationalist sentiment and racial jealousy and dislike, in order to embarrass the ministry in power. Factors which made this possible included the economic situation (the recovery of 1934–35 had not continued) and a tense and unsettled atmosphere caused by labour agitation and unrest fostered for political ends. The riots were not, therefore, a spontaneous outburst of nationalist sentiment; but their violence, once they had been detonated, showed once more what dangerous racial and nationalist pressures were building up.

A year after these riots the Second World War broke out in Europe. Just over two years later it spread to the Far East when the Japanese attacked Malaya, Pearl Harbor, Hong Kong, and the Philippines. For the Western observer the curtain dropped temporarily over the Burma scene. Life did not, of course, cease for the Burmese behind the curtain. But the break in relations with the British was such that it seems desirable to attempt some summary of the position reached at this stage.

In the course of some thirty years nationalism, previously inarticulate and dormant, had become conscious and vocal. It had become organized into political parties and had spread throughout the nation – not least into the Buddhist monkhood. From being treated

[1] Final Report Riot Inquiry Committee, p. 292.

as something little more respectable than sedition, at least by the British, it had emerged as a political movement the objects of which were openly and freely discussed. The establishment of the constitutions of 1923 and 1937 with instalments of parliamentary democracy opened a new field and a ready-made programme and purpose for political activity in the form of demands for further instalments, and indeed for complete independence. These demands obsessed the thought and action of all parties to the almost complete neglect of any other questions of principle. And as independence was seen to be drawing near, political life degenerated into a bitter and unconcealed scramble between the various political groups, which combined and recombined in a struggle to capture positions of advantage from which to seize power when the British left. The main groups before the Japanese invasion were U Saw's *Myochit* Party, Dr Ba Maw's *Sinyètha* Party, and various sections of what survived of the old G.C.B.A. The most influential of these sections adhered to U Ba Pe, but there was also some following for U Chit Hlaing. The least important group to all appearances was that of the *Thakin* Party. But it was to this group that, in the event, power was to pass.

Chapter 8

The Gaining of Independence

THE EXPULSION OF THE British by the Japanese in 1942 was the real end of British rule in Burma, notwithstanding the facts that the Allied armies which included British-Indian, British, African, and American forces, under Admiral Mountbatten and Generals Leese, Slim, and Stilwell, defeated the Japanese and drove them out of the country in 1945, and that the British for a while managed to re-establish their administration. The habit of being governed by the British, and habit is one of the strongest factors making for the acceptance of government, had been broken. It was never to be re-established, although there were still six years to run before the formal gaining of independence.

For the first three of these years, the Japanese were in occupation of Burma. But contacts between Japan and Burma had begun before 1942. It is probably not possible to say how long there had been spying. But in May 1940 a Japanese military officer was sent by the Japanese General Staff to Burma, in civilian guise and under the name of Minami. His task was to enlist the armed support of the Burmese in the event of a Japanese invasion of the country. He approached most of the Burmese political parties, holding out prospects of independence in return for their co-operation. He does not appear to have been in close touch with the *Thakins* – though they are believed to have had earlier contacts with other Japanese. Partly this may have been because the *Thakins* did not then seem at all influential; partly because the *Thakins*, with their communist leanings, held the Japanese at arm's length, preferring the thought of co-operation with Indian communists, with China, or with Russia. In September 1940 Minami learnt that Aung San had fled the country, because his arrest was imminent for anti-government activities, and that he was on his way, with a companion, Hla Myaing, to the international settlement of Amoy on the Japanese-occupied coast of China, whence he hoped to make his way to communist China. The Japanese intercepted these two and persuaded them, possibly under pressure, to go to Japan instead. Other Burmese were smuggled out to Japan in the following year, to a total number of thirty. These young men were given military training, against the time when they would be needed.

The Japanese entered the war on the night of 7–8 December 1941, when their forces struck, without warning, at Malaya, Pearl Harbor, the Philippines, and Hong Kong, in order to clear the way for their main offensive southwards. In the second half of December their forces entered Burma from Siam in an advance directed upon Moulmein, and thence upon the plains of Burma, and Rangoon. Meanwhile their offensive in Malaya prospered and on 15 February 1942 Singapore fell. The advance in Burma was now intensified, and on 7 March the British-Indian forces, under General Alexander, were forced to abandon Rangoon, breaking out northwards through the encircling Japanese. By now the assistance of Chinese Kuomintang forces had been offered to the British and accepted. These forces, advancing southwards, took over the eastern part of the front, across the Sittang valley, up which ran the main road and railway from Rangoon to Mandalay. The British-Indian forces so relieved, together with those that had made their way out of Rangoon, formed a western front facing south across the navigable Irrawaddy valley, up which ran an alternative road from Rangoon through Prome to the north. On both these fronts the Japanese drove back the British-Indian and Chinese forces, which by June had been almost completely driven out of Burma into India and China respectively. The British Government of Burma withdrew to India and the nucleus of a civil administration for Burma was established in Simla.

With the Japanese forces invading Burma came the thirty young Burmans. Their task was to raise guerrilla forces from amongst their countrymen to aid the invading armies. This they did, and fought alongside the Japanese with some bravery. They exercised an effect upon the British-Indian forces quite out of proportion to their numbers, being largely responsible, in one way or another, for the apprehensiveness of fifth-column activities by the Burmese which was felt by the British-Indian troops. In addition, as the Japanese penetrated into Burma, these young Burmans sought to set up a provisional administration behind the advancing forces, and in attempting to establish their authority sometimes used harsh brutality, particularly against loyal employees of the departed government. In due course the Japanese put down these attempts to usurp authority. They had their own plans for the administration of Burma.

The Japanese invaders sought to appeal to Burmese nationalism by promising independence for Burma. They also hoped to build a feeling of Asiatic solidarity by talk of the creation of a South-East

Asia Co-Prosperity Sphere. In either case the object was to enlist Burmese support for the Japanese against the white man. The Japanese also planned to raise, through the instrumentality of the thirty Burmans whom they had been training, Burmese military units, which would both stimulate, and afford an outlet for, nationalist feelings, and which might make some military contribution to the Japanese cause, though it was never contemplated that they would play a major part. These units came to be known at first as the Burma Independence Army, or B.I.A., but the name was later changed to the Burma National Army or B.N.A. Their commander was Aung San.

About April 1942, by which time the Japanese had expelled the British-Indian forces from Rangoon, Thakin Tun Oke, a member of the *Thakin*, or *Do-Bama*, Party, was appointed Chief Administrator under the Japanese. But when on 1 August 1942 a provisional government was formally set up, subordinate to the Japanese command, it was Dr Ba Maw, undoubtedly the outstanding political personality of the time in Burma, who became the chief executive. In the back-to-front fashion of totalitarian régimes a political party was then formed to support the government which had already been installed, by an alliance of the old *Do-Bama* Party with Dr Ba Maw's own *Sinyètha* Party. The new party was known as the *Do-Bama–Sinyètha* Party. Final authority remained firmly in the hands of the Japanese military administration, though in many fields of administration it had little interest, and allowed the provisional government a very free hand.

A year later, on 1 August 1943, an 'independent' Burmese government was established, of similar political complexion, still with Dr Ba Maw as Head of State. The independent government declared war on the Allies – this was part of the price to be paid for independence. The new government was much less subject to direct administrative interference, but Japanese political authority and, in the last resort, their military power, ensured that the Burmese government complied with Japanese requirements in all matters essential to the conduct of the war.

But while the Japanese were deliberately seeking to build up Burmese nationalism towards their own advantage, they did quite as much, unintentionally, to stimulate it, and of course in the opposite direction, by their arrogance and brutality. Disillusionment filled the Burmese from the earliest contacts. U Nu, later to become the first Prime Minister of Burma, has written of those days:

'The whole air was breathing rumours. "The Japanese are our great friends." "When a Japanese meets a Burman he greets him with our own war cry." "The Japanese will die for Burma's freedom." "A Burman prince is coming as a leader in the Japanese army." They all firmly believed the messages scattered down from aeroplanes and broadcast on the wireless that the Japanese were coming to help Burma, and rumour had swollen a handful of hope until it overflowed the basket. Now they were off to welcome their great ally the Japanese, and though it was close on noon under the scorching sun of Mandalay, the poor people were so keen to greet their great ally that they did not even notice the heat. We met them again in the afternoon about four o'clock. They were no longer marching in a procession but limping along in clumps of three or four. Their faces were no longer joyful and exultant as in the morning, and they seemed quite shy of facing the people who had stayed at home. . . . We asked what had happened. One of them replied in a surly tone. "Don't talk about it. We expected the Japanese Commander to be very thankful for our bowls of rice, but all he did was to take his hand out of his trouser pocket and give us a hard slap in the face." And then he suddenly broke out laughing.

And another man chipped in "Talk about rough treatment! After he had slapped our faces he made us drag logs and draw water; drag, draw; drag, draw. It almost broke our backs." Then they all burst out laughing . . . And I thought to myself whatever one may say there is nothing much wrong with Burmans who can see the funny side of things even in the most unpleasant circumstances. And from that time onwards the news spread like wildfire from one village to another that the Japanese were a tough crowd.

After a day or two we moved on to Kanbaing village where we met Tet-pongyi Thein Pe, and Kyaw Nyein. They had already started the resistance movement against the Japanese . . .'[1]

Steadily this grew until in August 1944 an all-party underground resistance movement came into existence, known at first as the Anti-Fascist Organization, or A.F.O., and later as the Anti-Fascist Peoples' Freedom League, or A.F.P.F.L. This had close links with the B.N.A. Indeed the League and the Army were the two aspects, political and military, of one movement.

Meanwhile it was not only the Japanese who were fanning nationalist sentiment. In July 1942 Tet-pongyi Thein Pe, mentioned by U Nu above, and Thakin Tin Shwe, walked out of Burma to India, where they got in touch with Indian nationalists, but also with officers of the British government of Burma. From this time on the British clandestine organizations did their utmost to foment and support the Burmese nationalist resistance movement against the Japanese. The climax to their efforts came in March 1945 when the

[1] Thakin Nu, *Burma under the Japanese*, London, 1954, pp. 20–21.

B.N.A. deserted the Japanese and came over to the British. This transfer of allegiance was facilitated by the work of the British clandestine organizations, but was basically due to Burmese recognition of the fact that ever since mid-1944 the probability of ultimate Japanese victory had been extinguished, and that there was no longer anything to be gained in the pursuit of independence from co-operation with the Japanese. Whichever side they fought on it was with the object of gaining independence for Burma. After the battles of Kohima and Imphal, the turning-points of the war, Japanese encouragement of nationalism in Burma was directed less to gaining the support of the Burmese than to bequeathing a difficult and dangerous problem to the returning British after Japanese withdrawal.

The tergiversation of the B.N.A., and with it of the A.F.P.F.L., was the starting-point for post-war political relations between British and Burmese. It had been long worked for by the British, but when it came it presented the military authorities with difficult problems. Politically, the acceptance of the aid proffered carried the danger that the A.F.P.F.L. would be put in a position of advantage and be enabled to trade upon its services to claim political control and immediate political concessions after the war. In fact it was not at all clear to the British that the League would, in any fair test of opinion, enjoy the support of the country at large, particularly of the more moderate and stable elements, those elements to whom the British felt under obligations, and whom it was particularly desired to encourage. It was the *Thakin* element in Burmese politics that, under the Japanese, had created the B.N.A. and the A.F.P.F.L. And in the latest test of public opinion, the last election before the war, the *Thakins* had gained only three out of 132 seats in the House of Representatives. They had been at that time in no sense representative of Burmese opinion. To welcome with open arms an army which had fought against the British on the side of the Japanese for just so long as it had suited them, all of whose members were technically guilty of treason, was a poor way in which to reward and put heart into those Burmans who had remained loyal to the British connection or who, without necessarily wanting the continuance of this connection, nevertheless were opposed to the communistic ideas and dictatorial attitudes of the *Thakins*, and at least were prepared to achieve their emancipation along the gradualist lines to which the British were committed. Militarily, on the other hand, although the co-operation offered by the B.N.A. was not likely to have much positive value in formal operations against the Japanese, its rejection carried the danger that a rebuffed B.N.A. would turn hostile and that the diversion of forces which this would necessitate, to deal with

them behind the advancing Allied front, would result in a subtraction from the Allies' main strength sufficient to jeopardize the
success of their advance upon Rangoon. This advance had become
a race against the breaking of the monsoon. Failure to win the race
might impose, not only a halt, but withdrawal of Allied forces to
Upper Burma, out of reach of the rains, and so cause a year's setback in their operations. It was decided to accept the military aid of
the B.N.A. but to refuse any political recognition, and so far as
possible to guard against the acceptance being used to gain political
leverage. (But, of course, this was in the event not possible, as we
shall see.)

Some at least of the B.N.A. units fought courageously on the
Allied side and suffered severe casualties in full-scale operations.
Most were employed only for scouting, guerrilla, and flank guard
purposes. These dispatched Japanese stragglers and committed acts
of sabotage against Japanese communications. Their contribution
was appreciable, but not comparable to the much greater aid given
by the Chins, Kachins, and Karens. But as the British advance swept
swiftly down onto Rangoon, most of the B.N.A. were left behind.
Together with the members of the civilian A.F.P.F.L. they sought
to terrorize the police, other employees of the Burma government,
village headmen, and members of the public. By exacting tolls, and
by setting up local headquarters allegedly 'to maintain order', they
attempted to set up an administration of their own and to prevent
re-establishment of the British government of Burma. Off the main
lines of the British military advance the B.N.A. forces arrived in
the villages in the guise of victors who had driven out the Japanese,
with, possibly, inconsiderable assistance from the Americans or even
the British, and acted accordingly. If the British were to resume the
government of Burma, whether through a military or a civil government, this was not a position that they could afford to tolerate. It
became urgently necessary to disband the B.N.A.

But the B.N.A. was Aung San's main weapon in his struggle for
independence and power, and he was determined to resist its destruction. The plan ultimately agreed to by him, under pressure and with
many attempts at evasion, was that those members of the B.N.A.
who were willing, and found medically fit, should be recruited into
the regular Burma army and that the rest should be disbanded.
Aung San tried to stand out for the recruitment of battalions of the
B.N.A. into the Burma army *as units*. This would have preserved
their allegiance to him but would have undermined the discipline
and loyalty of the Burma army. The British insisted upon recruitment *as individuals*, B.N.A. recruits being distributed among the
existing battalions of the Burma army, and the B.N.A. battalions

1   On the platform of the Shwedagon Pagoda

2   Monastery of Thibaw's queen, Supayalat, Mandalay

3   Rangoon: Sule Pagoda; City Hall; Law Courts;
    Independence monument; Rangoon river

4   Mandalay Palace shortly after annexation in 1886

5   The outer wall and moat, all that is left of
     Mandalay Palace

6 Pagan, showing Thatpyinnyu Pagoda and Mount Popa behind range of hills

8 Kyaukpadaung Pagoda with bullock-cart in the foreground

7 Chinthes (mythical animals) guarding the approach to the pagoda at Mingun on the Irrawaddy

9 Making umbrellas, an ancient Burmese craft

10 Monks and acolytes receiving alms

11   Wood-carving, another Burmese craft

12   The mountains of the Kachin State, with ricefields
       ploughed by buffaloes in the foreground

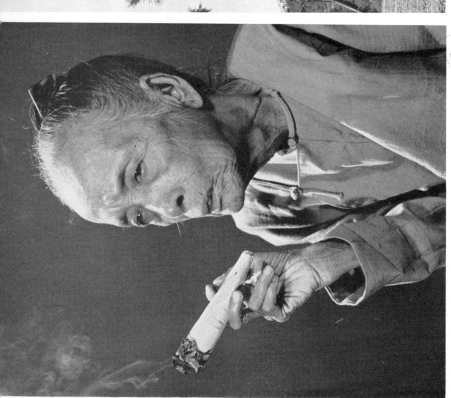

13 An old Burmese woman smoking a country cheroot

14 Mandalay Hill

15 Women transplanting paddy

16   Fishing on th
        Irrawaddy

17   Leg rowers on the Inle Lake in the Shan State

18 Hauling teak out of the Irrawaddy at Mandalay

19 Elephants hauling teak

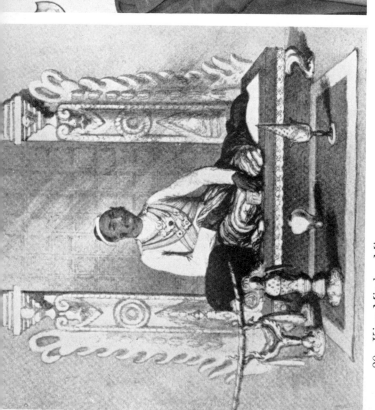

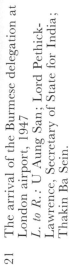

21 The arrival of the Burmese delegation at
London airport, 1947
L. to R.: U Aung San; Lord Pethick-
Lawrence, Secretary of State for India;
Thakin Ba Sein.

20 King Mindon Min

23 General Ne Win

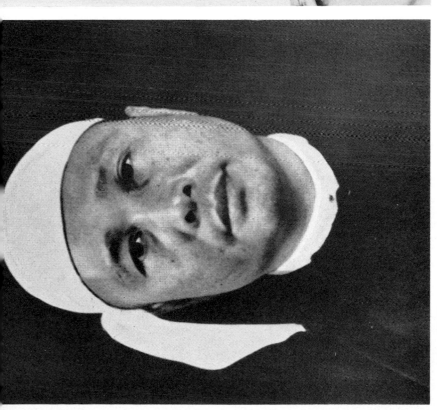

22 U Nu

24 An Anyein *Pwè*

25 A group of Burmans travelling to a monastery near Pagan for an Initiation Ceremony, bearing gifts for the monks

26   Shwedagon Pagoda, Rangoon

27   Sir Hubert Rance and U Aung San

ceasing to exist as such. Aung San was driven to agree to this, but he did not like it. The result was that although some 4,700 members of the B.N.A. were recruited into the Burma army, some 3,500 were not. At the same time the People's Volunteer Organization (P.V.O.) came into existence. Professedly an ex-service association for social work, there is no doubt that this included many of those who had not volunteered for the regular army. It began to appear that while Aung San had probably not relinquished his claims upon the personal loyalty of those members of his forces who had been recruited into the regular army, it was in the form of the P.V.O. that he and the A.F.P.F.L. executive had decided to preserve the flower of their private army. Not many months after the return of the civil government this ex-service association for social work was indulging in such military activities as dummy weapon drill and tactical exercises on the open spaces near the Shwedagon Pagoda in Rangoon. The existence of this private A.F.P.F.L. army, capable of use against the government or against other political parties, was to be a decisive factor in the months to come.

But it was the Governor of Burma in Simla and the British government in London who really had to face the political problems involved in the acceptance of aid from the B.N.A. In May 1945 the British government set out its policy for Burma in a white paper. It proposed that there should in the first place be direct rule by the Governor for a period that would probably not exceed three years and might be less. During this period the Burmese would be associated with the administration through a nominated executive council and later, perhaps, a small legislative council. In the next stage the 1935 constitution would be restored. At the same time steps would be taken to devise a new constitution for the third stage, which would confer upon Burma proper full self-government within the Commonwealth. The frontier areas, inhabited by the chief minority communities, would be excluded from these arrangements. When a form of government had been agreed upon it would be put into effect. No maximum period was prescribed for the second stage. The motives underlying these proposals were mixed. It was clear that Burma and her economy would be in a sorry state after two campaigns had been fought across the country. The British felt that responsibility for this lay heavily upon them since they had been unable to protect the country from the Japanese invasion. They felt, disinterestedly, that the least they could do was to restore order and administrative regularity, as an indispensable prerequisite to the reintroduction of democratic procedures. They also felt that they must revive the economy, before handing over the task of government to the Burmese. The white paper did not specify the means to be employed to this end, but it was known that it was proposed to do this through the instrumentality of the British and Indian firms that had previously operated in Burma. Here the motives were less disinterested since this would give British business the opportunity to re-establish its hold on the economy of Burma. But while Burma was a part of the British Commonwealth, Britons and Indians, no less than Burmese, enjoyed Commonwealth citizenship, and the government of Burma bore responsibilities towards them as well as towards the Burmese. In any case it seemed clear that the Burmese could not themselves revive their own economy – and later events have amply justified this assumption – so that there were in fact no other agencies available.

The Governor, Sir Reginald Dorman-Smith, explained the provisions of the white paper to a meeting of representatives of all shades of political opinion held on the cruiser H.M.S. *Cumberland* in the Rangoon river, on 20 June 1945. He emphasized that there was every hope that the period of direct rule would be less than three years, and said that he would establish without delay an executive council representative of all parties.

These proposals, reasonable, indeed generous, in relation to the pre-war British conception of a gradual progress to self-government, and to the need for economic rehabilitation, failed altogether to take into account the standing which the A.F.P.F.L. had won for itself, both under the Japanese and during the Allied invasion. They were not acceptable to Aung San and the A.F.P.F.L. They represented not more but less power and responsibility than the Burmese had enjoyed before the Japanese occupation. In particular, the scrupulous, and constitutionally proper, refusal of the Governor to accept the A.F.P.F.L. as representing the people of Burma until elections had shown this to be so, was quite unacceptable. The A.F.P.F.L. had claimed to be already the provisional government and still thought of themselves as such, and all that they were interested in was how to convert the 'provisional government' into the recognized lawful government of the country with the least possible delay. The white paper programme was far too slow for them – indeed it was not possible to say how long it would require. It put Burma further back constitutionally than she had been in 1939. And

> 'There is a tide in the affairs of men,
> Which, taken at the flood, leads on to fortune;
> Omitted, all the voyage of their life
> Is bound in shallows and in miseries.'

If power did not pass at once, it might not be to the A.F.P.F.L. or to Aung San that it would pass in the end. Worse than any specific constitutional or political provisions of the white paper were the known plans for reviving the economic life of Burma during the period of direct rule by means of 'projects'. These were themselves official or semi-official bodies, but the active agencies working under them consisted of, or were formed from, the foreign firms that had operated in Burma before the war, and the arrangements planned would clearly lead to the re-establishment of these firms. The A.F.P.F.L. felt that if they had learnt one lesson it was that political freedom was worth little if there was not also economic independence, and they were resolved to oppose the return of foreign business interests by every means available.

Four months later, in October 1945, the Governor resumed responsibility for the government of the greater and most important part of Burma. When forming his Executive Council he invited the A.F.P.F.L. to suggest candidates for seven seats out of eleven; to the remaining four he proposed to make appointments himself and it was known that Sir Paw Tun and Sir Htoon Aung Gyaw would get the Home and the Finance Departments, the two key portfolios which these old faithfuls (who had indeed accompanied the Governor into exile in India) had held before the war. The A.F.P.F.L. stipulated that all the League's nominees should be accepted or none, that the League should determine which portfolios they should hold, and that one of them must be that of the Home Department. Finally, they stipulated that all their seven members should be allowed to report to the A.F.P.F.L. and receive their instructions from the League. These conditions were rejected by the Governor and the British government; they could not have been accepted without fundamental modification of the policy in the white paper, which was that the British should remain responsible for the government of Burma until rehabilitation had reached a level that would permit of other arrangements, for under these conditions the League would clearly have become the *de facto* provisional government of Burma. The Governor's Council was therefore formed without any A.F.P.F.L. representatives. Aung San and the A.F.P.F.L. went into opposition – not parliamentary opposition within a constitutional framework, but unrelenting opposition to the temporary constitution itself, inspired by a firm determination to destroy the whole governmental and administrative organization, in order to replace it by something of their own devising.

There followed an eleven months' contest between the government and the A.F.P.F.L. In January 1946 the latter convened its first nationwide rally which consolidated support for the League and enhanced the standing of Aung San. At about the same time the Governor brought back to Burma Thakin Ba Sein and Thakin Tun

Oke who had been exiled to Malaya by the Japanese, and also
U Saw who had been imprisoned by the British. This was done not
so much with the object of creating an opposition to the A.F.P.F.L.
as to give to any opposition that existed the opportunity to build
itself up around them and so to test the League's claim, unsupported
by elections, that it represented the people of Burma. The British
were still far from convinced that the A.F.P.F.L. were representative
of general Burmese opinion. On 28 February, in the newly appointed
Legislative Council, Thakin Tun Oke accused Aung San of having
murdered, in 1942, a village headman, while the Burma Independence Army was aiding the Japanese invaders. Aung San did not
deny the accusation but claimed that the headman had been executed on the sentence of a 'court martial' for giving information to
the British and raising villagers against the Japanese. The government had received information of these events earlier, but no formal
complaint, and so had been able to avoid taking action. Now it was
not possible to avoid a decision whether to arrest and try Aung San.
Police and military in Burma were against arrest, mainly on the
ground that it would precipitate rebellion. The Supreme Allied
Commander, Admiral Mountbatten, was also opposed. The Governor's two senior British officials felt that rebellion was coming anyway and that since a police investigation had been ordered and
revealed a *prima facie* case, failure to arrest Aung San would bring
the law into contempt, and would in fact amount to an abdication
of power. These views carried the day and the British government
ordered arrest. Second thoughts led to the government counter-
manding these orders, just in time to prevent effect being given to
them. The result was to make it clear to the A.F.P.F.L. (who were
extremely well-informed of what took place in government circles
and could, in any case, have guessed without great difficulty) that
the British government did not dare to arrest Aung San. Con-
currently with these more dramatic events, the League continued,
on all possible occasions, its protests against the plans for the re-entry
of foreign business firms to Burma.

In the course of this contest it became clear that the A.F.P.F.L.
was supported, probably by a majority, possibly by a big majority,
of the country, and that in the circumstances of the time the League
would in any case, if not by fair means then by foul, win any general
election, whatever the real wishes of the people. It also became clear
that there were no other political parties or groups at all that could
hope successfully to oppose the A.F.P.F.L. Early in 1946 there was
growing disorder throughout the country and steadily the likelihood
of rebellion increased. It was forced upon the British government
that there was no other way out from the situation but to enlist the

co-operation of the A.F.P.F.L. It bears repeating at this point that the British were not opposing independence or going back on any promise of freedom; what they had been standing out against was the forcible seizure of power by an organization that was known to practise intimidation and was not known to have the willing support of a majority.

Implementation of this changed policy would be easier, and would have better chance of success, with a new Governor. Sir Hubert Rance replaced Sir Reginald Dorman-Smith, charged with the task of enlisting the co-operation of the A.F.P.F.L. But almost as soon as he had arrived, a strike of the police force broke out, on 2 September. There were crying economic grievances which the government had altogether failed to remove – wartime and post-war inflation had rendered police pay derisorily inadequate, but there is no reasonable doubt that the strike was instigated by the A.F.P.F.L., and there is no doubt at all that it was supported by the League. On 17 September a strike of other government employees followed, and on 24 September strikes of railway- and oil-workers completed the paralysis of the country. The People's Volunteer Organization, with brazen effrontery, took over the policing of Rangoon, and made a significant and very largely successful appeal to criminals to abstain from crime during the strikes in the national interest. The government was helpless. The new Governor had come with authority to reconstitute his Executive Council, but was in fact compelled by the strikes to do so. In the new Council there was a majority of A.F.P.F.L. representatives. Aung San, by the device of being appointed an official counsellor to the Governor, became deputy chairman and was given the Department of Defence and External Affairs, while U Kyaw Nyein took charge of the Home Department. From now on real power was in the hands of the A.F.P.F.L.

On 10 November 1946 Aung San, the Executive Council, and the A.F.P.F.L. presented a four-point demand to the British government:

1. There were to be elections for a constituent assembly in April 1947.
2. The elections were to include representatives of the frontier areas.
3. The British government was to proclaim before 31 January 1947 that full independence would be conferred within a period of one year.
4. There was to be a re-examination of the 'projects' scheme within the same period.

On 20 December 1946 the British Prime Minister, Clement Attlee, said in the House of Commons:

'We do not desire to retain within the Commonwealth and Empire
any unwilling peoples. It is for the people of Burma to decide
their own future . . . The day to day administration . . . is now in
the hands of Burmese members of the Governor's Executive
[Council] . . . For the sake of the Burmese people, it is of the
utmost importance that this should be an orderly – though rapid –
progress.'[1]

In January 1947 a delegation consisting of Aung San, Thakin Mya,
Ba Sein, Tin Tut, Ba Pe, and U Saw came to London. U Tin Tut
was the senior and most able Burmese member of the Indian Civil
Service which, after the separation of Burma from India, became the
Burma Civil Service, Class I. He had resigned in order to take a part
in politics. The delegation was accompanied by four advisers:
U Kyaw Nyein, U Aung Than, Thakin Chit, and U Ba Yin. Active
preparations continued for rebellion in Burma in case the delegation
did not gain its demands. But the principle of independence was
quickly conceded. There would be elections to a constituent
assembly in April 1947. Until a constitution had been worked out by
the assembly and agreed to by the British government, the Executive
Council of the Governor would be the interim government of Burma
and would be treated 'with the same close consultation and consideration as a Dominion Government and will have the greatest
possible freedom in the exercise of the day-to-day administration of
the country'. On one point only were the Burmese demands apparently not conceded outright. The Burmese had been insistent that
independent Burma must include the frontier areas, in which lived
most of the minority races of the country. What was conceded at the
London meeting was that 'it is the agreed objective of both His
Majesty's Government and the Burmese delegates to achieve the
early unification of the Frontier Areas and Ministerial Burma with
the free consent of the inhabitants of those areas'.

To understand what was at issue here it is necessary to look back.
When the first steps were taken towards self-government, in the
constitution of 1923, almost half the area of Burma, and about one-
third of the population, were excluded from the scope of the reforms, and continued to be governed much as they had been in the
past.[2]

When the next instalment of self-government came in 1937 the
frontier or scheduled areas, for the same reasons, still remained outside the scope of the new constitution.[3] The Burmese, who by now
had a very real measure of self-government within the predominantly

---

[1] Cady, op. cit., p. 540.
[2] See above, pp. 110-11.
[3] See above, p. 115.

Burmese part of the country, naturally resented this exclusion. To them it appeared as nothing but an example of 'divide and rule'.

Accordingly, when the A.F.P.F.L. took the political field against the British in 1945 it was a leading item in the League's demands that the scheduled areas must be included within independent Burma. For the British this was a difficult point to concede. They felt that history justified the minorities in their apprehensions that they could not expect a fair deal from the Burmese. By excluding the minorities from the reformed constitutions of 1923 and 1937 they had, by implication at least, recognized these apprehensions, and encouraged the minorities to believe that they would not be placed under Burmese rule. And through the war the minorities had greatly added to the obligations under which their loyalty had placed the British. The Chins, the Kachins, and the Karens all gave gallant and valuable military support to the British in the war against the Japanese. For much of the time that these people were fighting and giving their lives for the British cause, the Burmese fought on the other side. Only when it became clear that the British, not the Japanese, would win, and that there was more hope of independence to be got from supporting the British rather than the Japanese, did the Burmese change sides. Accordingly the British took the line with the A.F.P.F.L. that any arrangements for the inclusion of the minorities within an independent Burma must be acceptable to the minorities.

In January 1947 when the British government conceded the principle of full independence, they stipulated that inclusion of the minorities within independent Burma, which was an integral part of the demands presented by the Burmese, must depend on the 'free consent' of those affected. Joint efforts were to be made by British and Burmese to obtain this consent. The Burmese demands were backed by an implicit threat of rebellion, of attacks upon Europeans, and of the destruction of the government, if the negotiations in London were to break down. The only thing that separated the parties was the question of the minority areas. Failure to gain the 'free consent' of the minorities was unthinkable, for this could only result in the rejection of the offer by the A.F.P.F.L. In this case insurrection and chaos would result. In the circumstances both British and Burmese were deeply committed to obtaining that 'free consent'. Indeed it is pretty clear that the British government was not prepared to take no for an answer from the frontier areas. For the London agreement, although it referred to the 'free consent' of the inhabitants of these areas, went on to provide that the views of the inhabitants should be ascertained regarding the arrangements for the government of the areas both under the existing interim government and under the future independent government of Burma. The question that was to be put to the inhabitants about both these periods was not whether the frontier areas should or should not be unified with the rest of Burma. It was assumed that unification would take place. In regard to the interim government the minorities were to be asked 'to express their views upon the form of association with the Government of Burma which they consider acceptable during the transition period'. As far as independent Burma was concerned a committee was to be set up to inquire 'as to the best method of associating the frontier peoples with the working-out of the new constitution for Burma'. It is clear that it was not intended that the minorities should be consulted on the question that was really exercising them. In excuse for this burking of the real issue it may be argued that separate independent states for the minorities would not have been politically, militarily, or economically viable, and that the British could not in fact afford to oppose the Burmese on this point. The Shans could have opted for inclusion in Thailand whose people are of similar race, though they probably would not have done so. In the circumstances it may be felt that the unsophisticated leaders of the minority communities never had much choice or chance.

A conference was held at Panglong near Loilem in the Shan States in February 1947 to consider arrangements for the period of the interim government. Two or three months before this Aung San had met the leaders of the minorities, in the same place. He had then offered the minorities a separate status with full autonomy, participation in government at the centre, the protection of minority rights, and the right of secession. They were now promised, for so long as the interim government continued, a Shan counsellor, assisted by two deputy counsellors, one Kachin and the other Chin, to sit in the Governor's Council for the management of the affairs of the frontier areas. It is said that they were also promised that the first President of independent Burma should be a Shan, if they would agree to be a part of independent Burma, and in the event the first President, Sao Shwe Thaik, was a Shan Sawbwa. All the persuasiveness of Aung San and of the British representatives was brought to bear upon the leaders of the minorities. On 12 February 1947 these passed a resolution accepting that 'freedom will be more speedily achieved by the Shans, the Kachins and the Chins by their immediate co-operation with the Interim Burmese Government' and entered into various specific agreements with the interim government. British and Burmese heaved sighs of relief. The independence agreement could go through.

But whatever the minorities may have felt about becoming a part of independent Burma – and on this extremely difficult question for them they probably did not know what they felt – it is clear that they had not agreed to their inclusion. What they had agreed to was *co-operation*, and co-operation, not with independent Burma, but with the interim Burmese government, which still had a British Governor, and under which they were guaranteed that there would be no diminution in the independence they had hitherto enjoyed from control by the government set up under the constitution of 1937.

A month later a committee was set up, as provided in the London agreement, charged to inquire into and report on 'the best method of associating the frontier peoples with the working-out of the new constitution for Burma', so, once again, begging the question whether these peoples should be included within the new Burma and the scope of the new constitution at all. It quickly became clear to the committee that it was this question that was really exercising the frontier peoples, that it was extremely difficult for them to understand what was involved, that all desired separate status with the fullest possible autonomy, and that any agreement to enter into a federation postulated the right to secede. The committee in due course made its proposals for the inclusion of the frontier peoples in the new constitution.

But meanwhile, on 7 April 1947, elections had been held for the Constituent Assembly. The A.F.P.F.L., not unexpectedly, gained an overwhelming majority, and work began on the preparation of a constitution for an independent sovereign republic outside the Commonwealth.

It is now sometimes claimed by the Burmese that their departure from the Commonwealth was not of their own choosing but was forced upon them by the British. The argument runs that the Burmese leaders would have preferred to remain within the Commonwealth. On the other hand they felt that it was politically impossible for them to accept any status less than that of a fully sovereign republic, appointing its own Head of State, because anything less than this would have exposed them to allegations by the Burma Communist Party, and the people at large, that they had been duped by the British and fobbed off with less than real independence. But the construction then placed upon the Statute of Westminster was such that all countries within the Commonwealth must accept the British sovereign as their Head of State; this made it impossible for a republic to be a member of the Commonwealth. Only later, when more important countries, such as India, wished to remain within the Commonwealth, although becoming republics, was a formula evolved that made this possible. It was not evolved for Burma, since Burma was politically less influential. It was the failure to evolve this formula that excluded Burma.

There is no doubt that the British would have liked to retain Burma within the Commonwealth if this had been possible. And there seems little doubt that Aung San, Tin Tut, U Nu, and others of the Burmese leaders, began to think, but only at a late stage, probably after the negotiation of the Attlee–Aung San agreement in January 1947, that there might be advantages in remaining within the Commonwealth after all. Trust and mutual respect had grown up between Sir Hubert Rance and U Aung San, and the fair and courteous treatment accorded to the Burmese delegation in London had made its impression. But before accepting that it was merely the fact that Burma insisted upon becoming a republic that resulted in her exclusion from the Commonwealth, we need to consider whether, if the formula making possible the inclusion of a republic had been devised before Burma had to make her choice, it would in fact have been politically possible for her to choose to remain within the Commonwealth. There was widespread distrust of Britain's motives among the people of Burma, much of it whipped up by the propaganda of the A.F.P.F.L. leaders themselves. There was the ever-present need not to be outbid by the Burma Communist Party. There were influential unofficial British advisers who urged the Burmese 'not to make the mistake of opting to remain inside the Commonwealth' because this would only be 'sham independence'.[1] It may be seriously doubted whether it would have been politically possible for Burma's leaders to opt to remain within the Commonwealth at this time, republic or no. That this was the view taken by the British government would explain the scant attention paid by it, despite its desire to keep Burma within the Commonwealth, to last-moment overtures apparently made by U Nu when he visited London to execute the treaty of independence in October 1947.

However this may be, on 4 January 1948 Burma became an independent republic, outside the Commonwealth.

But the man who above all others had brought this about was no more. On 19 July 1947 two men with automatic weapons had pushed their way into the room in the Secretariat where the Executive Council was sitting, opened fire on those round the table, and made their escape. Aung San and seven other councillors were dead. The assassinations had been instigated by U Saw, possibly encouraged by irresponsible British elements, in the hope of creating confusion that would enable him to seize power. Whether he could ever have succeeded was not put to the test, for, in response to an appeal by the

[1] Vum Ko Hau, *Profile of a Burmese Frontier Man*, privately printed, 1963, p. 96.

Governor, U Nu instantly and courageously formed a new Council, so steadying the situation and preventing the disorders from which U Saw had hoped to profit. But Aung San and seven of the best and most dependable of his colleagues were dead, a loss from which Burma has not yet recovered, and from which it is probable that she never will recover.

Chapter 9

Independence

THE BRITISH HAD GONE. The future belonged to the Anti-Fascist Peoples' Freedom League. This was now a nationwide movement with little or no opposition apparent. It had been an independence movement. What would it become now that its objective had been gained?

Pre-war party groupings had become largely irrelevant, and what was left of the old parties had been incorporated into the League. In September 1945, however, a new party, the Socialist Party, had come into existence. This was numerically unimportant, and had little or no organization in the field, but it included in its ranks most of the intellectuals of the independence movement, men who had been students at the university before the war, many of them contemporaries and colleagues of Aung San. Most had belonged to the *Thakin* group before the war, and the party was, for practical purposes, the successor to the *Do-Bama* Party. They, more than any other groups, influenced the A.F.P.F.L. ideology. For them, and therefore for the League, socialism had become an article of faith. Indeed there was probably no party or group that could afford to take a contrary view.

The reasons for this 'compulsive' socialism are not difficult to discern. In the first place socialism, whatever view may be taken of its merits in practice, is a creed of ideals which appeal especially, and rightly, to the young. The *Thakins* were young when they began to think politically, and had remained young both in the ardour of their ideals and in the scantiness of their experience. Then everywhere socialism is the creed of revolutionaries. The *Thakins*, and then the A.F.P.F.L., were revolutionaries. It was almost automatic that they should become socialists. But in any case the *Thakins* had largely learnt their political thinking from English books and in these 'advanced' thought was seldom anything but socialist in flavour. Furthermore, as a revolutionary party the *Thakins* had been in touch with the left wing in India and had been both influenced and exploited by it. This left wing was for the most part communist and pushed the not unwilling *Thakins* along the same path.

But there was another, still more compelling, reason why socialism was accepted as the very air that the new Burma breathed. Quite simply, what every Burman nationalist most desired was to get the foreigners out of his country, to step into their jobs, and to gain for himself and for Burma control of the country's resources. In Burmese experience foreigners were equated with capitalists. It was scarcely to be expected that the Burmese should do anything but adopt a political creed one of whose central tenets was that the people must own the means of production and that, to achieve this, capitalists must be expropriated. Here was a screen of respectable academic doctrine behind which the Burmese could attain their very natural desires.

The constitution of the Union of Burma, framed by the Constituent Assembly before the departure of the British, borrowed details from the United States, from France, from Yugoslavia, but overwhelmingly it was derived from the United Kingdom. It rather curiously synthesized federal and unitary characteristics. In form Western parliamentary democracy as practised at Westminster was set up in Burma. But although democratic in form, the main intention underlying the legal phrases was not so much to enable the people of the country to choose the political ideology they preferred as to establish and safeguard socialism in Burma. Economic and social welfare was prominently written into the constitution itself rather than being a matter for contention between competing parties, and choice by parliament. The high aspirations of the time were set out in the preamble:

'We the people of Burma, including the Frontier Areas and the Karenni States, determined to establish in strength and unity a Sovereign Independent State, to maintain social order on the basis of the eternal principles of Justice, Liberty and Equality, and to guarantee and secure to all citizens justice social, economic and political; liberty of thought, expression, belief, faith, worship, vocation, association and action; Equality of status, of opportunity and before the law, in our Constituent Assembly this tenth day of Thadingyut waxing, 1309, B.E. (twenty-fourth day of September, 1947, A.D.) do hereby adopt, enact and give to ourselves this Constitution.'

Brave words indeed. But as we have seen earlier, no party had ever looked beyond the immediate task of ejecting the British, except perhaps to try to ensure that the mantle of the departing rulers should fall upon itself rather than upon another party. There had been no policy but the attainment of independence. And it was the resolve to work for this that alone had united the conflicting interests brought together within the Anti-Fascist Peoples' Freedom League.

As soon as the British had left and this unifying purpose had disappeared disintegration followed.

Pending the holding of a general election, U Nu's A.F.P.F.L. government, formed after the assassinations of July 1947, and the Constituent Assembly elected in April of that year, continued in existence as the government and parliament of the new Republic of the Union of Burma. The task that faced it was horrific. Indeed, a more experienced government would probably have been daunted. Even before the attainment of independence there were two groups in armed insurrection against the government. These were the 'Red Flag' (more intransigent but less numerous) communists and the *Mujahids*, Muslims in the north of Arakan. Within a few weeks of independence other groups and sectional interests also took up arms against the A.F.P.F.L. government. Within six months of independence the forces of violent opposition had still further increased to a point at which it is possible to enumerate the following groups in arms against the government – though there may well have been others:

Red Flag communists
Mujahids
The P.V.O.
White Flag communists
P.B.F. battalions of the army in mutiny
The Union Military Police, consisting largely of P.B.F. and P.V.O.
The Karen National Defence Organization
Some of the 1st Kachin Rifles in mutiny
The Mon National Defence Organization

The Shans may also have been in the field.

It is not difficult to understand why the racial minority groups, the *Mujahids*, the Karens, the Kachins, and the Mons, had taken to the jungle. Other racial minorities, spurred by apprehension regarding the treatment they might expect from the Burmese, were in due course to follow their example. But it is at first sight less easy to understand why the communists, the P.V.O., the P.B.F. battalions of the army, and the P.V.O. and P.B.F. members of the Union Military Police should have rebelled against the A.F.P.F.L., for the great majority of these were Burmese, and all had taken part in the nationalist movement – indeed the P.V.O. and P.B.F. had once been the B.N.A., and the B.N.A. and the A.F.P.F.L. had then been the two aspects, military and civil, of one organization, the nationalist movement of Burma. Why did they now fall out?

As for the communists, they were divided from the A.F.P.F.L. by ideological differences, but these were slight and could very easily have been reconciled if there had been any desire to do so. It seems that their defection under Than Tun was nothing but a move in the struggle for power. In the event it became clear that Than Tun had overestimated his strength against the A.F.P.F.L. But if he had displayed a little more leadership, and ability to make common cause with minorities, a little less bigotry, the outcome of the struggle might well have been different. As for the P.V.O. and P.B.F., the problem posed by them for the A.F.P.F.L., as soon as it became the government of the country, was the same problem that had troubled the British military administration under Mountbatten. Then the B.N.A., copiously armed and indifferently controlled, had lived on the country, had terrorized government servants and the public, and had sought to establish an administration of their own. British measures to disarm and control these troublemakers had been only partially successful, Aung San managing to retain much of his private army, whether in the regular Burma army or in the People's Volunteer Organization. Now the same thing happened again. The P.V.O. and the ex-members of the P.B.F. continued to live off the country, to terrorize the people, and to flout the government. Any attempt by the government to disarm the P.V.O. succeeded only in antagonizing the latter. The loyalty of the P.V.O. and P.B.F. to Aung San, which might have kept them on the side of the government if Aung San had still been alive, was personal to their old military leader and comrade-in-arms of the resistance and did not extend to U Nu. When it became clear that they could no longer exercise the influence to which they had been accustomed they went into revolt against the government. In September 1948 the government and country suffered a severe loss in the murder, for political reasons, of U Tin Tut, who had until a month before been a cabinet Minister, and had been a survivor of the assassinations of 19 July 1947.

The lowest point in the government's fortunes was reached in February–March 1949. Advancing rebel forces seized Insein, 11 miles from Rangoon; fighting took place at Thamaing, a suburb of Rangoon; and the following major towns (together with many lesser ones) were in the hands of rebels: Mandalay and Maymyo, Kyaukse, Meiktila, Yamethin, Toungoo, together with Pyinmana and Nyaunglebin, half of Pegu, Thaton, Pakokku, Myingyan, Magwe, together with Chauk and Yenangyaung, Minbu, Thayetmyo, Prome, Henzada, Tharrawaddy, Bassein, Loikaw, Papun, Rathedaung, and Buthidaung. Moulmein had been occupied by Karen rebels but handed back to the government. Geographically the greater part of the country and, with the single but important exception of Rangoon, by far the most important part, was in the hands of rebels.

This loss of territory naturally meant that there was no revenue coming into the government's treasuries. To counter this collapse in its finances, cuts were imposed on the salaries of all government employees. As a result, these employees came out on strike. Railway employees and students joined the strikers. At the same time, within what remained of the A.F.P.F.L., the socialists made a bid for power. When outnumbered and worsted by the joint action of the various independent groups in the government, they broke away into somewhat uncertain opposition.

In terms of human misery, there was fighting, looting, destruction of villages, burning of schools and places of worship, and great loss of life throughout the country. The fiercest and bloodiest clash was with the Karens. Tinker – who has gone out of his way to be generous to the Burmese – says: 'It would be profitless to attempt to establish who offered the first, and most, provocation.'[1] But virtually all the specific incidents he mentions are massacres of Karens by Burmese. In the Palaw township of the Mergui district Burmese auxiliary military police attacked Christian Karens while at worship in eight churches and murdered some eighty of them. At Taikkyi in the Insein district, twenty Karen houses were attacked and destroyed, 150 Karens were killed, thirty being deliberately murdered. In Ahlone, a suburb of Rangoon, the Karen quarter was set on fire, fire-engines were prevented from reaching the scene, and many Karens were killed as they tried to escape.

So desperate was the situation that a majority of U Nu's cabinet, socialists and P.V.O., wished to surrender to the communists. Indeed this might well have seemed the rational, perhaps the only, course to take. It was only U Nu's desperate determination and the support of the independent groups in the cabinet, many of them not in fact Burmese, that kept the fight going. And, indeed, it is almost inconceivable that a government could be so deeply engulfed in war and chaos and yet climb out of its difficulties.

Four factors saved the government. First and foremost, ironically, was the continued and altogether admirable loyalty, discipline, and courage of the Karen, Chin, and Kachin battalions of the army, although frequently fighting against their own people. These units took the shock of the communist rebellion in April 1948, the defection of most of the Burmese battalions of the regular army and of the P.V.O. to the side of the communists in July and August of the same year, and held fast in the later months of 1948, when trouble was brewing with the Karens. By the time this turned to open rebellion in January 1949, the communist rebellion had been largely mastered, and some of the P.V.O. had returned to the support of

[1] Hugh Tinker, *The Union of Burma*, London, 1961, p. 39.

the government against their old enemies the Karens. At the crunch of the government's fortunes, it was the Chins, Kachins, Gurkhas, and Anglo-Burmans, aided by some of the P.V.O., who saved the day.

A second factor was the total absence of any common organization, plan, or long-term purpose among the rebels. Had these not been lacking it is hard to see how the government could have survived. There was amongst them a common desire to destroy the government, but beyond that the purposes of the communists and the Karens, to the extent that they had been formulated at all, were entirely dissimilar.

A third factor was that the government held, and by the skin of its teeth continued to hold, Rangoon. This meant that it controlled exports of rice and was, by the sale of these, enabled to raise some funds when virtually all ordinary sources of revenue had dried up, and that it was able to pay for and receive material support from outside. It also controlled virtually the only channel for communication with the outer world, and so was able to present its case in terms that attracted the continuance of such support.

Lastly there were the facts that the government was actually in possession (albeit rather tenuous), that it controlled, or at least that no one else controlled, what remained of the administrative machine, and that it had been formally recognized by foreign states. From these facts flowed certain intangible, largely psychological, but not insignificant, benefits.

The government fought on and by November 1949 it had wrested the initiative from its opponents. The possibility began to appear that it might survive. Through 1950 and 1951 its forces, less numerous but better organized, supplied, and led than the rebels, slowly recaptured some of the lost towns and reopened some of the lines of communication. Mandalay, Insein, Kyaukse, Twante, Thaton, Yenangyaung, Nyaungu, Myingyan, and Tharrawaddy had already been taken earlier in the year. Taunggyi, Yandoon, and Danubyu were retaken in November 1949. Toungoo, the Karen 'capital', fell in March 1950, Prome in May, and Einme in the delta at the end of the year.

But even after these successes the government controlled probably less than half the country outside the towns and off the main roads, and that only in daylight. During the hours of darkness rebel gangs reasserted themselves, robbed and dacoited villages, exacted 'taxes' and protection money, and breached roads and railways as they liked. But the government no longer seemed in imminent danger of collapse, and its military forces had been expanded and better trained.

However, just when the internal situation showed these faint signs of improving, a dangerous external threat developed. In China at the end of 1949 the Chiang Kai-shek nationalist (or Kuomin-tang) régime collapsed. Its government and most of its military forces withdrew to Formosa, but some of the latter, probably about 2,500 in number, retreated out of China into Burma. Most entered Kengtung, but some crossed the frontier further north into the Wa states. Included in these forces would appear to have been remnants of the 93rd Army which had first entered Burma in 1942 in aid of the hard-pressed British-Indian forces. These Kuomintang forces, commonly known in Burma as the K.M.T.s, at first looked upon themselves as temporarily in foreign territory and behaved with circumspection and tolerable correctitude. In July 1950 a brigade of the Burma army (consisting in fact, of Kachins and Gurkhas, prob-ably the most effective of the Burma army units) attempted to expel the K.M.T.s. They achieved some success but these operations were made possible only by withdrawing troops from the civil war inside Burma against the communists. When the latter showed signs of resurgence the troops had to be switched back to the plains of Burma. In the following year the K.M.T. forces invaded China, entering Yunnan, but were repulsed and thrown back into Burma. A larger operation was now mounted by the Burma army, which drove the K.M.T.s out of the Kengtung plain into the surrounding mountains. But once again the Burmese forces had to be switched back to deal with revived communist activity inside Burma. By 1952 the K.M.T. forces had expanded to some 12,000, partly by local recruitment, probably of Shans, but almost certainly also as a result of reinforcement by air from Formosa. They invaded Yunnan for the second time but once again were defeated, this time heavily, and driven back into Burmese territory.

From now on the K.M.T. attitude changed. They appear to have renounced hope of any early re-entry into China and began to act as if they meant to stay in Burma. They issued counterfeit currency, levied taxes, impressed local inhabitants for military and other ser-vice. An airstrip was built at Monghsat, 50 miles south-west of Kengtung, and regular communication was established with For-mosa. There seems no doubt that in all this the K.M.T.s enjoyed American support. A war-lord's enclave was established within the boundaries of Burma. Its economy rested upon the cultivation of the poppy and the smuggling of opium abroad. Towards the end of 1952 the K.M.T.s expanded their occupation westwards across the Salween. By January 1953 they had penetrated to Yawnghwe, less than 20 miles from Taunggyi, the capital of the Shan State,[1] and a

---

[1] After independence the various Shan States were formed into the Shan State though the intended elimination of the chiefs did not in fact come about until 1959 under General Ne Win's caretaker government.

bare 50 miles from the boundary dividing Burma proper from the Shan country. Three brigades of the Burma army, under Brigadier Douglas Blake, an Anglo-Burmese officer, were sent to counter this invasion. The K.M.T.s were quickly driven back to Kengtung and defeated. By November and December, the K.M.T.s had agreed as a result of negotiations at the United Nations to evacuate their forces, to the number of 2,000, to Formosa. But in fact their forces were much more numerous than had been admitted, and they seem to have taken care to evacuate the least useful of them. There is no doubt that a sizeable group remained. This, reinforced from Formosa, necessitated the largest-scale operations yet undertaken by the Burmese in the next two years, 1954 and 1955. This campaign achieved some success, but nevertheless K.M.T.s undoubtedly remained, exercising acts of sovereignty on Burmese soil, and were to give more trouble in the years to come.

Turning back from the K.M.T. difficulties to the internal struggle, it has been said that the initiative passed to the government in November 1949. The government then lost no time in turning its attention to constructive measures designed to bring into being the kind of society envisaged in the preamble to the constitution. The adoption of such a policy when much, probably most, of the country was still in rebel hands displayed idealism, courage, and a great confidence in the future, if it was not merely naïve. It was also largely forced upon the government by the need both to outbid the rebels in holding out prospects of early realization of a socialist Utopia, and to silence the impatient grumblers within its own ranks. In retrospect it may be felt that the government would have been wiser not to divert its energies from the task of decisively defeating the rebels and re-establishing order and its authority before attempting to bring the new Burma into being. But it may instinctively have realized that this would mean putting off the adoption of constructive measures for ever, or for so long as would come to much the same thing. The continuing disorder during the twenty years that have passed since Burma became independent certainly suggests that the re-establishment of order and governmental authority are beyond the powers, or perhaps the will, of any Burmese government that has so far emerged, whether civil or military. And indeed throughout the whole of Burmese history it has been only very rarely, and for very short periods, that any government has controlled the whole country. It is scarcely to be wondered at, therefore, if the absence of such control does not seem so serious to the Burman as it does to the more orderly and ordered European.

For the establishment of a socialist state, however, the absence of control was, and could surely have been foreseen to be, disastrous.

In any case the government clearly had not the slightest conception of the difficulty of the task it was undertaking. Its experience of politics was confined to the comparatively simple field of the struggle for independence and power; of administration Ministers had no practical experience whatever. They held genuinely the belief that Burma was a rich country, most of whose riches had been sucked out by foreigners – British and Indian. Having got rid of these foreigners, it seemed to them that it was the simplest and speediest of matters to take and use these riches for their own people. It may well be right to hold that the British and Indians took away a disproportionate share of those riches, but this view overlooks the vital fact that it was the British and Indians who converted potential into actual wealth by providing capital, expertise, hard work, responsibility, and judgement.

The initial optimism of the Burmese government was reinforced by the fact that it had plenty of money and that it did not seem difficult to raise more. Over the period 1945–48, that is to say before independence, the British government had made some £75 million available on loan to pay for the cost of the Burmese government and for the measures of rehabilitation it was undertaking. These advances were to meet the cost of policies conceived for the benefit of Burma, but conceived by the British. At the time of independence there were grants and transfers of material. In June 1950, after the rebellion had made it impossible to collect more than an infinitesimal proportion of the land revenue, hitherto the main source of government income, a loan of £6 million to the Burmese government was provided by the British Commonwealth jointly. At about the same time the United States somewhat reluctantly undertook to make economic aid available to the amount of $8 to 10 million. There was also the more remote prospect of reparations and possibly of a loan from Japan. Furthermore, and for a while, a certain amount of foreign private capital had been attracted into the country, though not without difficulty, by joint ventures, foreign undertakings permitted to operate on condition that the government of Burma was allowed to hold a substantial proportion of the shares, shares never punctually and seldom fully paid for. If money was easy to come by at this period, there was much to give confidence also in the rice export trade, the backbone of Burma's economy. Production and export of rice had not regained pre-war levels, but they had greatly improved since the disastrous years of the war, and gave promise of still further recovery. The outbreak of the Korean War in June 1950 led to a great demand for rice, with the result that the price in world markets rose from £40 per ton in mid-1950 to as much as £80 at one time in 1952. With such prices for her main export, Burma's reserves of foreign currency steadily increased until in 1953 they reached their peak with a total of K.126.9 crores,[1] or about £95 million. It is not surprising that optimism flourished and that the government believed that Utopia was only round the corner, and to be had almost for the asking. And if Utopia was so near, the best way to stop criticism and disarm opposition was surely to bring it into existence at once, notwithstanding the existence of a state of civil war.

But if the government's first intention was to break the hold of foreigners on the economy as it stood, or as it had stood before the war, it also wished, in the second place, to change the whole nature of the economy itself so that this should not depend exclusively on the export of raw materials – in practice, the rice crop – alone. Continuation of this typical 'colonial economy' would still leave the country dangerously at the mercy of the foreigners. Nationalization, diversification, industrialization, were the principles that must inspire planning for future development. A Ministry of National Planning and an Economic Council were established. But there was a desperate shortage of economists, still more of business or technical experts. Certainly none of the political leaders had any practical experience in these fields. It became necessary to look outside the country for advice.

Those technically best qualified to give this would undoubtedly have been members of the firms operating in Burma, some for a long time, before the war, or members of the British administration. It may be wondered whether or not they would have proved able to perform the psychological gymnastics involved in adopting the new attitudes required. But, whether or not they could have made the necessary adjustment, for the Burmese government, it was politically out of the question to call them in. The whole of the independence struggle had been conducted to achieve the expulsion of the British. It was a prime article of political faith that the British had been sucking out the wealth of Burma. Having got them out it would have been unthinkable to bring them in again on any terms. And any recommendations made by them would have been suspect, as machinations to re-establish their economic control. So, disastrously, Burma went elsewhere.

First, a group of economists visited Burma under United Nations auspices – a group that was in fact British, drawn from Oxford. This conducted a broad survey of the economy, reached the not

[1] The *Kyat*, abbreviated to K., is a silver coin that replaced the Indian rupee current in Burma under the British and then worth about 1s. 4d. sterling. Its official exchange rate is now lower and its real value still less. Crore is Hindustani for ten million or 100 lakhs.

unexpected conclusion that the real income of the people of Burma
was little more than half what it had been before the war, and made
certain general recommendations regarding the rehabilitation and
development of the economy. Next, a United States firm, the
Knappen–Tippetts–Abbett Engineering Company of New York
(which came to be known in Burma as K.T.A.) was called in to prepare
more specific plans. K.T.A. established a mission in Burma of 150
persons, on U.S. rates of pay, the cost of which was debitable against
the advances made to the Burmese government. The dollar costs
recoverable from the Burmese were nearly $2 million, and there
were also extensive costs in Burmese currency. K.T.A. produced a
preliminary report in 1952 and a comprehensive report in 1953. The
reports were constructed on the foundations of extensive ignorance
of Burma and the Burmese, and of complete faith in the almost
automatic benefits of capital investment. Tinker summarizes their
attitude: 'A beneficent circle is envisaged: the increased employment
of more Burmans in new enterprises at higher rates of pay will both
increase national productivity and increase demand, and so stimulate a better standard of living.'[1] The reports were also based on the
confident assumption that the export price of rice would never fall
below £55 or possibly £50 per ton. They proposed capital investment of K.750 crores or £562 million over a period of some seven
years, and the creation over a longer period, by three five-year plans,
of three industrial concentrations – in the Rangoon area, in Akyab,
and in Myingyan. They recommended a number of particular projects towards giving effect to these proposals.

A World Bank mission visiting Burma in 1953 had this to say of
the K.T.A. proposals:

'A considerable part of the K.T.A. project rests on assured re-
lationships among projects which may or may not materialize.
For instance, the soundness of a project for establishing mineral
processing facilities and a number of related installations at
Myingyan will depend, among other things, on the technical and
economic feasibility of developing the Kalewa coal deposits and
on the size and nature of zinc deposits at Taunggyi which are not
entirely certain. A market for a proposed hydro-electric power
project at Saingdin depends on the establishment of the pulp and
paper mill which is being considered for the same region, and on
the type of heat generator to be used at the mill . . . justification
of portions of the transport programme rests on execution of other
projects which may or may not materialize.'[2]

Some of these projects had been investigated in the past and dis-

[1] Tinker, op. cit., p. 109.
[2] Quoted, ibid., p. 111.

carded as economically not feasible. The mission also said more generally:

'The principal limitation of the planning activity so far, appears to be a pre-occupation with the engineering and financial aspects of individual projects without adequate consideration for Burma's limited administrative, managerial and technical capacities. Personnel limitations make it improbable that Burma can undertake any large number of new development projects within a short period.'[1]

But even if the administrators, the managers, and the technicians had been available, there was another factor that a visiting mission would find it delicate to discuss. Political leaders were inexperienced, compelled by circumstances to exercise authority, some intoxicated with power, unfortified by indigenous custom or tradition against venality. It was corruption almost more than incompetence that was to result in loans being wasted and misused and poured away with little more effect on the economy than water upon sand.

But K.T.A. were not the only foreign advisers. When the United States agreed to make economic aid available to Burma it was a condition of the loan that a technical and economic mission from the U.S.A. would administer and very largely control the application of this aid. The mission was sixty strong and once again its cost was to be debited to the advances taken by Burma. No comparable attempt was made by the British to govern how loans should be spent; it would have been politically impossible to do so, for the same reasons which had rendered it unthinkable that Burma should call in British advisers after independence. But it is doubtful whether the close control understandably sought by the Americans was successful in effecting any real restraint on the waste and misuse of the period.

On the invitation of the Burma government there was also a United Nations mission in Burma to make recommendations for development in the field of social welfare. This did not lead to such disastrous waste of money, but it had even less impact upon conditions than the economic and technical missions.

Finally, two missions came to Burma from the World Bank when this was approached by the Burmese government for loans. The World Bank did not seek to exercise any detailed control over the utilization of the loans made, but it did understandably specify the purposes to which they might be applied. In contrast with some of the other planning advisers, its recommendations were realistically related to the circumstances and potentialities of Burma.

To revolutionize the economy and to handle all this aid, the

[1] ibid., p. 111.

Burmese government set up vast and frequently overlapping planning machinery. There was the Ministry of National Planning and under this an Economic Council and a National Planning Board – these two later being amalgamated to form the Economic and Social Board. And there were the Nationalization Commission, the State Timber Board, the State Timber Extraction Organization, the National Housing Board, the Supervisory (Cabinet) Committee on Mingaladon Airfield, the Agricultural and Rural Development Corporation, the Industrial Development Corporation, the Mineral Resources Development Corporation, the Social Planning Commission, the Economic Planning Commission, the Social and Economic Advisory Council, the Planning Projects Implementation Mission (to Europe), and probably others.

In the event, the prospect of giving effect to the grandiose planning of the foreign advisers rapidly decreased and soon disappeared altogether. For a great deal of the resources upon which it depended had to be poured into defence expenditure for the conduct of the civil war against the rebels, whose activities had made it impossible to collect the vital land revenue. Much must also have been diverted into expenditure resulting from the decision to make education free for all, with effect from 1 April 1951, and to embark upon other welfare projects at the same time – gestures of socialization undertaken because of the approach of a general election and because of the need not to lose ground to the communists. There was some investment by the government in joint ventures with foreign, in fact British, firms, for example to work the silver-lead mines at Namtu and the oilfields. This might have proved successful if these firms had been offered any assurance of security of tenure, of working, of life and limb, and of some reasonable return on their own investment. In the absence of such assurance the firms soon abandoned or restricted their operations, and the government investments bore little fruit, even when the government shares had been paid for. A staggering amount of the resources available to the government disappeared in connection with projects for the development of the economy. The projects were often themselves ill-conceived and unrealistic, incapable of producing the results intended, incapable even of completion. There was gross extravagance and waste of funds because of failure or unwillingness to exercise proper technical and administrative control. There was plain malversation and misappropriation. Two examples may be adduced – the notorious cases of the Mingaladon airfield and the Thamaing textile mill, the facts concerning which were ascertained by public inquiry presided over by a judge of the High Court.

The Mingaladon airfield, Rangoon's airport, was badly damaged in the war, was repaired by the R.A.F. in 1945 but only temporarily, and had in any case become too small for modern aircraft. It became necessary in 1948 to build new runways. When the Public Works Department reported that it was unable to undertake this, a Danish firm was called in to prepare a survey and estimate. The estimate was K.27 lakhs[1] or £200,000. The cabinet sanctioned construction and a sub-committee of the cabinet called for tenders. Ignoring other competitors the contract was awarded to the Danish firm in October 1950. An American supervising engineer was appointed as the government's watch-dog. 'The firm went straight ahead, seventy Danes were taken on the pay-roll, with lavish transport and accommodation facilities; no plans had been drawn up, no proper accounts were maintained, 50 per cent errors in some works were reported.'[2] K.T.A. were called in to advise but without effect. Frightened by mounting costs and multiplying defects, the American supervising engineer resigned in October 1951. The government began to investigate and then set up the public inquiry into the scandal. Full figures have never been published, but losses must have exceeded K.6 crores or £4 million. The contractors returned K.8 lakhs, say £60,000, on account of a building that had completely collapsed.

The textile mill was built during 1948 and 1949 at Thamaing just outside Rangoon. An American manager and assistant were employed and spinning- and weaving-machines were bought from America and Japan. For eighteen months after completion the mill could not be used because it was necessary to recruit and train Japanese overseers to operate it, but still more because it was found that the machines installed were unsuitable for Burma cotton. The import had to be organized of appropriate types of cotton from America and other foreign countries. For years the mill had to be operated at only 25–33 per cent of capacity, and of course at a loss. The quality of cotton produced has never been anything but the poorest. The cost of building this white elephant is admitted to have been approximately £2 million – apart from losses incurred in its operation.

In the course of 1953 Burma began to move out of the period of honeymoon optimism into a completely different atmosphere. Under the momentum of the previous period of confidence the K.T.A. comprehensive report was submitted to the government and various missions were sent abroad to place orders, and negotiate contracts for projects, which would involve the spending of well over £6 million, the greater part in the United Kingdom. But at the same time the tide was beginning to ebb. The two disastrous scandals

[1] Lakh is Hindustani for 100,000.
[2] Quoted Tinker, op. cit., p. 102.

mentioned above greatly shook confidence in the government, and
the government's confidence in itself. They shook confidence also in
foreign advisers. The inquiry report on the first was published in
July 1952, but time was needed for its full impact to be felt. Then
in 1953, with the ending of hostilities in Korea, the export price of
rice fell sharply and continued to decline for a number of years. As
a result, foreign exchange reserves, which reached their peak in
1953, then began to fall. As for foreign private capital, the government had tried to attract this into Burma in 1949 with some success.
Any hope of support from this source was destroyed by a spate of
nationalizations through 1953 and 1954. In the first year the Arracan
Flotilla Co., the Rangoon Electric Tramway and Supply Co., and
the Sooratee Burra Bazaar were taken over by the government. In
the second year the Burma Cement Co., the Dyer Meakin Brewery,
and the Zeyawaddy Sugar Factory were nationalized. In all cases
compensation was assessed on the basis of original cost less deprecia-
tion – derisory in terms of market value, albeit excessive to the
doctrinaire nationalist and nationalizer. It was scarcely surprising
that foreign capital could not be induced to flow into the country.
As for inter-governmental loans, or loans from the World Bank, the
early days of indulgence to enable the newly independent country
to get started were over. Burma had shown so little sign of getting
started with what had been advanced that further help from these
sources was extremely unlikely.

There were immediate difficulties, too. The tap of current economic aid from America had been turned off in March 1953 – this
not by the U.S. government, but by courageous decision of the
Burmese government itself. The situation created by the presence of
Chinese nationalists in the Shan States has already been mentioned.[1]
The Burmese had for some time suspected that support for the
K.M.T., with reinforcements and material from Formosa, was
organized, and ultimately made possible, by the U.S.A., hoping to
establish a bridgehead on Burmese soil for the invasion of communist China. In the operations begun in March 1953, suspicion
turned to certainty. After an engagement near the Salween river the
Burmese found, among the enemy killed, the bodies of three white
men and on these, letters bearing American addresses. Outraged and
incensed by this abetment of dangerous violation of its territorial
sovereignty, the Burmese government at once announced that
American economic aid was no longer acceptable.

Suddenly the whole outlook became bleaker. Optimism and confidence leaked away. It began to be realized that the welfare state was
perhaps not just round the corner, that it might not after all come

---

[1] See above, pp. 145–7.

simply as a result of dispossessing the foreigners, indeed, that a great deal of hard work would be required to bring it into existence.

During the first years of the struggle for survival against the rebels, there had been no time for politics. But when, in 1950, it had gradually become clear that the government was likely to survive (although not yet by any means victorious) and when, in 1951, the first general election had been held, political life began to revive. It is possible, but one must admit improbable, that if there had been an effective opposition in parliament, an opposition that could credibly aspire to provide an alternative government, politics might have been concerned with questions of ideological or other principle. But unfortunately, even disastrously, for Burma, the only real opposition to the A.F.P.F.L. consisted of the communists, who were unrepresented in parliament because they were waging rebellion in the jungle. The opposition forces that were represented lacked numbers and influence, and it was perfectly clear that if ever the government weakened it would not be they who took its place. Proceedings in the house accordingly lacked reality and urgency. Nor was there any fruitful clash of ideologies, for all were socialists, differing only as to the degree or tempo of application of the nostrum. Politics became nothing more than a struggle for power, as it had been in the last years of the British period. And since there was no real opposition, except in the jungle, the struggle was played out within the ranks of the A.F.P.F.L. and its allies, not between them and the parliamentary opposition.

As confidence ebbed and discontent increased, so did those forces weaken which had at one time held the government together – the earlier concentration on the gaining of independence, the certainty and excitement of, as Ministers believed, realizing the Utopia of the welfare state, the overriding need to unite in order to preserve the existence and the fruits of the revolution, if not their own lives. The centrifugal, disruptive tendencies of Burmese political life reasserted themselves. Through 1954 disillusion grew and there was much dissatisfaction and criticism regarding the operations of the numerous top-heavy and incompetent government corporations that had been set up to take over the functions of the foreign firms or to develop new areas of the economy. There was a major scandal concerning the State Agricultural Marketing Board – expenditure of K.1½ crores (£1 million) could not be accounted for, and 200,000 tons of rice had disappeared from its stores. Towards the end of the year U Nu made the startling revelation that out of K.10 crores (close upon £7 million) spent on construction work, only K.4 crores was actually producing any buildings or plant. No less than K.6 crores was being wasted in 'bribes, excess profits, barren projects, and other non-productive expenses'.[1] It was obvious to all that corruption and incompetence were rife throughout the government's economic undertakings.

Had there been any effective opposition in parliament, the administration would have been lucky to survive, and at the least it would have been necessary for the A.F.P.F.L. to close its ranks. But without an opposition, the only result of these scandals and discontents was to intensify sectional manoeuvring for power within the A.F.P.F.L. itself.

In the second general election, held in 1956, the A.F.P.F.L. secured a comfortable but nevertheless reduced majority. An opposition had emerged that could not altogether be disregarded, consisting largely of the National United Front, or N.U.F., composed of various elements with little in common except their dislike of the A.F.P.F.L. This, however, did not lead to any closing of the ranks. For the time being the government's majority was sufficient for survival. But on a longer view the results suggested that U Nu and the A.F.P.F.L. coalition were losing their grip, and this led to a further intensification of the power struggle within the League. U Nu relinquished the premiership for one year to reorganize the League and to try to reduce corruption, but could do nothing to lessen the internal conflicts of the party, for the three chief contenders for power were among the Prime Minister and three deputy Prime Ministers appointed to carry on during U Nu's year in retreat. The influence that went with the holding of these offices was inevitably used to build up personal support.

U Nu resumed the premiership in June 1957 but this only exacerbated the contention for power. In January 1958 at the third All-Burma Congress of the A.F.P.F.L. he suddenly and startlingly rejected socialism as a political creed, declaring that 'the A.F.P.F.L. rejects Marxism as a guiding philosophy or as the ideology of the A.F.P.F.L.'[2] There had been, in fact, little ideological difference between him and the leaders of the Socialist Party, U Ba Swe and U Kyaw Nyein – whether Marxists or not, they had all been socialists – and this seems to have been nothing more than an opportunist move on U Nu's part. It was designed, in the first place, to make a direct appeal to the rank and file of the A.F.P.F.L., banking on his undoubted personal popularity. Secondly, it was designed to isolate the socialists. Lastly, it was designed to attract to himself the support of the parliamentary opposition, which consisted mainly of groups of independents of more moderate or middle-of-the-road views. In June 1958 the socialists resigned from the government.

[1] Tinker, op. cit., p. 120.
[2] Quoted, ibid., p. 91.

Fifteen Ministers, including U Ba Swe and U Kyaw Nyein, and twenty-two Parliamentary Secretaries went out, representing the hard core of the original A.F.P.F.L. U Nu managed to improvise a coalition consisting of the rump of the League that had remained loyal to him, of elements of the opposition, and of representatives of the minority communities. On a motion of no-confidence he mustered a majority of seven. But U Nu was now dependent upon his old enemies, his influence was greatly weakened, and his position was rapidly becoming untenable. He announced that a general election would be held, but then changed his mind. The contenders for power were mobilizing and organizing their supporters. U Ba Swe had the support of the Trades Union Congress (Burma). Thakin Tin relied upon the All-Burma Peasants' Organization. U Nu's support was to be found mostly among religious, cultural, and educational bodies. U Kyaw Nyein, having no comparable power base, began to organize the students. 'Private armies' became important once again. The socialists could generally rely upon the backing of the Auxiliary Union Military Police. Thakin Tin and the All-Burma Peasants' Organization had their 'peace guerrillas'. The regular army was very far from a-political and if it became involved in the scramble for power it might very well split and support different factions. Crime and general lawlessness were increasing all over the country. With another and worse civil war (in addition to the chronic war against the K.M.T.s) staring him in the face, U Nu on 26 September 1958 broadcast to the nation that because of the disturbed and dangerous conditions in the country, he had invited General Ne Win, the head of the army, to take over responsibility for the government in order to restore security and law and order, and to create the conditions necessary for the holding of a free and fair general election as soon as possible. Western parliamentary democracy as operated in Burma had brought the country to the very brink of disaster. A military commander and his army were called in to save the situation.

Parliament assembled on 28 October 1958 and General Ne Win took over as Prime Minister. It was originally hoped that he would be able to restore the situation sufficiently to hold a general election by the end of April 1959. But in February 1959, when he reported that order had not been sufficiently re-established, he was requested by parliament to continue as head of the government, the provisions of the constitution being modified to allow him to do so without being elected a member of parliament. In the event, the election was held a year later, on 6 February 1960, bringing to an end the period of army responsibility.

During this fifteen-month period the army claimed to have set itself three tasks: to restore peace and the rule of law; to implant democracy; and to establish a socialist economy. In practice it was forced to confine itself almost exclusively to the first of these objectives. Fifteen months was little enough time for the restoration of order, which in any event was at this stage the best possible contribution towards the other objectives. The method was to place army officers in the Ministries; in the Central Security Council; in the police force; in the departments, corporations, boards, projects, industries; in the railways, waterways, and airways administrations; in the Port Commission; in all parts of the general administration of the country. These officers might be young and inexperienced, but they injected a sense of urgency, imposed a certain discipline, and displayed a firmness that had been lacking among the politicians. And they were far less corrupt. It is probably too much to say that they purged the administration of politics, but they went some way towards this.

A vigorous campaign was initiated against crime. The number of senior police officers, free from the routine commitments inseparable from charge of a district police force, was trebled or quadrupled by the creation of fifteen posts of Deputy Inspector-General. Some sixty-four new police stations were opened in remote parts of the country to which the police had been unable to extend their operations without active army support. Police morale was revived by training courses, but above all by the co-operation and support of the army and by the cutting-down of interference by politicians. Army operations against insurgents were stepped up, being continued (for the first time, it was claimed) without intermission through the monsoon season. A scheme for resettlement of surrendered persons, and their reintegration into the community, which had been allowed to peter out through incompetence, lack of determination, and what were described as 'political complications',[1] was revived. It was claimed that the number of insurgents in the field had been reduced from somewhere between 9,000 and 15,000 to only 5,500, close upon half of whom were Kuomintang trespassers. The figures can be little more than guesses, and even if reliable would have little significance. The methods employed in these campaigns were not new. But the tightening of administrative control, the intensification of a sense of purpose, and the greater realism displayed, undoubtedly pulled the country back from the anarchy and lawlessness that had threatened to engulf it.

The fact that the government set up by the army was not dependent for its survival upon the votes of any party or group, that it was not always being driven to outbid the communists for public

[1] *Is Trust Vindicated?*, published by Burmese government, p. 35.

support, meant that it was able to undertake certain measures, the necessity for which had long been clear, but the unpopularity of which had deterred the government of the politicians. Among these was the removal of the squatters who since the war had progressively covered most of Rangoon's open spaces with squalid, insanitary, and poverty-stricken huts. In part these unfortunates represented a natural increase in the population of Rangoon, in part they were refugees who had fled from the danger and discomfort of the disturbed countryside to seek some measure of security in the city. Their presence created a threat to the cleanliness, hygiene, and health of the capital and posed grievous problems for the fire and police services. No previous government had dared evict them, or been sufficiently firm in attempting to provide sites to which they could be moved – without such action the problem was virtually insoluble. Little enough was done by the new government, but at least an effort was made to clear sites for three 'satellite' towns on the outskirts of Rangoon; to drain the areas; to provide roads, water, and electric lighting; and to provide police stations, fire stations, schools, and other essential services. There was room in these new towns for some 150,000 to 200,000 persons to build, or rebuild, their houses, although it was admitted that conditions were pretty harsh. But at least there was somewhere for the squatters to go, and the government successfully removed them from the open spaces and road verges of the city.[1]

Another task successfully undertaken was the cleaning-up of the city which had been allowed, by general inertia, to become dirty and insanitary. Every Sunday for six months, under what was described as 'Operation Sweat', 25,000 troops and some 100,000 civilians (including many government servants) turned to and collected rubbish and garbage. Over 11,000 tons of rubbish, and a threat to the health of the city, were removed.

In a different sphere, the government had been seeking since 1952 to deprive the Shan chiefs of their hereditary rights to extensive administrative, judicial, and revenue powers – these privileges being considered incompatible with a democratic socialist state, and a potential threat to the authority of the Union government. Little success had attended their efforts. The new government quickly applied the screw and on 24 April 1959 the chiefs signed an agreement relinquishing their powers.

In all these matters it is clear that the assumption of power by General Ne Win and the army involved no change of policy or ideology. The new government genuinely considered itself a 'caretaker' administration and merely pushed forward with greater

[1] ibid., pp. 386 *et seq.*

determination and efficiency what the old had failed to do. Its decision to put a stop to the nationalization of land might give the impression of a change in policy. But, in fact, it was taken because the previous government's measures had been ineffective and corrupted by political chicanery, and with a view to resumption of nationalization when the methods had been cleaned up and revised. In foreign affairs there was no change in the policy of neutrality and non-alignment. By its firmness and impartiality, and by the tightening-up of administration, the caretaker government had undoubtedly achieved a marked improvement in the security and orderliness of life in Burma. There were inevitably grumbles about military high-handedness, but it had certainly earned the gratitude and respect of law-abiding persons in Burma, anxious to go about their everyday affairs in peace and safety.

As 1960 approached it was felt that order and stability had been sufficiently restored to make a general election possible. This took place on 6 February 1960. Meanwhile electioneering had started. It had been the defection of the socialist component in the government that had precipitated the crisis leading to the army takeover. The chief contenders for power now were the socialists and their allies, under the leadership of U Ba Swe and U Kyaw Nyein, on the one side, and U Nu and his non-socialist allies on the other. Internal rivalries and dissensions within the socialist camp were put aside in the hope of gaining power. The group had a better party organization than its opponents, but no coherent programme.[1] Since there were to be found within its ranks most of the survivors of those who had originally started the A.F.P.F.L., it tended to claim that it was in the direct A.F.P.F.L. succession, and it had come to be known as the 'Stable' A.F.P.F.L. Its opponents, relying mostly on the personal popularity of U Nu and his Buddhist appeal, emphasized the need to reform the A.F.P.F.L., to fight corruption within the party, and had come to be known as the 'Clean' A.F.P.F.L.

The result of the election was an unexpectedly overwhelming victory for U Nu. The 'Clean' A.F.P.F.L. won 156 seats and its supporters among the minority communities 10 seats. The 'Stable' A.F.P.F.L. won only 34 seats and its allies four. The Arakan National United Organization won 6 seats. There were 16 other independents. Disturbed conditions made it impossible to hold elections for 24 seats. But looking back, perhaps this victory was not really so surprising. If the 'Stable' A.F.P.F.L. was associated in the mind of the ordinary Burman, the man in the village, with anything other than the jungle war of politics, it can only have been the idea of socialism. To many this idea must have been repellent; to most it

[1] Tinker, op. cit., p. 92.

cannot possibly have meant anything. And the 'Stable' A.F.P.F.L. appears to have been associated in the public mind with the period of military rule and with totalitarian tendencies. U Nu enjoyed tremendous personal popularity and the 'Clean' A.F.P.F.L. appealed mainly to Buddhist sentiment and tradition, offering to make Buddhism the state religion. Here was something that every villager knew about, whether or not he understood a great deal, something that was, apart from the need to earn his living, by far the most significant thing in his life. If, as is probably proved by the results of this election, present-day political jargonizing has left the villages virtually untouched, then perhaps this result can be quite easily explained. In addition, where there were no National United Front candidates, the communists gave their support to the 'Clean' A.F.P.F.L., as the lesser of two evils.

Back in power with a handsome majority, U Nu severed his somewhat tenuous and largely nominal connection with the A.F.P.F.L. and formed a new party, the *Pyi daung su* or Union League Party. The 'Stable' section of the A.F.P.F.L., with the goodwill, now perhaps not a very apt description of their inheritance, of the A.F.P.F.L. before it had split into 'Clean' and 'Stable', alone continued to use the party name. U Nu and the *Pyi daung su* Party announced a moderate policy, notable in that there was to be gradual state withdrawal from economic activity in view of the limited resources of technical and administrative manpower.[1]

The administration carried on for a while under the momentum imparted by the caretaker government, but this soon began to fail. It became clear that there had been no change of character or spirit among the politicians. The promises made by U Nu in his election campaigns began to crowd in upon him. He had said he would make Buddhism the state religion. But legislation to this end not only antagonized the minority religions but also gave offence to certain staunch Buddhists who could not accept anything that might be construed as subordination of Church to state.[2] In his search for support against the socialists he had made statements that could be interpreted as an offer to consider creating separate Mon and Arakanese states. And now the Shans were agitating for more federalism and more independence in the curiously mixed unitary–federal constitution. Indeed, under the constitution, the Shan States (and the other subordinate states of the Union except the Kachin state) enjoyed the right, subject to compliance with certain procedures, to secede from the Union ten years after introduction of

[1] ibid., p. 92.
[2] See F. N. Trager, *Burma – From Kingdom to Republic*, London, 1966, pp. 193–4, 197.

the constitution. There is little doubt that without the incorporation of this safeguard, the minority communities would never willingly have become a part of the Union of Burma at all. The Shans would appear to have had considerable constitutional justification for their demands for a measure of autonomy, if that was what they wanted.

Operations against rebels continued with success in some directions, but the Karens and Shans were active as ever. Large-scale operations were undertaken against the K.M.T. forces near the Thai border during the 1960–61 cold season. It was reported that the Burmese army used heavy artillery and tanks, and suffered considerable casualties. Just as the A.F.P.F.L. coalition of 1945, and the A.F.P.F.L. itself in 1958, had disintegrated, so now the *Pyi daung su* Party, once in power with a decisive majority, developed internal tensions and gave every sign of approaching fragmentation. The danger of civil war, so real in 1958, once more threatened the country. When it appeared that U Nu might be ready to let the Shans secede, General Ne Win and the soldiers took fright.

It is said that early in 1962 General Ne Win went to U Nu and offered him the help of the army in these dangerous circumstances but that U Nu declined the offer, on the grounds that he had the situation under control. The army, however, thought otherwise. There was always present in their minds the fear that the Kuomintang forces in the Shan State[1] might be used and supported by the Americans to establish a bridgehead on the mainland from which to threaten or invade communist China, so creating another Korea or Vietnam on Burmese soil. The soldiers decided to act.

[1] See above, p. 146.

Chapter 10

Military Dictatorship

IN THE VERY SMALL hours of 2 March 1962 tanks, guns, and lorries loaded with troops, moved down the Prome Road onto Rangoon from their barracks and camp in the northern outskirts of the city. By 3 a.m. the houses of Ministers (which had already for a long time been ringed by barbed wire and protected by military sentries), and of other important political personalities, were surrounded. The Prime Minister, U Nu, five of his Ministers, Sao Shwe Thaik, the first President of the Union of Burma but a vociferous Shan nationalist, and a number of others were seized and imprisoned. Others, including the Minister for Chin Affairs, were released after questioning at army headquarters, where General Ne Win, Chief of Staff of the Army and head of the defence services, was present in person. As daylight came it was realized that troops had seized the central telegraph office and the Law Courts. In the course of the day they also took possession of the Rangoon police stations. There was no opposition and little disturbance. The man in the street noticed little difference; indeed he may well not have been aware of what had happened. The only known loss of life occurred when Sao Shwe Thaik's house was surrounded. A shot was fired, whether deliberately (though this is unlikely), or accidentally, or provoked by resistance, is not known, killing a son of the former President.[1]

On the afternoon of the same day General Ne Win broadcast to announce that 'in view of the deteriorating situation in Burma' a Revolutionary Council had been formed with himself as Chairman to take over the government of the country. The Council consisted of himself; Commodore Than Pe and Air Brigadier Clift (heads of the navy and the air force); Brigadiers Aung Gyi, Tin Pe, San Yu, Sein Win, and Colonels Thaung Kyi, Kyi Maung, Aung Shwe, Than Sein, Kyaw Soe, Saw Myint, Chit Myaing, Khin Nyo, Hla Han, and Tan Yu Saing. A new government was formed; less than half the Council became Ministers; and the Ministries were distributed as follows:

[1] *The Times*, 3 March 1962.

Defence, Finance, Revenue, Judiciary	General Ne Win
Commerce and Industry	Brigadier Aung Gyi
Agriculture, Forests, Co-operatives, and Supplies	Brigadier Tin Pe
Education and Health	Commodore Than Pe
Foreign Office, Housing, Mining	U Thi Han
Home Affairs and Immigration	Colonel Kyaw Soe
Information and Culture	Colonel Saw Myint
Transport and Communications	Colonel Ba Ni

The only civilian was U Thi Han who had been director of military supplies and accustomed to working with the military authorities. It was the army that had taken over the country, by resort to force.

The head of the civil service instructed the permanent heads of the Ministries to carry on with their work under the new Ministers. Colonel Saw Myint, who had taken over the Ministry of Information, spoke to a meeting of journalists about freedom of speech but appealed to his audience not to write anything that might cause alarm. Schools had already begun their end-of-year examinations and a special request was broadcast to teachers and students to carry on with these. Parliament was not in session, was dissolved, and has never met again.

The end of the pretence at Western parliamentary democracy, of the mis-employment of the forms and procedures of Westminster in a kind of jungle warfare in pursuit of power, came quite quietly, with less dislocation to public business than would have been caused by the holding of a general election, and with less hurt to anyone – except, of course, to the one fatal casualty and to those, initially few, who suffered incarceration.

After the arrest, and in some cases imprisonment, of the Ministers of the government of U Nu, power rested firmly and absolutely with these seventeen military officers of the Revolutionary Council, fifteen from the army, one each from the navy and air force. The so-called new government set up at the time of the *coup* was no government at all, in any constitutional or democratic sense, being merely a sub-committee of those persons, whether themselves members of the Revolutionary Council or not, through whom the Council imposed its will on the departments of the administration. The real government was the Council itself. Parliament was not even mentioned. It had in any case never enjoyed any real power. The administrative machine was called upon to continue functioning and the people were exhorted to remain calm. Legislation was by decree of the Revolutionary Council. Existing laws were maintained until modified or repealed by decree.

The occasion for this *coup* was the demand of some of the Shan

Sawbwas for a looser form of federalism that would assure to the Shans a measure of independence. It was believed that the Shan separatists had backed their demand by a threat of secession if their request was not granted. It was to preserve the Union of Burma that the soldiers stepped in, they were able to claim.

But there were more deep-seated reasons. There was widespread dissatisfaction with the politicians. It quickly became clear, after they had received power back from the caretaker government of General Ne Win, that they had not learned anything. They talked much but did nothing. They had not the courage to tackle unpopular tasks. Their energies were consumed in the endless combining, re-combining, and intriguing for power. They had no grip of the administration. Corruption was rife. More generally, there was much disappointment with the results of socialism, at least as so far applied by the politicians. This disappointment resulted in a demand not for less but for more socialism, which came just at a time when U Nu, in his attempt to rally moderate opinion, was showing signs of becoming less Marxist in attitude. Above all, however, if the politicians would not or could not effectively exercise the power supposedly entrusted to them, it was too much to expect, in the fluid, amorphous political circumstances of the time, that the only group in which power in fact realistically resided, the army, should not find itself sucked into the vacuum left by the politicians, and feel impelled to assume leadership.

But although the confrontation with the Shans was the occasion, rather than the cause, of the military *coup*, it was no idle fear that the Union might disintegrate. All the important minority communities were in more or less open revolt. Shans and Karens each had several insurgent organizations. Kachins had the Kachin Independence Army, Chins the National Progressive Party. There was the New Mon State Party. In much of the territory inhabited by these peoples the Union government's authority was scarcely recognized – certainly not off the main roads. But this was not the end of the matter, for even in the Burmese homeland there were the communists, themselves divided into two rival parties, the Burma Communist Party (the 'White Flag' communists), and the Communist Party of Burma (the 'Red Flag' communists), to say nothing of the Arakan 'Red Flag' communists with racial undertones to their ideological propaganda, all, as ever, in active rebellion against the government. The first task for the new government and the army (and fortunately these two were the same) was to repel and subdue the rebels in all parts of the country in order to hold the power it had seized.

The situation was comparable to that facing U Nu at the time of independence. There was a change of régime and the incoming government had to prove its right to govern. At no time, however, was General Ne Win in such desperate straits as his predecessor. Mainly this was because the army at his disposal was a better established, more cohesive, and more effective weapon. Whereas U Nu had had to fight for the survival of his government, it was for the preservation of the Union that General Ne Win had to fight – the continued existence of his government was never seriously in doubt.

Of the several threads that must now be taken up, it will be convenient to follow this one first, the efforts of the government to put down insurgency. We shall return later to the question of what sort of a government it was that the army had set up, and what it was seeking to do.

Military operations were at once stepped up, but little could be achieved before the break of the monsoon largely closed down the campaign. It was ironical that the first publicized action by troops was when they were called in to break up demonstrations by communist-led students at Rangoon University. This they did by opening fire upon demonstrators and university buildings. Seventeen students were killed, thirty-nine wounded.[1] This was a tragic outcome of the unscrupulous manipulation of students, and of student indiscipline, for political ends, tactics which had first been introduced to Burma some forty years earlier, in the British period, and had been further exploited after the lapse of sixteen years by the *Thakin* Party, to which General Ne Win had belonged. A few days later, on 11 July 1962, special courts were set up with power to inflict the death sentence on persons found guilty of insurrection or other acts against the state.

As the rains abated, field operations were resumed and the government claimed that on 12 October its forces had destroyed the Shan rebels' main base. Little or nothing has been revealed of the campaign during the succeeding months of the dry season, but on 18 March 1963 rebels blew up a passenger train in the neighbourhood of Toungoo. Then on 1 April 1963 the government offered an unconditional amnesty to all persons convicted of offences other than murder, rape, or crimes resulting in injury to the person, or loss of or damage to private property. The amnesty was also extended to all rebels who surrendered their arms before 1 July. U Nu and members of his government who had been detained in custody were excluded from the benefit of this amnesty.

Two months later the government took further steps. On 11 June it invited representatives of all rebels to peace talks, on 22 June it withdrew all offers of rewards for information concerning rebels or

[1] *Observer*, 15 July 1962.

for their capture. On 26 June it extended the time before the closing of the amnesty offer, which eventually did not expire until 31 January 1964. But there was very little response. However, the advent of the monsoon imposed a lull on operations.

About the beginning of July communication was established with leaders of most of the rebel organizations – the Burma Communist Party, the Communist Party of Burma, the Arakan Red Flag communists, the Karen National Defence Organization, the Kachin Independence Army, and the Mon and Shan insurgent organizations – and at various times and in various ways during the next few months, negotiations began, sometimes with individual organizations, sometimes with groups such as the National Democratic United Front, which included the Burma Communist Party, the Karen National United Party, the New Mon State Party, the Karenni National Progressive Party, and the Chin National Party. But one after another all these negotiations broke down, except only those with the Karens, and by the end of November 1965, with the monsoon over and another campaigning season approaching, the negotiators had returned to their jungle fastnesses and rebel activities were reviving all over the country. In the case of the National Democratic United Front the breakdown was followed by the arrest and detention of some 420 of its members.

Negotiations with the Karens continued after expiry of the amnesty offer until, on 12 March 1964, an agreement was signed by the government and the Karen National Defence Organization. Under this it was provided that the government would summon a national convention, to include not only the Karens but all the indigenous races of Burma, with a view to adopting a new constitution on the basis of the government's manifesto, *The Burmese Way to Socialism*.[1] The Karen state would be renamed Kawthoolei, and the inclusion within this of the areas of Karen population in the predominantly Burmese Irrawaddy and Tenasserim divisions of Burma would be considered at the convention. The Karen National Defence Organization would be given representation on the executive and administrative councils in the Irrawaddy, Tenasserim, and Pegu divisions. A joint committee would be set up to superintend the cessation of hostilities. On this basis an uneasy peace was established with the Karens.

If only one set of negotiations was to succeed, clearly that with the Karens was the most important and the most advantageous. For if the Karens were less numerous than the Shans, they were more homogeneous, better organized, far more experienced in warfare, and in every way a more serious threat. They were a great deal more

[1] See below, pp. 169–71.

numerous than any of the other groups in rebellion. Furthermore, the Karen areas were far closer to the vitals of Burma, and some were interspersed among areas of Burmese population. Finally, the Karen areas included much of the best rice land and some of the best of the teak forests. While these were denied to the Burmese the economy of their country was gravely threatened.

The other rebels remained in the field and hostilities continued much as before. The government has claimed few successes. Releases of political prisoners in February 1967 and again in February 1968 (when it was claimed that all political detainees had been set free) suggest that the government may be feeling more secure. And in September 1968, Than Tun, leader of the White Flag communists, was shot dead, not by government forces, or by any of their supporters, but by one of his own guerrillas, a Chin, who had apparently found his own name in a list of persons to be liquidated. On the other hand much other evidence suggests the reverse. Crime increases. Insurgency does not decrease. In 1967 there were disturbances that could be described as food riots. Naga guerrillas receiving arms and probably other support from China to be used against India, seem able to travel back and forth across northern Burma despite anything that the Burmese government does, or can do. It is probably fair to say that while the disintegration of the Burmese homeland and the secession of the Karen areas has been averted, the government has not had any significant success in establishing its authority over the remoter hill areas. Economically, this is probably no great loss, provided that production from the Shan silver-lead mines reaches Burma. Control has been established over these and over their lines of communication, though it may not spread much further afield.

Inevitably the question arises whether the government, or perhaps the government forces, really want to bring the operations against the insurgents to an end. It always seems that they should be able to do so, but they never do. Here it must be remembered that an ever-increasing number of the senior and more experienced military officers are continually being seconded away from the army into the administration and into the nationalization of economic life.[1] The war against the insurgents has to be left to junior and inexperienced officers who, despite superiority in equipment, are no match for veteran guerrillas. Behind these physical difficulties, however, the Burmese government is faced with a fundamental dilemma that will be more fully considered later. In essence it is that the insurgents are for the most part communists. Unfortunately it is the communist ideology that is professed by Burma's powerful and near neighbour,

[1] See below, pp. 196–201.

China. The Burmese government cannot but be inhibited in its attempts to suppress insurgency by the fear that all-out effort could easily provide the Chinese with a pretext for invading the country in support of the communist opposition in Burma. Lastly, one is tempted to ask, does the army perhaps prefer things as they are? If hostilities were to cease, the army would lose a great deal of its importance, and its priority in regard to resources. Its numbers might be reduced, and those retrenched might find themselves out of a job. It is probably much pleasanter, particularly to the Burmese temperament, to swashbuckle through villages and live off the countryside and its inhabitants in the course of generally not very dangerous operations, than to lead the restricted, routine life of barracks. And the fluidity of a never-ending state of war offers unrivalled opportunities for smuggling or other occupations on the side. Perhaps these are unworthy suspicions. But far more unexpected things have happened in a country with a flair for coming to commonsense terms with inconveniences of all kinds.

At the same time as the Revolutionary Council was waging war against the rebels, in order to preserve the unity of Burma and to assert its own authority to govern, it was busy with the consolidation of the political powers it had seized by force, with the establishment of its control over the administrative machinery, with the formulation of its policies, and with the mobilization of popular support for these policies, and for itself.

As to its policies, on 30 April 1962 the Revolutionary Council issued a declaration, entitled *The Burmese Way to Socialism*. This was in the first place a profession of belief in traditional Marxist socialism – which the Council conceded would need to be adapted to the circumstances of Burma. It may seem to be putting the cart before the horse to decide upon the policy to be followed by a government before deciding what kind of government is to put the policy into effect, particularly whether that government is to be democratic in form with a consequent obligation to sound public opinion. But the policy was inescapable, for a socialist ideology was so much an article of political faith in Burma that it made all this seem perfectly natural. Had not the independence movement that drove out the British been a socialist movement? Had not socialism been written into the constitution that followed? And in any case, the question of the kind of government that was to put this policy into effect had also been decided already, for it was quite clear that real power resided in the soldiers and that it would continue to reside in them, however this might be disguised by verbiage. Whatever system of government the Revolutionary Council might have in mind for the more distant future, it would not be democracy of a

kind recognizable as such in the West. Still less would its plans for
the immediate future be so recognizable.

There was a definite flavour of communism about *The Burmese
Way to Socialism*. Partly this was merely verbal, with the Revolutionary Council undertaking to '. . . strive for self-improvement by
way of self-criticism. Having learnt from contemporary history the
evils of deviation towards right or left the Council will with vigilance
avoid such deviation.' Partly, however, it was the determination of
the Revolutionary Council to impose its own Marxist solution for the
ills of Burma by force, in defiance, if needs be, of the wishes of the
people, in defiance also, it has sometimes seemed, of the promptings
of commonsense. And always there was the need to pre-empt bids by
communism on the extreme left. The intention to impose socialism
was accompanied by a firm commitment to a policy of nationalizing
the means of production – 'agricultural, and industrial production,
distribution, transportation, communications, external trade, etc.'

Support for these policies, and for the Revolutionary Council,
was to be sought primarily from the peasants and workers. These
were to be wooed at the same time as expectations of material gain
were held out to them. They were described as 'the vanguard and
custodian' of a socialist democratic state, and the Revolutionary
Council, in its march towards socialism, proposed to '. . . base its
organization primarily on the strength of peasants and other working
masses who form the great majority of the nation'. At the same time
the prospect was held out of an improvement in the standard of
living, which was to result from the common ownership of the means
of production, and there was to come into being '. . . a new Society
for all, economically secure and morally better, to live in peace and
prosperity'. Nevertheless 'the middle strata and those who will work
with integrity and loyalty for the general weal' were also to be
allowed to participate in the new socialist state. The reference to
'middle strata' postulates the existence also of an 'upper stratum',
but these expressions are largely irrelevant in a Burmese context
where there is in fact little stratification. In the British period there
were officials and non-officials. It might at one time have been
possible to speak of an upper stratum consisting of those with a
Western education and a partly Western orientation. But these are
disappearing and many of those who survive were imprisoned under
the Revolutionary Council. The only sector of society that could
possibly be described as an 'upper stratum' in present conditions, is
the army – and clearly it is not, except only in the exercise of political power. The only useful division of society now is into the less-
educated (mostly, but not exclusively, peasants) and the more
educated (mostly town-dwellers). In fact the reference to 'middle

strata' does little more than give a further flavour of communism to
the Revolutionary Council's manifesto. And in practice little has
been done to attract the middle classes. It is 'the masses' that provide the real target for its propaganda and for such benefits as it can
distribute.

As to the kind of government that was to bring about this desirable
state of affairs, offered to the peasants and the workers, there was in
the first place a conscious and explicit rejection of parliamentary
democracy on the Western model. The Council's manifesto began:
'. . . in some countries the Parliament has been so abused as to have
become only the means by which the opportunists and propertied
people deceive the simple masses'. It went on:

> 'In the Union of Burma also, Parliamentary Democracy has been
> tried and tested in furtherance of the aims of socialist develop-
> ment but also, due to its very defects, weaknesses and loopholes,
> its abuses and the absence of a mature public opinion, lost sight of
> and deviated from the socialist aims, until at last indications of its
> heading imperceptibly towards just the reverse have become
> apparent.'

The manifesto finally said: 'The nation's socialist aims cannot be
achieved with any assurance by means of the form of Parliamentary
Democracy that we have so far experienced.' For this conclusion
there was justification and to spare both in the abuse of the tentative
Western parliamentary régime introduced by the British as a step
towards self-government, and in the years of increasing misrule
through supposedly parliamentary forms that had preceded the
military seizure of power. And one cannot but respect the honesty
with which the conclusion was reached and stated. In so many
'emergent' countries the rulers have preferred to continue to pay
lip-service to the idea of parliament, finding the forms of Western
democracy convenient to their own ends, and using them cynically
as a cover for every sort of internecine struggle and exercise of
power. Burma was to be spared this degrading sham.

But as to what was to be put in the place of parliamentary
democracy, the Revolutionary Council was less explicit – understandably so perhaps, since, as we have seen, the short answer was
without doubt the Revolutionary Council itself. In general terms,
the manifesto announced that 'the Revolutionary Council therefore
firmly believes that it must develop, in conformity with existing
conditions and environment and ever changing circumstances, only
such a form of democracy as will promote and safeguard the
Socialist development'. The manifesto went on to speak of 'Socialist
democratic' administrative machinery and of 'Socialist democratic
education and democratic training'. In the constitution of the

Burma Socialist Programme Party,[1] there is reference to the 'principle of democratic centralism' and even to the election of the leading committees of the party by popular vote. But not yet. All this was to happen only 'when the party constructional work is done and the Cadre Party blossoms into the Party of the entire nation'. Clearly it has not blossomed yet. Whether all this was mere word-spinning or whether there was any real intention to establish a 'Socialist democracy' is not clear. If there was any such intention the course of events and the passage of time, particularly the insecurity of the government's control of the country, have compelled or are likely to compel its abandonment. In any case 'Socialist democracy' is clearly very different from anything that the West would recognize as democratic.

But whatever the future may hold, the present is clearly still the transitional period of the construction of the party. For the present the government is the Revolutionary Council which seized control by force, perhaps could not help seizing it because no one else was endowed with sufficient power to govern. In greater detail, the Revolutionary Council announced its intention to 'reorientate all erroneous views of our people'. It would further 'carry out such mass and class organizations as are suitable for the transitional period, and also build up a suitable form of political organization'. And again: 'When political organizational work is carried out Socialist democratic education and democratic training will be given to the people so as to ensure their conscious participation.' They were to be well indoctrinated in the ways that their masters wanted them to follow. In the concluding section of the manifesto the Revolutionary Council 'believes that the people will, with an active awareness of their duties and responsibilities, play their part in full in this national Revolutionary progressive movement and programme under the leadership of the Revolutionary Council'.

The last thing that the new 'democracy' was intended to do was to enable the people to express views on how they should be governed or to choose those who should govern them. Its function was rather to mobilize support for the new government and its socialist policy, both arbitrarily imposed by the military, and at the same time to generate amongst the people a sense of identity with their new rulers, to foster the illusion that they had, perhaps, some control in the formulation of policy. It may well be that the forging of a hard core of support for authority is a necessary measure in an 'emergent' country, particularly in Burma which had drifted so perilously near disintegration. But to call this process democracy is not appropriate.

It is, nevertheless, sometimes claimed that even in this transitional

[1] See below, p. 174.

period a new kind of democracy, presumably 'socialist democracy', is being built up. It may serve to make clear what those who make such claims have in mind if we examine what happens at the lowest level. Village headmen, and the elders who form the village committees, are now appointed, whereas before they were elected. Formally, their appointments are made by the appropriate Security and Administration Committee.[1] But before this happens local members of the Burma Socialist Programme Party[2] have visited the village, have talked things over with the inhabitants, found out who would be willing to serve, formed their own opinion of the competence of the candidates and of the degree of popular support they could hope to enjoy, have at the same time explained to the candidates what their task would be, what would be expected of them in the way of 'correct attitude', and doubtless made sure of their readiness to support the government. On the strength of these inquiries the party members place a short-list of recommended candidates before the Security and Administration Committee. This makes its selection after such further inquiries as its members care to undertake. There is envisaged here a two-way process, a kind of government by suggestion and consultation. The government authorities are anxious to put forward their views and to press these upon the people. But at the same time they want to feel their way, to test popular feeling and attitudes, and to ascertain how far the views advocated are acceptable. At its best, it can be appreciated that such a system might offer a sounder, more sensible, more realistic, and in essentials a more democratic form of government than the bare counting of heads under a Western-style democracy on issues which rarely, if ever, involved any question of principle; which, if they did, were beyond the comprehension of the voters; but which were, in fact, nothing more than a struggle for power, to be settled by appeals to the pocket or other practical advantage of the voter. At its worst, however, the system is all too liable to incorporate many of the least desirable features of one-party totalitarian government – the propagandizing, the withholding of rights or privileges, the covert pressures, the spying and tale-bearing, the blackmailing, in order to enforce compliance with the party line and support for the government. These are often sought to be excused as being due to excessive zeal under a new system. But, in fact, they are the natural concomitants of such a system. How often the system works at its best, how often at its worst, can only be guessed. The optimism of those who seek to introduce it seems somewhat naïve. It requires no cynic to lean to pessimism.

[1] See below, pp. 178–80.
[2] See below, p. 174.

The Burmese Way to Socialism had promised the building-up of 'a suitable form of political organization'. The first step towards this came on 4 July 1962 when the Burma Socialist Programme Party was formed by the Revolutionary Council. At headquarters the organization of the party was to consist of three committees. The chief of these was the Central Organizing Committee with five departments under its control – for Peasants' Affairs, Workers' Affairs, Mass Organization Affairs, Administrative Affairs, and Educational Affairs. The other two committees were the Party Discipline Committee and the Socialist Economy Planning Committee. For 'the transitional period of its construction' the Revolutionary Council was to be the supreme authority with absolute control of these three committees. Indeed, the members and chairmen of the committees were to be appointed by the Council, and in the cases of the Central Organizing Committee and of the Party Discipline Committee, the members and chairmen must be drawn from among Council members. In the case of the Socialist Economy Planning Committee an admixture of non-members of the Council was permissible – there was an extreme dearth of soldiers who had even a nodding acquaintance with economics, socialist or other. In the field, organization was to consist of party units recruited for territorial areas or industrial centres as required. Between these cells in the field and the headquarters organization it was planned to interpose Divisional Supervision Committees.

It was contemplated that at some time in the future, 'when the party constructional work is done and the Cadre Party blossoms into the Party of the entire nation' (in other words, when the nation had been drilled and could be trusted to do what the Revolutionary Council wanted), ultimate authority would pass to a Party National Congress and a Political and Central Committee thereunder, and that then the headquarters committees would be elected by popular vote, presumably of the Congress. But that time has not yet come and the Revolutionary Council is, and is likely to remain, in absolute power. The party organization is under its tight control. Admission of members to the party requires the concurrence of the Council, and a member is required to 'accept out of conviction *The Burmese Way to Socialism*'; to abide by the constitution of the party; 'to carry out unswervingly the tasks assigned to him by the Party'; and 'to be prepared to submit to the scrutiny of the Party Discipline Committee'. Membership is of a political *corps d'élite*, rather than of a political party.

The Burma Socialist Programme Party was no party in the Western parliamentary sense – naturally enough, since parliamentary democracy had been explicitly rejected as inappropriate to the needs of Burma. It was, rather, an instrument of government of the kind the world has become familiar with in the single-party, totalitarian states, whether Fascist, Nazi, or communist in flavour. It was required not to ascertain or give effect to the will of the people, but to tell them what they ought to want and to make sure that they supported the Revolutionary Council.

There was at this stage no prohibition of other political parties – that was to come later. But they had been largely reduced to impotence by the imprisonment of their leaders. And arrests continued of others known or believed to be potential leaders – arrests that received little or no publicity, but which, for that very reason, were multiplied by rumour and so became the more terrifying.

The Council of Ministers of the government was treated more or less as a fourth committee in the headquarters organization of the party, under the Revolutionary Council. Indeed, in the organizational chart appended to the formal constitution of the party, it is shown in the same manner, and given the same standing, as the committees, and in the party constitution itself it is provided that 'the Chairman of the Revolutionary Council of the Union of Burma shall form the Council of Ministers of the Revolutionary Government either with members of the Revolutionary Council only, or with members of the Revolutionary Council and other suitable persons in combination . . .'. And it was laid down that the Revolutionary Council 'shall ensure that there is close and appropriate co-operation between the Central Organizing Committee and the Council of Ministers of the Revolutionary Government . . .'. There was no parliament to which the Ministers would be held responsible or to which they would be required to explain their policies.

As to the Revolutionary Council itself, the real government, there was no provision in the constitution for changes or replacements. The time was envisaged, as we have seen, when it would be subordinated to a Party National Congress. But until that time change and replacement would presumably result and have, in fact, resulted, from the natural interplay of political and personal forces, and changes in the grouping and balance of power within the military cabal that had seized authority in Burma.

It bears repeating at this stage that the system sought to be imposed by the Revolutionary Council is not to be condemned outright merely for what it is, however repugnant this may be to those soaked in the ideas of Western democracy. In a country such as Burma, where the electorate is as yet comparatively uneducated (albeit less so than in many other emergent countries) and politically inexperienced, where parliamentary candidates are also inexperienced and frequently irresponsible, voters are more than ever liable to be carried away by facile appeals to emotion or self-interest. There is no reason why the 'democracy' of the Revolutionary Council should not work to the advantage of the people it is governing at least as well as the democracy of the politicians, if it can be honestly administered. The advantage claimed for a democratic régime, that the voters can in the last resort throw out a government, was largely illusory in the circumstances of parliamentary democracy in Burma. Since the only alternative government, the only real opposition under the democracy of the politicians, was under arms in the jungle and not available to be elected, any vote to displace the government was likely to result in nothing more than a routine shake-up of the existing groups into some apparently fresh, but basically unchanged, combination. The Revolutionary Council needs to be judged not by what it is, but by what it does.

Meanwhile, the party was drawing up a statement of the philosophy of the Burma Socialist Programme Party, which was approved by the Revolutionary Council and published in January 1963 under the title of *The System of Correlation of Man and his Environment*. It is difficult to take this seriously. It seems to be a very peculiar grafting of Marxist principles, or perhaps only of Marxist terminology, onto the stock of Buddhist metaphysics. Some of it is platitudinous. Much is totally at variance with ordinary experience. In either case it is quite inconsequential. It may serve to encourage the converted. It can impress no one else – except with the naïveté of the régime. It is difficult to understand for whose benefit it can have been concocted.

In March 1963 the Burma Socialist Programme Party began to enrol members. There was no very great response. On 9 August 1963 a further step was taken towards the obliteration of all opposition when eleven well-known political leaders were arrested, to join U Nu and his chief supporters in prison. This time the Revolutionary Council struck at the parties which had been in opposition to U Nu; U Ba Swe and U Kyaw Nyein were among those taken into custody. The official reason given for these arrests was that those apprehended had attempted to 'sabotage' the peace negotiations then taking place with the Karens. The real reason presumably was that the Burma Socialist Programme Party was encountering opposition and making insufficient progress in building up support for the Revolutionary Council. If there was any attempt by these leaders to influence, or interfere in, the negotiations, it can have originated only from a common hostility to the Revolutionary Council. Nothing else would have brought the Karens and such political figures into the same camp.

Two months later, on 7 October 1963, further steps were taken to build up the Burma Socialist Programme Party, when it was announced by the Revolutionary Council that the party would be subsidized by the state to enable it to carry out its programme successfully.

Then in November, when all the peace negotiations except those with the Karens broke down, there was another wave of arrests. Some 420 of the leading members of the National Democratic United Front, leaders of the White Flag communists, of the Mon and of the Chin rebels, were seized. In the following month, when negotiations with the Shans broke down, many of their leaders suffered the same fate. By the end of the year it was estimated that at least 1,400, and possibly twice as many, political prisoners had been taken into custody since the arrests began in August.

Also in December the universities of Rangoon and Mandalay and the colleges at Moulmein and Bassein were closed down *sine die*, after anti-government demonstrations and riots.

On 28 March 1964 came the next step in the destruction of opposition, when all political parties, other than the Burma Socialist Programme Party, were dissolved and proscribed, and their property and assets confiscated. A few days later it was decreed that all organizations, other than the political parties already dissolved, must apply to be registered by the government. This requirement extended even to religious bodies.

The apparatus of the single-party state was now complete. Since then the usual pressures, largely covert but nonetheless powerful, have been applied to stimulate the growth of the party. In government service promotion tends to be easier for party members and to be withheld from non-members. Outside the services the enjoyment of amenities tends to follow the same rule. When, as in Burma at the present time, there are widespread shortages of consumer goods, with consequent attempts at rationing and licensing, the range of amenities that may become dependent upon the favour of the party or the government is extensive. The same applies to the as yet rudimentary welfare services that are being introduced. And yet, as far as is known, the party still does not command wide adherence. Membership is largely confined to the armed services, together with a sprinkling of other government employees. To the public it has made no wide appeal. It has certainly not yet blossomed into the party of the entire nation.

From the political apparatus we turn to the framework of day-to-day administration. The old territorial divisions continue. The old manuals and old procedures survive and are observed – except that references to such matters as leave to Europe for officers of the

Indian Civil Service are treated as expunged. The old hierarchy of
officers still exists – but in name only. For the Revolutionary Council
found it hard to trust the administrative services not to water down
its policies. These services, like all administrations, had developed a
momentum of their own which it was difficult to deflect. Their
members for the most part were of better standing and education
than their new masters and prone perhaps to fall into an attitude of
knowing better. The Revolutionary Council also believed all civil
servants to be corrupt. At all levels of the administration, therefore,
from the Secretariat in Rangoon down through commissioners,
deputy commissioners, subdivisional officers, township officers, to
village headmen, there have been constituted Security and Administration Committees (S.A.C.s) which have taken over real responsibility from the old officials. The composition of these committees
was initially improvised as the army sought to seize control and
varied considerably, but has settled down to a standard form. Their
chairmen (except only of the village committees) are army officers of
appropriate rank. The civil officials listed above, who once had full
administrative responsibility in their own charges, are now no more
than committee secretaries. In the case of the Central Committee
the chairman is the Home Minister and the secretary is the Chief
Secretary to the Government – the permanent non-political head of
the Home Department. Members are the heads of departments
represented at the particular level – police, public works, forests,
medical, education, and so on. The secretary and the departmental
members of a committee are responsible for providing technical
information and advice. Whether it is the chairman who decides,
using the secretary and the committee as the chief of staff and staff
of a military commander – which, of course, the chairman is – or
whether the committee decides corporately, depends probably on
personalities. Some chairmen are known to have established excellent relations with their committees. The chances of this happening
have probably been improved since 1966 when it became the practice for army officers seconded for civil work to receive special
training in civil administration before taking up their appointments.
Burma Socialist Programme Party members are not formally members of committees, but tend to be associated with the S.A.C.s when
it is a matter of persuading or influencing the public, of mobilizing
support, or of rounding up recruits for voluntary or other work. The
village committees consist of the headman, who is chairman, and of
village elders. These are appointed, not elected, probably on the
recommendation of local Burma Socialist Programme Party members and after inquiry by the S.A.C. concerned. If it has done nothing else this has at least terminated the anomaly, introduced by the

British and continued under the U Nu régime, of the village headman being at one and the same time the agent of the government
for the preservation of order and the collection of the revenue, and
the elected representative of his village. The obvious incompatibility
of these two functions had frequently been demonstrated.

The establishment of the S.A.C.s resulted primarily from the need
to establish military control of the civil organization, a process which
necessarily had to involve diminution of the very extensive powers
and prestige of the general administrative officers, particularly of
the deputy commissioners, upon which to a very large extent the
working of the system had previously depended.[1] But there was also
in the minds of the soldiers the idea that the committees would
deter from corruption civil officers and clerks, since all business
would have to be transacted in the presence of other officers and
under the eyes of the chairmen. Not all civil servants were corrupt,
but many in the lower grades could be obstructive if no sweetener
had passed, and the army tended to take an excessively pessimistic
view of the integrity of civilians. And the committees also had the
merit that they would cut out the kind of time-consuming and
responsibility-evading correspondence to which even the best of
civil services are prone. Given the circumstances of the time, there
were great advantages in the establishment of the committees, and
indeed it is difficult to see what else the army could have done.
Much depended of course upon the character and abilities of the
chairmen. It would be too much to expect that all were good but
there were undoubtedly some, possibly many, who were imbued with
a desire to make the administration work for the good of the public,
who succeeded in establishing good relations and a good atmosphere
in their committees, and were notably free of the hectoring character
often attributed to military men.

In the broadest of terms the work undertaken by the S.A.C.s is
still recognizably that which was the responsibility of the officers of
the general administration in the British time. But there have been
great changes, so great that the similarity is really superficial and
misleading. There has been one large subtraction. In the British
period land revenue had for long been the main source of government income – just before the Second World War customs revenue
had overtaken land revenue, these two forms of taxation accounting
for 23 per cent and 22 per cent of government income. The largest
and most complicated aspect of the general administration had been
the assessment and collection of land revenue, but collection broke
down almost completely during the worst of the disturbances following independence, and has never been satisfactorily revived. The

[1] See above, pp. 79–81.

elaborate, some would say over-elaborate, machinery of survey and inspection set up by the British to ensure fair assessment has fallen into decay. Other taxes have become more important. And in any event the present government of Burma depends for its revenues more upon trading profits, especially from the export of rice, than upon taxation. The revenue work which once took up most of the general administrative officer's time, and constituted a great part of his expertise, has largely disappeared. But if there has been this large subtraction from his work there have been at least two major additions. In the British time it was government policy to build up a system of local self-government, partly as an education towards democracy in a wider field, by handing over the administration of certain matters of purely local interest to popularly elected municipalities and rural district councils. These local authorities, which had employed their own administrative staffs, operating quite separately from the staffs of the central administration, disappeared during the Japanese occupation and were not revived by the British during their brief period of post-war responsibility. Under the U Nu régime popularly elected municipal committees were revived; the rural district councils were not, pending introduction of a reformed scheme for democratic decentralization to rural authorities. Under the present régime the local authorities are no longer popularly elected and are just as directly under the control of the central government as any other part of the administration. The point of maintaining separate local authority administrative staffs has accordingly vanished and there is a general tendency to place these staffs and the work for which they are responsible under the officers of the general administration, so adding to their work and to that of the S.A.C.s. The other addition to the responsibilities of general administrative officers flows from the nationalization of trade and industry, particularly of the retail trade. The commercial functions assumed by the government have led to the establishment of trade offices throughout the country. These, like other technical departments, have their own direct channels of communication with headquarters in technical matters and are expected to make their own decisions. But the S.A.C.s inevitably acquire a certain responsibility for ensuring that there is no scandalous misconduct by the trade officers. And where public convenience and the preservation of order are concerned, the trade officers come under the control of the S.A.C.s. Thus nationalization has added not inconsiderably to the responsibilities of the administrative officers.

But there is a much more fundamental difference between the ways of government now and those during British rule or even under the régime of U Nu. Real power has shifted. It used to be exercised, subject to the law, and subject to instructions from above, by the general administrative officers of the civil service. The rule of law may not always have been fact, but it was the accepted ideal. Power now resides in the army (overtly in the officers as chairmen of the S.A.C.s, covertly in the Military Intelligence Service, which spies on everyone else) and in the Burma Socialist Programme Party. To ask whether in the last resort it is in the army or in the Burma Socialist Programme Party that power resides is to establish a false antithesis, for at the highest level these two are the same: the party heads are top army officers, and the top army officers are party heads. In theory the party will one day supersede the army; in practice there is no sign of this happening; and if it happened it would make no difference, with the party as it is now constituted. It forms the army's civil wing, a useful auxiliary for propaganda and civil administration. But in the last resort, it is the army that has the arms. Over-zealous party busybodies help the Intelligence Service in its task of spying. Government employees find themselves under observation at their work and watched at leisure, to see what they do with their spare time and what company they keep. Persons of education and standing, and therefore suspected of liberal tendencies, may find themselves followed if they go for a country walk with a friend. Members of the press, persons concerned in trade or industry, are particularly liable to attention. Even the Military Intelligence Service is liable to be spied upon by yet other organizations. And occasionally, not often, but often enough to have its effect, someone is seized by military patrols in the night and carried off into detention. In Rangoon police are said to go off duty at 12.30 p.m. From then until dawn the army takes over and is understood to be far less considerate than the police. To assemble these points (for which there is in fact evidence), in one paragraph, undiluted, probably conveys an excessively pessimistic impression. Life in Burma is not all like that. But these things happen, and the result is a general atmosphere of fear, which immediately strikes most visitors to the country. This is why people look over their shoulders before speaking of anything that might not be agreeable to the government.

But it is not only the people who suffer. Within the government and the government services the same spying and tale-bearing goes on, and as a result fear rules there too. And this is one (though only one) of the causes of the widespread unwillingness to take responsibility, the continual seeking for orders from above, upon which most observers comment. It is a cause also of the proliferation of committees, where personal responsibility can be avoided, the channels of responsibility can be blurred, and the opportunities for spying can be multiplied. The system is perhaps not efficient enough or ruthless enough to deserve the label of a police state. But the spirit in which it is run is quite certainly that of such a state, or of an oriental despotism, in which the will and the whims of the tyrant are enforced by arbitrary orders and fear of the sharp consequences.

Real power lies with the army, or rather with a military junta. It is often exercised sensibly and humanely, given the disturbed conditions of the time, and the need to build up some governmental authority. It is often exercised in excessively doctrinaire fashion, particularly with regard to economic policies. Sensible or doctrinaire, however, it is strictly arbitrary, and its exercise is subject to error, to individual bias, to corruption, and to the ever-changing needs of the internal struggle for power. Burma is back to government by king and court as in the days before the British annexation.

Chapter 11

The Economy

THE KEY TO THE economy of Burma is rice.[1] Rice is the staple food of the country; some 70 per cent of the people gain their living from the cultivation or handling of rice; and rice has until recently provided some 60 per cent of the value of the country's exports, though this contribution, as we shall see, is now getting less, with the result that exports are dwindling, if not disappearing.

Dr Tinker, writing of the policies of the U Nu government for the resuscitation of Burma after the war, says:

'Burma might . . . perhaps have overhauled the whole machinery of rice production, storage, transport, shipment, and marketing: in that way she could have regained her pre-war position as the world's foremost rice exporter. Or she might have gone all-out to diversify her agriculture, to become less dependent on the price movements of one crop. In the end, the pattern of Burma's economy is the same today, in 1956, as it was five years ago: a pale imitation of the same economy fifteen years ago.'[2]

Now, fourteen years later, it is even paler. The government of General Ne Win has been no more successful than that of U Nu in making Burma less dependent upon the cultivation of one crop. Exports of rice have shown a steady decline. The economy is stagnant and probably failing. The prescription of U Nu and his government for the ills of Burma was socialism. It clearly did not work. But the only treatment that Ne Win and the soldiers around him could devise was to increase the dose. This has been no more successful.

Before the Second World War the rice trade of Burma was firmly in the hands of a number of European firms who by combination had established a near-monopoly. This, as a result of post-war circumstances, was converted into a state monopoly, first under the British, then under the Burmese. For after the expulsion of the Japanese from Burma, world food shortages made it a matter of the greatest urgency to revive the rice trade. In the absence of civil transport and other facilities this could initially be done only under

[1] See above, p. 86.
[2] op. cit., p. 127.

military auspices. There were obvious political objections to the re-establishment by the military authorities, as one of their first acts, of the virtual monopoly of the rice trade by a few British firms, a monopoly that was deeply unpopular amongst the Burmese. Accordingly, revival was effected by an official organization under military control, largely recruited, however, from the staffs of the British firms, which looked forward to the time when they could resume operations on their own account. But in 1946, by which time Burmese opposition to the reintroduction of such firms was vocal and able to make itself felt, this organization was developed and made permanent, to become the State Agricultural Marketing Board, which supplanted the firms, and to which was entrusted broad responsibility for the whole process of rice marketing. The near-monopoly of the firms had become a state monopoly which, as we shall see, was later to become virtually complete.

After independence in 1948, the State Agricultural Marketing Board continued. To a government professing Marxist principles, which had placed nationalization of the means of production high on its programme, no other course would have been conceivable. By 1950 the Board was handling 80 per cent of the export trade, and it was not long before it had become responsible for virtually all exports. By 1952 the internal buying of rice had largely been taken out of private hands, 98 per cent of this business being handled by the State Agricultural Marketing Board or its agencies. It is possible that there was some revival of private buying in the internal trade in subsequent years, for in February 1963 when the Revolutionary Council embarked on its policy of out-and-out nationalization,[1] the government announced, as if this were a novelty, that the State Agricultural Marketing Board would become the sole buyer of rice and that private dealers would no longer be permitted at all. The Board would for the time being make use of private rice mills, but these also would be taken over by the government in due course. This takeover of the rice industry had now become just one aspect of the government's determination to nationalize everything. (The lengths to which this policy was pushed will appear later in this chapter.) The buying and marketing of rice, both for export and for internal consumption, had now become a complete government monopoly. Later the State Agricultural Marketing Board was re-named Trade Corporation No. 1, taking its place, with some twenty other corporations, under a Trade Council.

The encouragement of cultivation and improvement of outturn by technical and other measures in regard to rice and other crops

---

[1] See below, pp. 196–201.

has been the responsibility since 1952 of the Agricultural and Rural Development Corporation. This, like Trade Corporation No. 1, is under the absolute control of the revolutionary government.

The results of this monopoly, while not so disastrous as at one time seemed probable, are not such as to afford much comfort.[1]

The area of land under rice cultivation before the Second World War and through the 1930s was pretty steady at around 12 million acres. The war and the Japanese occupation reduced this by almost half. In 1945–46 the area rose again to 6,983,000 acres. Over the next three years it increased by roughly a million acres each year to 10,128,000 acres in 1948–49. The British, and later the independent Burmese government, offered bounties for land brought back into cultivation. The gradual re-establishment of more orderly and secure conditions encouraged the cultivation of areas remote from villages. Above all, the reopening of foreign markets and the keen demand for rice were responsible for this steady increase in cultivation. The worst of the insurgencies and civil war caused little decrease in the area under rice – though they cut actual rice production very considerably. From 1952 to 1960 the area remained very steady at just below or just above 10 million acres. Between 1961 and 1964 it increased once more until in 1963–64 it reached 12,475,000 acres, just over the pre-war area. The Revolutionary Council can justly claim credit for this improvement, which was brought about mostly by reclaiming the 'lost' lands of the Pegu and Irrawaddy divisions through jungle-clearing, drainage, flood protection, and minor irrigation projects. These areas had gone out of cultivation mostly because of insurgent attacks, but even these were being better contained in the two divisions. In 1966–67 the area reached the record figure of 12,787,000 acres, just over a 6 per cent increase on the pre-war average.

The total area under cultivation for both rice and other crops in 1966–67 appears to be about 25 million acres. Of this some 5,600,000 acres have been left fallow.[2] This is, in fact, the same area as that left fallow in 1964–65, and a good deal less than that for 1961–62,

[1] At this point it is desirable to enter a warning. The available figures are, almost without exception, the figures compiled and published by the Burmese government – indeed, there are no others. It is not suggested that these are falsified, though it would not be surprising if the convenience of the government had played some part in their presentation. But the question that does arise concerns the reliance that should properly be placed in them. Can the Burmese government itself know what the facts are? Its authority does not extend to more than some 60 per cent of the country. Its officers probably cannot tour and inspect even so much. It is doubtful whether with the best will in the world any reliable figures can be compiled. However, there are no others and they must be used – but with this reservation.

[2] *Far Eastern Economic Review*, 23 March 1967.

which was 7,220,000 acres. It is, however, almost half as much again as the area normally fallowed before the war – some 3,838,000 acres. It seems that the acreage of land brought under rice cultivation has become stabilized at a point somewhat above 12 million acres, and about 6 per cent more than the pre-war figure; but it is probable nevertheless that an abnormally large, and possibly an increasing, area is being left fallow. This is ascribable not to the needs of good husbandry, but to insecurity and danger from rebels or criminals, which deter cultivators from working at a distance from the protection of their villages.

Pre-war production of rice from the area of 12 million acres was 7,785,000 tons. Of this, a little over 3 million tons was exported. During the Japanese occupation production fell by almost a half and barely sufficed to feed the people of Burma and to meet the demands of the Japanese armies. In 1945–46, while ploughing and planting had to be undertaken at the time when the Allied forces were driving the Japanese out of the country, it was only 2,822,000 tons. Apart from a setback in 1948–49 and 1949–50 caused by the civil war, production has steadily increased, reaching 6,798,000 tons in 1961–1962, and in 1964–65 exceeding the pre-war figures with what has until the present day remained the record outturn of 8,373,000 tons. For this the Revolutionary Council can fairly take credit. There was a slight but not significant drop in 1965–66 to 7,928,000 tons, and a disastrous year in 1966–67, notwithstanding the fact that the area cultivated in this season was the highest ever. In 1967–68, however, the figure was up again to 7,592,000 tons, barely less than the pre-war outturn. It seems that production has stabilized at about the same level as before the war. There has not been an increase in production to match the 6 per cent increase in the area under rice.

Before returning to consider the disaster of 1966–67 it is desirable to look at the rice export figures, for they are a part of that disaster.

Pre-war	3,123,533 tons
1961–62	1,840,000 tons
1962–63	1,619,000 tons
1963–64	1,495,000 tons
1964–65	1,309,000 tons
1965–66	900,000 tons[1]
1966–67	550,000 tons[2]
1967–68	350,000 tons[3]

Exports were raised during the U Nu régime, after the complete interruption caused by the war, to the level inherited by the revolu-

---

[1] *Financial Times*, 5 July 1967, and private information.
[2] Private information. *Financial Times* gives figure of only 600 tons.
[3] Article in *Far Eastern Economic Review*, 16 January 1969.

tionary government – 1,840,000 tons. Since then they have decreased, at first steadily, but in the last two years at an accelerating speed, culminating in a fall of almost 40 per cent during 1966–67.

We now need to turn back to the year of disaster, 1966–67. After two exceptionally good years, 1964–65 and 1965–66, in which production of rice reached 8,373,000 tons and 7,928,000 tons, the 1966–1967 crop totalled only 6,500,000 tons, a fall of 18 per cent. Exports collapsed to 550,000 tons – even lower figures have been mentioned, and this figure was only achieved by diverting stocks required for internal consumption. This brought about an actual shortage of rice which led to food riots in some towns. The government was forced to introduce rationing, an unheard-of measure in Burma.

The alarm caused by this dramatic collapse of production set everyone, both the government and its critics, at home and abroad, searching for causes. The official explanation was bad weather, destructive pests, and insurgency. The season was indeed unfavourable. There was a pest of locusts. Insurgency undoubtedly was a reason. Villagers dared not till fields at a distance from their villages for fear of being molested by rebel bands or dacoit gangs. But many felt that although there was undoubtedly substance in these causes, they were not the whole of the explanation, that there were more fundamental reasons for the crisis that had overtaken the country.

The revival of outturn in 1967–68 to the more than respectable figure of 7,592,000 tons has to some extent given the lie to the government's critics, and shown that some of the near-panic of the previous year was unwarranted, that there was more substance in the explanations given by the government for the fall in production than its critics had been willing to concede. Correspondingly, there is perhaps less force in the other causes put forward by the critics. And yet it is difficult to feel that these are not valid and that if they are not removed, or in some way neutralized, they will inevitably operate to hold back a much-needed expansion in production, even if by themselves they are not sufficient to reduce production. It is for this reason desirable to examine them – particularly as to do so will throw a good deal of light on the present state of the economy in Burma.

Two main reasons were put forward, the first of which is the disappointing share in the profits from the cultivation of rice which the cultivator receives. Throughout the period of the U Nu régime the price received by the cultivator for his paddy was controlled by the government at K285 per 100 baskets. This was about three times the pre-war average but was in real terms probably less, since the prices of other commodities had risen even more. It was the equivalent of about £10 per ton and was never increased, even

when the price at which the government sold this paddy abroad
rose to £60 or £70 a ton as the result of the demand created by the
Korean War. Since then the price abroad has slipped back gradually
to something between £32 and £36 a ton. The price paid to the
cultivator was increased by K.10 in October 1963. In July 1964 it
was further raised to K.310–325[1] and by the end of 1966 it was up
to K.330, at least for early sales.[2] This represents about £11 a ton
as compared with some £35 received by the government for any
paddy that it succeeds in exporting. But the crux of the matter is
that at this level the price paid to the cultivator covers his costs of
cultivation barely, if at all, and does not cover the cost of fertilizers
and other adjuncts to improved cultivation. The prices fixed by the
government, even after the recent increases, offer no incentive to
the cultivator. But the situation is even worse than this. Since the
government established its complete monopoly of the rice trade it
has required that all rice be brought into government stock before
being sold, even for internal consumption. The cultivator who sells
100 baskets of paddy to the government, receives after inevitable
deductions K.318 at the most. When milled this quantity of paddy
will produce 40 baskets of rice. For this the cultivator, at government prices, has to pay K.448. The small cultivator who grows little
more than enough rice for his own needs is heavily penalized for his
efforts, unless he can escape the clutches of the government agents –
and fortunately for him there can be little doubt that he is largely
successful in doing this. For the revival in outturn in 1967–68 has
not been matched by any revival in exports. And the official explanation is that cultivators are withholding and storing their rice.

The other main reason advanced for the fall in production is that
whatever money the cultivator receives for his crop is worthless if he
cannot buy anything with it. And there are now in Burma serious
shortages of many commodities. Onions, chillies, pulses, are difficult
to obtain. Even rice was rationed in the 1966–67 crisis for those who
did not grow it. *Longyis* are rationed to two a year, but not every-
body succeeds in getting his allocation. Charcoal and firewood for
cooking, and bamboos are scarce. Soap and imported goods are very
short. The black market flourishes and prices run at five to six times
the official rates. The basic necessities of life are hard to obtain,
luxuries, even the small luxuries, are virtually unobtainable. Accordingly, with so little upon which he can spend his money, there is
little incentive to the cultivator to grow more rice, or even to maintain his production. These shortages, at least in respect of goods
produced within the country, are largely ascribable to incompetence

[1] *Far Eastern Economic Review*, 30 July 1964.
[2] *Working People's Daily*, 25 April 1967.

and dilatoriness in storage and distribution. With tempting black markets round the corner, corruption is certainly also a factor. (They will be more fully discussed later in this chapter in connection with internal trade.) In the case of imported goods, and of goods manufactured in the country but dependent on imported materials, the course of the balance of external trade also affects the position. This also will be further discussed later in this chapter, but we have already seen that the main export, rice, has seriously decreased, forcing a contraction of imports.

If the main reasons for the failure of rice production to increase are the poor price of rice fixed and the absence of 'incentive' goods, it is possible that there is also a third factor – difficulty in obtaining finance. The members of the revolutionary government are on record[1] as saying that the cultivators of Burma require from K.500 million to K.600 million to finance their agricultural operations for a season. They pointed out the grievous inadequacy of the agricultural loans made by the U Nu government, the highest amount being only K.90 million in 1960–61. They claimed a far better record for themselves, asserting that whereas 'the total amount of agricultural loans issued by the former government in 1961–62 was K.243 million only', they themselves have disbursed K.512 million in 1962–63, K.849 million in 1963–64, and earmarked K.1,030 million for 1964–65. In fact these figures represent not the loans disbursed during these years, but the cumulative totals of agricultural loans put into circulation by the end of these years. The amounts actually disbursed are much less:

	Loans Disbursed	Total Loans Outstanding
1961–62	K.152,200,000	K.243,600,000
1962 63	K.358,400,000	K.512,100,000
1963–64	K.357,500,000	K.710,900,000
1964–65	K.324,300,000	K.741,300,000
(Estimates) 1965–66	K.157,300,000	(Estimate) K.571,700,000

If only the annual amounts disbursed are available to finance cultivation, then, on the government's own showing, the loans made are not adequate for the purpose. If the cumulative total of loans put into circulation for agricultural purposes is assumed to be still available for the financing of cultivation, then there is finance and to spare in the hands of the cultivators. But in fact it would be extremely unsafe to make any such assumption. Much of the money will have been spent or gambled away, and is much more likely to have gravitated into the hands of the richer, of the more astute, or of those who have favours to dispose of. It is safe to assume that it is then lent back to the cultivator, 'under the counter', to finance his

[1] *Forward*, Vol. III, No. 14, 1 March 1965, p. 23.

operations, since the loans made by the government annually are not sufficient to finance the whole crop.

What is clear is that the amount of agricultural loans outstanding has increased from K.91,400,000 at the end of 1960–61, to K.153,700,000, K.353,400,000, and K.417,000,000 at the end of the following years, and that ever since 1962–63 the proportion of loans that has been recovered out of the amounts actually due to be repaid has been steadily falling, from 82 per cent in 1962–63 to 65 per cent in the following year and to 60 per cent in the year after that.

It is this disappearance of money into the sand that has forced the revolutionary government to take a second look at its agricultural loan policy. With effect from 1965–66 '. . . disbursement of agricultural loans has been tied to stricter terms such as collective security or joint guarantee and other conditions . . .'. Since then conditions have been still further tightened so that no fresh loans are made unless the cultivator has repaid at least 75 per cent of earlier loans taken by him. This stiffening of conditions has naturally led to a fall in the amount of advances taken to less than half that paid out in any of the preceding three years.

But it is also reported[1] that cultivators are in any case finding that the red-tape, the delays, the inefficiency, the corruption, that they encounter when applying for government loans are such that the ultimate cost of these loans is no less than that of loans obtained from private moneylenders, and that the government loan is in any case likely to be so long in coming that it will be too late for its purpose. Cultivators are increasingly tending to borrow from private lenders, into whose hands, presumably, the outstandings of government loans have gravitated. The attempts of the British government of Burma to make official loans available for agriculture at modest cost had run into similar difficulties, and cultivators generally preferred to borrow from the Chettyars, although on paper these charged a much higher rate of interest. It is clear, however, that there is plenty of money about at the present time.

Here another factor comes into play. In March 1963 the government enacted the Peasant Rights Protection Law under which land and other possessions of a farmer were exempted from attachment for debt. This measure, designed to protect the cultivator from harassment by the wicked moneylender, has worked quite otherwise – to deprive the cultivator of the only security he can normally offer in order to obtain a loan. As a result, private moneylenders, like the government, have become more chary of financing cultivation.

Another influence may be a reduction in the average area of agricultural holdings, to an uneconomic size. In this connection it is

[1] *Far Eastern Economic Review*, 23 March 1967.

necessary to look at the present status of the cultivators of the land. The pre-war problem, which had baffled the British administration, of agricultural indebtedness and absentee landlordism – as we have seen earlier, 47·51 per cent of occupied land in Lower Burma and 13·66 per cent of occupied land in Upper Burma had passed into the ownership of non-agriculturists, and 38·76 per cent and 7·94 per cent into the ownership of non-resident non-agriculturists[1] – was largely solved by the war. Most Indian landlords fled to India in front of the Japanese advance and in 1944 their abandoned lands were distributed to cultivators. Indigenous landlords, and those Indian landlords who had remained, found it increasingly difficult to maintain their rights, partly because of the collapse in the price of rice that followed the cutting-off of Burma from her pre-war markets and the resultant inability of tenants to pay rents, partly because of the ideological unacceptability of landlordism to the Marxist convictions of the government of the time. After independence the complete collapse of law and order meant quite simply that landlords did not dare collect rents or otherwise assert their ownership. The cultivator in possession continued to cultivate without payment of rent or, for the most part, even of land revenue. At the same time, in 1948, the government introduced the Land Nationalization Act, which, although it almost totally failed in its purpose of resuming land from non-agriculturists for distribution to agriculturists, was a warning to landlords that they could expect no government support. Five years later, in 1953, a better thought-out Land Nationalization Act was passed. Under this, very broadly speaking, and subject to various exceptions, particularly in regard to religious domains, land was to be resumed from non-agriculturists (of whom there cannot by this time have been many in effective ownership) and from agriculturists owning land in excess of what they could work themselves, to be distributed in holdings of a size that could be worked with one yoke of oxen (about 10 acres). It was of course realized that such smallholdings were doubtfully viable economically. Accordingly, longer-term plans were that every five agriculturist families should be grouped into one mutual aid team, that four mutual aid teams should form one agricultural producers' co-operative, and that co-operatives should be incorporated into collective farms of 800–1,000 acres.

It is difficult to know, and the government itself probably does not know, what has been the result of this redistribution. During the U Nu régime it was negligible.[2] The Revolutionary Council has

[1] See above, pp. 86–9.
[2] Hugh Tinker, op. cit., pp. 241–3; Manning Nash, *The Golden Road to Modernity*, New York, 1965, p. 286.

undoubtedly been more successful in asserting its authority and imposing its policies. Indeed the result has been to bring down the average size of agricultural holdings to an estimated 5·4 acres in 1964–65.[1] Such holdings, and the many smaller holdings concealed by an average figure, are economically too small for successful working. The new tenants (many of them previously landless men) lack experience and capital, and naturally have difficulty in borrowing any. As a result, many are discouraged from making use of their opportunity to cultivate, or at the best cultivate incompetently. It is certain that little has been done to bring into being the structure of mutual aid teams, co-operatives, and collective farms planned to counterbalance the fall in size of holdings.

If there are now no incentives to cultivate, if there is no longer a carrot to coax the donkey, it seems that the stick has also been removed. For since 1963, when the Revolutionary Council enacted a Tenancy Law to provide that landlords should not be permitted to select their tenants, but must accept those allocated to them by the local Land Committees, it has been virtually impossible for a landlord to get rid of an unsatisfactory tenant.

Then in 1966 the government enacted a law which resulted in the total abolition of land rent.[2] These apparently revolutionary measures in fact did little more than accord official recognition to an existing state of affairs in which almost all landlords had disappeared and cultivators of land had become for all practical purposes the owners of the land they worked. What exactly their status is under the law is not clear, but few if any pay rent, and not much land revenue is collected. These measures were intended to encourage the cultivators. The government feels that it has done everything it can for them, freed them from landlords, from moneylenders, and from foreign exploiters, provided them with tractors, seeds, and fertilizers, and raised the price of rice; the government says 'No pains are spared that the peasants may be free from want, from debts and from diseases so that they may concentrate on the vital task of ploughing the land without worries.'[3] But they do not respond and the government does not understand why. A number of reasons have been given earlier, but the very abolition of landlords and rent is surely another. The good, dedicated cultivator will profit by these concessions to improve his outturn. But the others, and there are many more of these, will react differently: if they are not being pressed by the landlord or the village headman to pay rent or revenue, why bother to grow more than they need for their own use?

[1] *Report to the People*, 1966–67, p. 13.
[2] *Far Eastern Economic Review*, 1966.
[3] *Far Eastern Economic Review*, 23 March 1967.

With reference to the disastrous year 1966–67, the government is probably right in claiming that the main immediate causes were the weather and the pests. But although the various inhibiting factors that have been considered in the preceding paragraphs may not have been the main causes, they doubtless contributed. They will certainly operate to hold back rice production in the future. But the real reason for the alarm in 1966–67, for the continuing fall in exports of rice, and for the certainty that food crises will recur, is much more deep-rooted and much more serious. The briefest glance at the population figures will show what is happening. For a pre-war population of 17 million the total outturn of $7\frac{3}{4}$ million tons of rice was used, as to 3 million tons or just over, for export, as to $4\frac{3}{4}$ million tons for internal consumption. Since then the population is estimated to have increased by 50 per cent. A comparable increase in the amount of rice required to be retained for internal consumption gives a figure of over 7 million tons. These are the roughest of figures, but the general trend is all too clear. There is now barely enough rice to feed the country, and there never will be enough in the future unless revolutionary changes take place in the methods of agriculture in Burma.

In the face of this threatening situation it is obviously urgently, critically, necessary to increase production, whether by bringing more land under the plough, or by increasing outturns from land already cultivated, or by both these measures. As for bringing more land under cultivation, apart from exhortation at peasant seminars, it is not clear that any measures, such as the grant of subsidies, have been taken to encourage the cultivator. The reclamation of new rice land can be a formidable task and has often broken several pioneers before one has succeeded. The total estimated cultivable area in Burma if compared with the area actually cultivated shows an impressive acreage of some 16 million acres still available to be brought under the plough. But this figure should be treated with the greatest reserve. Very little of it is likely to be suitable for rice (whatever may be the case in regard to other crops), and such of it as can be brought under rice is in any case likely to be only marginally cultivable. It is doubtful whether, with the best will in the world, there is scope for any significant expansion here.

As for increasing the productivity of the land that is under cultivation, there is theoretically great scope. Rice yields are less than 33 per cent of those obtained in Japan. Ground-nut yields are only 20 per cent to 30 per cent of those obtained in Egypt, Nigeria, and Italy.[1] Great expansion should be possible. But to change the ways

[1] *Far Eastern Economic Review*, 19 January 1967, L. F. Goodstadt, 'Sad Harvest'.

of peasant, often illiterate, cultivators is a formidable task. The government has indeed imported, and is now manufacturing on a considerable scale, chemical fertilizers and insecticides. But since cultivators are required to pay for these, since the price paid to the cultivator for his rice does not cover the cost of using fertilizers, and since all distribution is haphazard, unpunctual, and likely to be dependent upon the greasing of palms, the quantities used are infinitesimal. Something like one ton of natural fertilizer (cow dung) is used on one acre of ploughed land. For the same area 2 to 3 lbs of chemical fertilizer are used. Reluctance to use chemical fertilizers springs not only from their cost, but also has a basis in prudent commonsense. Techniques of use are unfamiliar and by-effects, particularly in new conditions, are not always predictable. If there are instructors, they are generally more gifted with ideological enthusiasm than practical experience. It is the cultivator, not they, who will be left to grow the crop and bear the risk of failure. The use of insecticides is on an even smaller scale. There has been considerable distribution of improved seed, but it now appears that modifications are being made to the programme for this which look very much like abandonment. The area of land under irrigation has been increased by some 50 per cent over the past five years, and doubled as against the pre-war figure, but the percentage of irrigated land in the total sown acreage has been pushed up only from 7 per cent in 1961–62 to 8·6 per cent in 1965–66. There is plenty of scope for small, local irrigation projects, or improvements, but schemes for irrigating large new areas are likely to encounter far more intractable practical difficulties than their enthusiastic but often inexperienced advocates admit. The sad fact remains that the rates of outturn per acre are actually less than they were before the war.

The Revolutionary Council makes much of its programme for the utilization of tractors in agriculture, but it is difficult to discern any justification for this policy, at least with regard to the cultivation of rice. The number of plough cattle is not insufficient. The average number of acres of ploughed land to a yoke of plough cattle has fallen from just over to just under 12, and 10 acres is a normal area for working by one yoke. Cattle are increasing faster than the amount of land under cultivation. Tractors cost a great deal more than cattle and together with the spare parts required, consume foreign exchange. They are too costly to be privately owned (and anyway this would offend against Marxist principles), so they are state-owned and maintained. In theory they are hired out to cultivators. In practice only the rich can take advantage of such an arrangement, since the drivers will not work for those who cannot make it worth their while. Maintenance is spasmodic and often

incompetent – breakdowns are therefore frequent. And it is clear
that failures of distribution and organization have led to disastrous
under-use of tractors. In any case, their use for rice cultivation
presents technical problems which are unlikely to have been entirely
solved. It is difficult to resist the conclusion that the policy of using
tractors is more an expensive political prestige symbol than an
agricultural necessity.

In foreign trade it is once again rice that is the key to Burma's
prosperity, since rice provides some 60 per cent of the value of her
exports. We have already seen the alarming fall in the amount of
rice available for export. Virtually the only other exports are of teak
and minerals. These have shown an upward tendency which, however, since they are so small in comparison with exports of rice, can
do little to offset the disastrous decrease of rice exports. The down-
ward curve of the total value of Burma's exports is shown below:

1961–62	K.1,265,700,000
1962–63	K.1,263,800,000
1963–64	K.1,128,700,000
1964–65	K.1,057,600,000
1965–66	K. 915,000,000[1]

A further sharp fall is inevitable during 1966–67, and there is at
present no prospect of reversing this trend.

Imports over the same period have been:

1961–62	K.1,043,600,000
1962–63	K.1,097,000,000
1963–64	K.1,086,600,000
1964–65	K.1,413,100,000
1965–66	K. 803,300,000[2]

A slight upward tendency turned into a sharp rise in 1964–65,
resulting, for the first time since the *coup*, in an adverse balance of
K.355,500,000. The rise was accounted for mainly by an increase in
imports of food (plus K.174,700,000), but also by greater industrial
imports (plus K.91,500,000). The main increases of imported foods
were ground-nut oil (K.84,950,000), other cooking oil (K.58,393,000),
dairy products (K.51,926,000), sugar (K.26,296,000), and coconut
oil (K.24,662,000). Foreign exchange reserves accordingly fell.
Severe cuts were made in imports. In the course of 1966–67 foreign
exchange reserves dropped again sharply and the government imposed further extremely drastic cuts on imports. All budget allocations
of foreign reserves to the various Ministries are reported to have
been slashed by from 30 per cent to 50 per cent. These cuts have
been imposed even on the Ministry of Defence, hitherto exempted

[1] Provisional figure, *Far Eastern Economic Review*, 9 March 1967.
[2] Provisional figure, *Far Eastern Economic Review*, 9 March 1967.

from such squeezes. Besides affecting defence expenditure, they
have made serious inroads on imports of machinery and construction stores. They have drastically reduced imports of consumer
goods and are the main reason for the lack of incentive goods which,
as we have seen is in turn one of the main reasons for the unwillingness of cultivators to grow more rice.

Turning from statistics to the human scene, the first impression
experienced now by any visitor to Burma who knew the country in
the past is apt to be that life is dull, that colour, sparkle, and variety
have been drained from the towns. Where previously shops and
market stalls proclaimed a variety of names (though more often
Indian, Chinese, or European than Burmese), where shopkeepers
vied with one another in attracting customers, and where an endless
choice of goods from all over the world was displayed, there are now
only People's Shops, distinguished by nothing more characterful or
interesting than a number, institutional and drab in appearance,
with generally inadequate stocks of drearily uniform and often unappetizing commodities. It is, of course, the nationalization of the
retail trade that has wrought this change. And clearly it is not only
the visitor who is affected by it. This was, however, only the last step
in the doctrinaire application of the Marxist panacea of nationalization to the not very receptive body politic of Burma.

The seizure of power by a military junta need not have been
accompanied by the complete dedication to the nationalization of
trade and industry that the Revolutionary Council in fact has
shown. If it was merely the golden eggs that the Council was after,
it might seem that it would have been far simpler, and probably
more profitable, to allow the geese to continue laying under suitable
socialist restrictions. And indeed in its manifesto of 30 April 1962
the Revolutionary Council, although it had stated its resolution to
march unswervingly towards the goal of socialism and, explicitly,
that this would involve the nationalization of the means of production, had also said that '. . . national private enterprises which contribute to national productive forces will be allowed with fair and
reasonable restrictions' and that

'on the full realization of Socialist economy the Socialist Government, far from neglecting the owners of national private enterprises which have been steadfastly contributing to the general
well-being of the people, will even enable them to occupy a worthy
place in the new society in the course of further national development'.

But 'national' in this context presumably meant 'Burmese', and the
emphasis was in any case on nationalization.

This policy grew partly out of the Marxist ideology that Aung

San and the other early *Thakins* had imbibed from their reading of English books at university, during the British period, and had assimilated from their contacts with communists in India. It had since become a part of the aura of the founding fathers of the independence movement. It was an indispensable article of faith for any political movement in Burma. It owed more, however, to straight national feeling. Since most of the trade and industry of Burma was in foreign hands, nationalization meant not only compliance with Marxist theory, but also the seizure for Burma and the Burmese of the control, and of the profits, of these undertakings. That the latter would probably grow less, scarcely weighed in the balance against the fact that they would be retained in Burma. As long ago as 1951 U Ba Swe, when advocating Marxism, had said 'Politically we are independent, economically we are being dominated by Imperialist Capital. Economically we are in bondage.'[1] To the Burmese, nationalization was essential to the completion of their independence movement, a respectable way of dispossessing the foreigners, who had established such a hold on the economic life of the country. In this respect there was no difference between the policies of the revolutionary government and those of their predecessors of the U Nu period.

For the rest of 1962, however, no overt steps were taken towards further nationalization of the economy. It seems that the Revolutionary Council was divided as to the extent and pace of nationalization that were desirable. Brigadier Aung Gyi, Vice-Chief of Staff to General Ne Win, and at this period very generally believed to be the power behind the throne, headed the moderates who wished the government to feel its way, act with restraint, and not reject outright the benefits to be gained from accepting controlled foreign investment. Brigadier Tin Pe led a more left-wing, not to say communist, faction within the Council.

On 1 January 1963 the government, which already held 51 per cent of the shares of the Burmah Oil Company, acquired the remaining 49 per cent and also all the remaining interests of the smaller oil companies, the Indo-Burma Petroleum Company and the British Burma Petroleum Company. For these acquisitions the government agreed to pay £4,687,500 in London. They represented the not unexpected completion of a process already begun, rather than any fresh wave of nationalization. But on 8 February 1963 Brigadier Aung Gyi resigned. He had lost his battle against the extremists. On 15 February the Revolutionary Council announced the following measures designed to implement the policy set out in *The Burmese Way to Socialism*:

[1] Quoted Tinker, op. cit., p. 63.

(1) All economic enterprises relating to the procurement, production, distribution, import, and export of goods would be taken over by the government.

(2) The State Agricultural Marketing Board would be given a monopoly of the buying of rice, no private dealers being permitted. Until such time as arrangements could be made to take them over the Board would employ private rice mills. But these also would be nationalized in due course.

(3) No more permits would be issued for new private enterprises in this field.

The earlier idea that Burmese private enterprises might be allowed to continue, subject to restrictions, had gone. It was clear that moderate socialism of the British parliamentary kind had been thrown overboard. For the next twelve months and more there was a spate of nationalizations which showed clearly that Burma was being swept away into communist courses – although not formally communist, perhaps even hostile to communism, and still unaligned in her foreign relations.

On 23 February 1963 all banks, whether foreign or Burmese (but the Burmese banks were few and small), were taken over by the government and renamed People's Banks. Compensation was promised in three months' time. In fact it was not until more than two and a half years later, on 9 September 1966, that the government decided to pay compensation to ten nationalized banks. And whether compensation was actually paid is not known. In the case of the Burmese banks it was said that it would be calculated so as to reimburse all subscribed capital, plus compensation for fixed assets, minus an allowance for unpaid debts. In the case of the foreign banks all capital brought in from abroad would be repaid in the original foreign currency plus, as in the case of the indigenous banks, compensation for fixed assets, minus an allowance for unpaid debts. Since technical knowledge for the operation of the People's Banks was lacking, it became necessary to employ foreign advisers. It might have been expected that these would have been recruited from the foreign banks nationalized, whose staff had knowledge and experience of local conditions and of banking in South-East Asia. It is symptomatic of the resentment and distrust felt towards foreign capitalists that, rather than do this, the aid and advice were sought of a bank that had never operated in Burma at all. The takeover of the banks was quickly followed, on 26 February, by nationalization of the several foreign firms that made up the timber industry. On 6 June 1963 the News Agency Burma was set up to take over all private wire news services, though this was less a measure of economic nationalism than a means of controlling the outflow of news that might not accord with the propaganda line of the moment, or the impression sought to be created by the Revolutionary Council. On 14 June the Anglo-Burma Tin Company was nationalized. Apart from a late takeover, on 29 January 1965, of Burma Unilever Ltd., the great expropriation was now virtually complete. The means of production were in the hands, supposedly of the people, actually of the Revolutionary Council, and the army.

In February 1963 the Revolutionary Council had announced its unreserved acceptance of the principle of nationalization, not only for the means of production, but also in respect of the retail trade, and had set about taking powers for this purpose. In the second half of 1963 and the early months of 1964 the big formally constituted firms, mostly Indian-owned, which handled by far the greater part of the internal wholesale and retail trade, were expropriated. People's Shops were established to replace them. It was not altogether unknown for the original owners to be retained in charge as government employees remunerated by a salary, but this did not often happen in the case of foreigners. Even in the case of the smaller Burmese-owned shops it was more likely that someone would be appointed who was a good party member, or who had otherwise earned the gratitude of the authorities. In the two years following the decision to nationalize the retail trade some 100,000 Indians[1] and some 12,000 Pakistanis left Burma for their homelands.

By March 1964 the new system was considered well enough established to permit a further step to be taken by making it illegal for certain essential commodities to be marketed *except* through People's Shops and the government distributing organization. Sales were to be at prices fixed by the government. These commodities were said to be 'controlled'. On 16 January 1966, by which time the number of People's Shops had increased, this control was extended to cover almost all essential and many other commodities (the list totalled 426 items). This meant that the multitude of small retail shops, all bazaar-sellers, even the peripatetic vendors of bazaar-produce, could no longer legally carry on their business unless they became People's Shops or were otherwise incorporated into the governmental retail trade organization, and remunerated as government employees. It was apparently the intention of the government that they should actually be so incorporated, but there seem to have been no plans or preparation for this formidable, not to say impossible, administrative task. The effect of the extension of control was to throw out of work, at least temporarily, a vast number of persons,

---

[1] Keesing, *Contemporary Archives*, 21–28 August 1965, gives figure 'more than 98,000' from April 1963 to 19 July 1965, 11,768 Pakistanis in same period.

possibly as many as 2 million, many of them the poorer people whom the government professed itself most anxious to help.

This ill-conceived attempt to control the minutiae of the retail trade caused great ill-feeling among the dispossessed shopkeepers. More importantly, it also led to the withholding of commodities from the government controlled markets, to the growth of a black market, to the demand of extortionate prices in this market, and to great intensification of the evasion of the nationalized system. Such was the discontent aroused that General Ne Win was driven to give the matter his personal attention. He confessed that 'nationalization of private business was something like having caught hold of a tiger's tail and there was nothing else to do but hang on'.[1] Nevertheless discretion was allowed to have its effect, the General bowed to the storm, and, in September 1966, thirty-four items of essential commodities were 'decontrolled' and allowed to be handled by private traders and co-operatives again. In the following month forty-five items of forest produce, mainly fuel and house-building materials, were decontrolled. It was expected that more than 500,000 persons would regain employment as a result of these measures. It was also hoped that black-market prices, and indeed black-market activity, would be reduced. This unfortunately does not seem to have happened to any appreciable extent. Shortages in the legitimate market, originally due mainly to the incompetence and rigidity of the government system, are now real, and black marketeers see no urgent reason for allowing them to disappear.

People's Shops are stocked by the highly centralized Trade Corporations established by the government, which like all other governmental functions are under military control. The army attitude seems to be that since it can satisfactorily feed itself through its quartermaster organization, it can equally satisfactorily look after the civil population by the same methods. There is here also a certain puritanism and contempt for more sophisticated ways and more cultivated, less ascetic, tastes. There is little variety in the commodities supplied to the People's Shops, and consequently little choice for the consumer. There are often shortages. Sometimes these are real because of the clamping-down on imports or because of failure of internal production. Sometimes they are due to maldistribution resulting from excessive centralization, failure of transport, or plain inexperience and incompetence in operating a highly complex process made all the more complex by its excessive centralization. In 1966–67 the shortages in towns extended even to rice and it became necessary to ration this and other commodities. If maldistribution leads to shortages of some commodities it leads also to a

[1] *Far Eastern Economic Review*, 1967.

glut of others for which there is no demand at the given time and place. At once, where there are shortages and a monopoly, favouritism and corruption enter into the process of distribution. And at once the black market appears. There do not seem to be large organized rings, but everyone indulges in the minor traffic. If anyone doesn't want what the People's Shop tells him he can get on the ration he buys and sells to someone who does, and with the proceeds goes and buys what he really wants round the corner. Since the shopkeepers are paid a salary, with little prospect of promotion or removal, there is no incentive whatever for them to attract or consider the customer and there are frequent complaints of high-handed and arbitrary behaviour. Consumer committees have been appointed to safeguard the interests of the people and to keep a watch over the workings of the People's Shops. Sometimes they are effective. But sometimes, predictably in an atmosphere of shortages, they merely use their position to ensure that they get first pick of the distribution of the rarer commodities. The final impression left is of naïve idealism combined with doctrinaire obstinacy and complete administrative incompetence – a dangerous mixture.

Here may be mentioned a curious stretching of the Business Enterprises Nationalization Law of 1963. In July 1966 this was used to 'nationalize' all foreign mission hospitals – the Seventh Day Adventist Hospital and the Ramakrishna Mission Sevasharam Charitable Hospital, both in Rangoon; the Namhkam Hospital in the Shan State; and the Ellen Mitchell Memorial Hospital in Moulmein. A little later the Bishop Bigandet Home for Incurables, the Rangoon Leprosy Home, the St John's Leper Asylum, and the Leper Hospital and Home were also nationalized. These institutions were most certainly not business enterprises. Nor can they in any way have sucked profits out of the country; they must, on the contrary, have channelled foreign charity into Burma. Perhaps this was their offence. They can hardly have been centres of proselytization, though they probably did provide a rallying point for the minorities professing their various religions. This was an example of simple xenophobia and of religious rather than economic expropriation.

As the flood of nationalization abated in mid-1964 another ideological measure was introduced. On 17 May it was decreed that 50-kyat and 100-kyat notes were no longer legal tender. This might have been done as a measure to combat inflation, but at no time was it suggested that this was the reason. It seems to have been largely designed to impoverish the better-off classes (there were by now few persons who could be described as wealthy) and to attract the support of the poorer classes, the 'peasants' and 'workers'. But, as with the policy of nationalization, the great majority of persons hit by the new measure would be foreigners. This appeal to Burmese resentment against foreign economic domination, and to the poor, against the rich, ensured popularity for the measure and for the government enacting it. By heightening xenophobia it also conveniently distracted attention from the failures and the less popular repressive policies of the Revolutionary Council. The decree demonetizing the larger-denomination notes announced that smaller-denomination notes would be paid out in exchange for the demonetized notes, but only up to an amount of K.500 for any one person, on application to centres that would be set up for the purpose. There was much delay in establishing the centres, and on 13 June 1964 the government further announced that it would be necessary to distinguish between capitalists and *bona fide* working people. For the former there would be no exchange of notes at all, even below the K.500 limit. Not until 3 September 1964 did payments begin of the smaller-denomination notes in exchange for the demonetized higher denominations. Refund centres were then opened in Rangoon and throughout the country.

The Revolutionary Council makes much of the need to establish and expand industries in Burma, in order to reduce or eliminate dependence upon imports while trying to raise, or at the least maintain, the standard of living of the people – having regard to the present economic trend the Council would probably be prepared to settle for the latter, and will be fortunate if it achieves even that. Industrialization has not gone far. Less than 10 per cent of the population are employed in industry. The proportion was actually higher as far back as 1931 in the British period, since when the big foreign firms that employed the only considerable aggregations of industrial labour have disappeared. In the case of many persons, it is very small-scale village industries in which they are employed, not large-scale industrial undertakings. The statistics published include any undertaking earning an annual income of more than K.4,200 – say £300 a year. On the other hand, at first sight, industrial production appears to account for 50–55 per cent of the total value of production in Burma, whereas agricultural production represents only about 30 per cent. But in fact more than half of the industrial production represents the milling of rice, and is therefore properly a part of the rice trade. These percentages have remained remarkably steady since 1961–62, with a very slight swing towards industry. There is no clearly discernible upward trend in industrialization and certainly no great leap forward. This is attributed by the government to three causes. The first is poor industrial relations. If the facts elicited by the commission appointed to inquire into the decline of production at the State Jute Factory can be taken as typical of conditions elsewhere, then poor industrial relations include the following: indiscipline on the part of the workers; incompetence and negligence on the part of the management; and the fact that the management was politically powerless to resist the demands of the trade unions that higher posts should be filled not by persons with proper qualifications but by promotion from the ranks of the workers. The second reason, and in view of what has been written above this will not be unexpected, is that there has been a contraction of imports because of the fall in exports and consequently a shortage of raw materials for manufacture. The third reason is that the State Trading Corporation concerned failed to make satisfactory distribution of commodities manufactured by private concerns. This was doubtless ascribed to ideological or other jealousies. But from such other reports as come out of Burma it does not seem that the failure in distribution is altogether confined to the products of the private sector. In the nationalized sector there are transport difficulties, because transport is not available, or because, owing to lack of co-ordination, it is not available at the right time and place, or because rebels interfere with movement. There is lack of storage or poor storage both for industrial raw materials and for the products of industry. There is lack of information regarding demand and supplies available. Above all there are delays because of administrative muddle, because of the refusal to take responsibility,[1] because of the need to meet rake-offs all down the line.

To summarize, the economy of Burma is stagnating and appears to face an inevitable decline. Rice production is stationary at pre-war levels. Since before the war the population has increased by 50 per cent and continues to increase at a modest but steady rate. In other words, population has overtaken, or is overtaking, food supplies. There is little or no rice, Burma's chief export in the past, for foreign markets. There is therefore no foreign exchange and consequently there are virtually no imports. The standard of living is falling and will inevitably fall further. In the very near future Burma may even be faced with the need to import rice to feed her own people, and the question arises how she will be able to pay for such imports.

[1] See above, p. 181.

Chapter 12

Welfare

EDUCATION AND PUBLIC HEALTH are the major – indeed, for all practical purposes, the only – welfare services. The Revolutionary Council often asserts that it is building a welfare state, but in fact there is little or no other 'welfare' in Burma. In 1966–67 expenditure on education ran at around K.219,485,000[1] and on health at K.89,857,000. The total of expenditure on all other social services was only K.3,184,000. These figures compare with K.461,918,000 on defence.

The social services, other than education and public health, can be dismissed in a few words. They include social security insurance, which is claimed to cover 469,254 people working in 3,916 industrial establishments. These persons are responsible for 2,115,491 out-patient attendances in workers' hospitals, where they receive prompt treatment for injuries or sickness not serious enough to necessitate treatment in general hospitals, and quick attention in such routine matters as applications for sick leave. The remaining social services consist of twenty-three day nursery schools, four training schools for boys, and one each of the following: child care centre, training school for girls, girls' home, blind school, home for women, women's remand home, training school for social services. Apart from the twenty-three day nursery schools, most of these institutions, or comparable ones, existed long before Burma became independent – though many of them were created and administered by foreign religious missions with the aid of grants from the government.

The writer can scarcely help being influenced by his experience in 1961 when he went to revisit a house he had once inhabited as a senior government official in Moulmein. He found the compound and the house neglected, and derelict. Windows were broken and weeds grew over the drive. There was no one in the house. But there was a notice board. It proclaimed that this was the local welfare office. This, of course, was before the *coup* and the assumption of power by the Revolutionary Council. But the writer finds it difficult

[1] Report to the People on the Revolutionary Government's Budget, Estimates for 1966–67.

to believe that conditions are so very different now, out of Rangoon. In Rangoon there is a shop-window to keep up, and consequently a good deal more to see. However, Buddhist charity and the tradition of family responsibility have in the past rendered unnecessary, and probably still render unnecessary, much of the care which must be officially organized and provided in the supposedly more advanced countries of the West, because if it were not so provided it would not be provided at all.

But in regard to education this picture is a little less gloomy and in regard to public health very much brighter. In education, there has been, at least in point of numbers, a remarkable expansion since independence.

To take primary education first, immediately before the war, at the culmination of the British period, education from the first to the fourth standard for children from six to eleven was provided in about 6,000 schools. The great majority of these were vernacular schools in which Burmese was the medium of instruction and English was not taught. Some thirty-six were English schools where teaching was in English. Some 240 were Anglo-vernacular schools where teaching was in Burmese, but English was taught as a subject. The great majority were private, not state, schools in the sense that they were the result of local enterprise (though possibly stimulated and encouraged by officers of the government); that the buildings did not belong to the state; that the staff were not formally employees of the state; and that about a third of the funds required for maintaining these schools came from the public. On the other hand, the remaining two-thirds of the funds were derived from government sources, one-third from the government, one-third from local authorities, municipal and rural. (This proportion applied to total expenditure over the whole field of education; in the case of primary schools the share borne by the state must have been greater.) These subventions from the state were dependent upon the schools being inspected and recognized by government inspectors.

There was, therefore, in fact a very strong measure of government control. A very few schools (some 143 of all the primary, middle, and high schools) were state schools staffed and directly administered by the government's education officers. Pupils in all these schools numbered some 500,000, about 5 boys to every 4 girls. In addition there were close on 20,000 monastic schools, the indigenous Burmese system of education, surviving from before the British period. These were attended by some 200,000 pupils, all boys. Education was not compulsory. Only a few schools charged fees which in any case were extremely low. Almost all boys and most girls attended either the recognized or the monastic schools. But only one pupil in five stayed in the recognized schools long enough to go beyond the second standard – for more than one or two years. In the monastic schools perseverance was no better – some pupils attended only for a few days. This great majority of early leavers acquired little more than the bare ability to read, write, and count, if indeed they acquired that, an ability that was often lost in after-life. In 1940 56 per cent of men were literate (the criterion was that they should be able to write a letter and read the reply). The figure for women was only 16·5 per cent, and for the whole population 36·8 per cent, leaving 63·2 per cent illiterate.

The first change in this system came immediately after the war, and applied to the whole field of education, not only to the primary schools. During the Japanese occupation education had come practically to a standstill. The British military administration had to rebuild from the beginning and managed during its short period of responsibility to reopen 2,060 primary schools. These, in tune with the policy of the returning civil government that would in due course take over, were all state schools, directly maintained and administered by the government. When the civil government in fact returned many of the foreign missions reopened their 'private' schools. In the primary field the mission schools were not of great significance.

After independence the Burmese government, in view of its socialist outlook, naturally adhered to the principle of state education. It also made education free in all state schools. The civil war inflicted a disastrous setback, the number of primary schools falling from 4,328 in 1948 to 2,186 in 1949. However, by 1952 the number was up again to 3,335 and since then there has been consistently striking expansion, totals rising to 8,951 in 1955, 11,935 in 1961–62, and 13,903 in 1965–66. The number of pupils in these schools has risen from 382,000 in 1949, to 392,398 in 1952, 1,096,000 in 1955, 1,394,091 in 1961–62, and 1,886,335 in 1965–66. The number of primary schools has been more than doubled, and the number of pupils attending them almost quadrupled since 1940. If this increase of almost 300 per cent in the number of primary school pupils is compared with the population increase over the same period of about 50 per cent, it is clear that many more children are getting a longer period of schooling than in the past. In the primary field there is no reason to suppose that this vast expansion has involved any lowering of standards. Now, as before, the main objective is to teach children to read, write, and count.

The second important change in primary schooling (the first was the decision that all schools should be directly administered by the government) was made by the revolutionary government: the decision that English, already taught throughout the middle and high schools, should also be taught as a subject in the fourth (last) standard of all primary schools. There is, however, great difficulty in providing staff qualified to teach English even to the modest levels envisaged.

In sum, there has been a striking advance in the field of primary education, an advance reflected in the fact that illiteracy has dropped from 63·2 per cent of the population to something like 40 per cent. The credit for this would appear to be fairly evenly shared between the U Nu régime and the revolutionary government.

The field of secondary education is covered by middle and high schools. Here, during the British period, the most important part was played by the English and the Anglo-vernacular schools. In the former all teaching was in English. In the latter, teaching was in Burmese in the lower standards, in English in the higher standards; but English was taught as a subject throughout. These schools were in fact outnumbered by the vernacular schools (of the high schools twenty-two were English, 117 Anglo-vernacular, and 191 vernacular; of the middle schools ten were English, 117 Anglo-vernacular, and 909 vernacular), but the English and Anglo-vernacular schools gave the broader and better education, and they led to the university. Moreover, of the two the English schools stood out as best. The vernacular schools led to little but primary school teaching or appointments as revenue surveyors in connection with the assessment of land revenue. These 330 high schools and 1,036 middle schools were attended by some 200,000 pupils. The outstanding fact about them was that almost all the English schools, high and middle – almost all the best schools – were Christian mission schools, and that of the aggregated English and Anglo-vernacular high schools about half were of this type. Of the remaining Anglo-vernacular schools, three-fifths were government schools, two-fifths national schools, started under the influence of the political nationalism that emerged in the 1920s.

After the disasters of the war and of the civil war, there was a steady revival in the numbers of high and middle schools and of pupils attending these, but it was not until about 1961–62, just before the revolutionary government seized power, that the number of these schools rose once again to the pre-war total – though the number of pupils had regained the pre-war level a few years earlier. The revolutionary government has kept the number of schools steady at about the pre-war figure, but has quadrupled the number of pupils attending them, bringing this to over 800,000.

To recapitulate, in the middle and high schools there have been three important changes as compared with the pre-war British system. First, all these schools are now state schools, a policy in fact introduced by the British after the war, but at first not applied with such rigour as to exclude the foreign mission schools. Second, English is now taught in all schools, so ending the gulf that yawned between the English and the Anglo-vernacular schools on the one hand and the vernacular schools on the other. This reform is clearly desirable in principle, but it is also clear that it has not proved possible in practice to provide teachers of English in the requisite numbers. The third change is the disappearance of the English schools – the foreign mission schools. That the best and most influential schools in the country should teach in a foreign language, should inculcate, or at least offer, a foreign religion, should be controlled and in part staffed by foreigners, and should in this way tend to create a community within the community, was obviously not a situation that the Burmese government, or indeed any government, whether of an emergent country or not, could long tolerate. These schools escaped the first wave of conversions into state schools immediately after the war – the British authorities were more ready to permit their continued existence, particularly having regard to their high quality. The first step towards their elimination was taken in 1955 when the government of U Nu withdrew the option, hitherto allowed to candidates for matriculation, of taking their papers in English, and ruled that all such examinations must be taken in Burmese. This immediately created difficulties since all teaching was in English and many of the staff were not competent to teach in Burmese. These difficulties were added to in the succeeding years. The next definite step was not taken until 1965, when the revolutionary government 'nationalized' the schools, taking over control of their staffs as well. Expulsion of all foreign missionaries in 1966 ended an obviously impossible situation. One can sympathize with the desire of the Burmese to be masters in their own house. Unfortunately the best schools have been destroyed or damaged. And real mastery of English, with all that this can mean in the way of access to present-day knowledge and thought, is likely to be put out of the people's reach.

The destruction of the English schools and the attempt to teach English in all middle and high schools have seriously lowered academic standards throughout the secondary system. With this has gone a weakening of discipline, largely because of the intrusion of politics into the schools, which has affected university education more disastrously and will be further discussed in that connection. But it has contributed to the collapse in academic standards in the schools also.

Immediately before the war the University of Rangoon consisted

of the two colleges which had originally been joined in 1920 to form
the university, University College and Judson College, together
with the Medical College, the Teachers' Training College, and the
College of Engineering, all in Rangoon. There were also the Agricultural College and Intermediate College, both in Mandalay. The
total number of students in these seven colleges was about 2,700.
Teaching was in English and many of the staff were English, some
with international reputations in their subjects. A brave attempt
was made to create a university in the image of the Oxford and
Cambridge of the day – highly selective, residential, aiming at high
academic standards, mainly concerned to train an élite for government service and the professions. From the beginning there was
external political pressure by the nascent political parties, to whom
academic standards meant nothing and who were seeking to capture the support of the young, for an easing of those standards
and an increase in the number of graduates. During the U Nu
régime the number of colleges remained the same, but the university
student population rose to 10,000 in 1955 and then to 18,000 in
1961–62. Most of the English staff had left. Teaching was mainly in
Burmese, but as textbooks were still in English, and Burmese lacks
the terms or the precision required by modern knowledge, such an
arrangement was inevitably unsatisfactory. To remedy this, the
Burma Translation Society was established in 1947 with the main
purpose of translating foreign works into Burmese, and of providing texts in Burmese for use in schools and especially university.
Knowledge of the English language had worsened. Standards fell
grievously. Dr Tinker, who worked in the university himself, says:
'In theory the university remains the apex of intellectual efforts
in Burma; in fact it has flung its doors open to a crowd of low-
grade trainees who block the path of the really talented youth of
the country and waste the time and energy of Burma's leading
scholars. The pressure upon the university reflects the prestige of
a degree as a symbol of status and a passport to superior employment. Other avenues of technical and professional training remain
undeveloped.'[1]
Towards the end of 1958 Dr Hla Myint of Oxford was appointed
Rector of Rangoon University. While the caretaker army government tightened up the general administration, he made a courageous
attempt to re-establish genuine university standards, by reducing
the intake of students and raising the standard of qualifications
required from those admitted. The use of English was revived.
But as soon as the politicians returned to power, the old pressures
mounted up again. Hla Myint's position was made impossible and

[1] op. cit., p. 212.

he returned to Oxford. The inflation of numbers and devaluation of degrees were resumed.

The revolutionary government is probably less aware than the politicians of what a university should stand for, and although it need not, as did the politicians, fear to lose the votes of 'the masses', yet it has in fact chosen to use the masses as the foundations of its political power. Academic inflation and devaluation have been accelerated. Since the government came to power student numbers have risen from 18,000 to 25,000. The number of constituent colleges has been increased from seven to seventeen and now includes, besides the original Rangoon University of Arts and Sciences, three institutes of medicine, a dental college, institutes of animal husbandry and veterinary science, of agriculture, of education, of economics, of technology, the Mandalay Arts and Science University, a defence academy, a workers' college, and colleges (some only intermediate) at Moulmein, Bassein, Taunggyi, Myitkyina, and Magwe. This fragmentation of the universities into independent colleges appears to have been part of a deliberate policy designed to weaken the university vis-à-vis the government. In so far as it implies diversification and confers emphasis upon medicine it is to the good. Possibly it also springs from recognition of the undoubted fact that, at least until the advent of the revolutionary government, there was too much supposed university education and too little technological training. But this is not clear. It is certain that the increased demands for teaching staff must have outrun the supply of qualified graduates. This, together with the increase of students, has led to a further debasement of standards. Some texts having become available, teaching is now mostly in Burmese. With effect from 1965–66 English has ceased to be a compulsory subject for degree examinations. Whether this will in fact result in any significant decrease in the number of those gaining a real proficiency in English remains to be seen. If it does, it will tend still further to cut Burma off from the main stream of modern thought and knowledge. Medical training may constitute a partial exception to this gloomy picture. The medical authorities seem to have managed to keep up, perhaps even to raise, standards by concentrating their efforts upon the abler students and accepting that the rest do not have first-class potential. In general, however, the ideal of a university has been lost. In its place has come nothing more than a degree factory with maximization of output as its main objective, without regard to quality.

But perhaps the most tragic feature about university education in Burma is the part played by politics, whether by pressure from without or by student politics from within, often also instigated from without. The very birth of the university in 1920 was attended,

as we have seen, by a boycott fomented from outside in order to
bring pressure to bear on the government for political ends in
connection with the reforms introducing a small measure of self-
government. In 1928 there was constructed the Students' Union
building which was to become the centre of agitation. In 1930 the
Students' Movement and the *Thakin* Party came into existence. In
1936 Thakin Nu, Thakin Kyaw Nyein, and Thakin Aung San provoked a battle with the university authorities, and when disciplinary
counter-measures were inevitably imposed, brought the students out
on strike. This would appear to have been one of the few occasions
on which trouble originated internally, without fomentation from
outside. But once it had broken out, the political parties were quick
to support and make capital out of it. The Education Minister,
Dr Ba Maw, speaking for the government, largely conceded the
strikers' demands. In 1928 there was a school strike, into which
university students were drawn. A demonstration by them outside
the Secretariat was dispersed by the police who inflicted injuries on
one student that unfortunately led to his death. After the war the
depressing sequence was quickly revived and there were strikes in
1946, 1947, and 1949. In 1953 the communists organized a more
determined boycott. The government brought in police and military police and the demonstrators were only dispersed after what has
been described as 'a pitched battle in front of Ava Hall in which
a thousand students fought it out against tear-gas, fire-hydrants,
and (according to eye-witnesses) bullets'.[1] The culmination (or perhaps it is not yet the culmination) of this tragic story came in July
1962, when there were once again communist-organized student
demonstrations. The newly established revolutionary government
moved the army in, blew up the Union building, always the centre
of agitation, and opened fire on the demonstrating students. Thirty-
nine students were wounded; seventeen were killed and the bodies
were removed in army lorries. Less than eighteen months later there
was yet more trouble, with further anti-government demonstrations.
This time the government closed all universities and colleges for six
months. Since then there has been no overt disaffection, and order
has been maintained. But any shreds of academic freedom that had
survived the régime of U Nu have disappeared.

Nearly all these disturbances were instigated from outside the
university. The formal demands in all were for easing of examination requirements or for greater permissiveness in a society already
lacking discipline. The real objective underlying probably all of
them was to embarrass the government of the day. To assist students
in demands for the removal of grievances, real or trumped-up, is a

[1] Tinker, op. cit., p. 208 (*Nation*, 4 October 1953).

simple and effective way for a political party to enlist support. It is
also a safe and effective way to harass the government. Students,
who readily attract the sympathy of the public, are thrust into the
front line and take such knocks as come. The real instigators keep
out of view and it is very difficult to bring any responsibility home
to them.

U Nu, as premier, took the soundest of lines against this evil and
besought students to leave politics to the politicians, declaring 'Our
Union underwent a complete transformation at [independence] . . .
Every one of us need not take up politics . . . as before . . . The duty
of the students is to try to become educated.'[1] But, as Tinker says,
'the students do not heed U Nu's admonitions: his own student
example is more powerful'.[2] It is always easier to breach than to
mend the defences against lawlessness and disorder. When U Nu
took the lead in fomenting the 1936 disturbances at the university,
he was already some twenty-nine years of age, having returned to
the university, after a period of schoolmastering, to read law. He
was almost ten years older than Aung San and Kyaw Nyein, and
the others who took part in the troublemaking – for troublemaking
it undoubtedly was – and himself bears a heavy responsibility for
the disasters that have followed.

During the régime of U Nu political pressures and activities
spread even to the schools where pupils found themselves enrolled
in one of two competing unions, one sponsored by the A.F.P.F.L.,
the other by the communists, which through their political affili-
ations at the centre, brought pressure to bear upon headmasters to
make concessions, or even to accept, promote, or reject particular
pupils.

A tragic commentary on the general state of academic life under
the revolutionary régime is furnished by the summary expulsion
in 1964 of Professor G. H. Luce, then nearly seventy-five years
old, and his wife, a Burmese lady. When Professor Luce, a great
lover and champion of Burma and of her people, probably the
most erudite and distinguished scholar in the country, retired from
Rangoon University he settled in Burma, for the rest of his life
as he hoped, and continued to play an important part in intellectual
life. He was refused permission even to take his books and notes,
the irreplaceable record of a lifetime's work (though these were, a
year later, and as a result of pressure by the British Foreign Office
and Embassy, restored to him). No reasons were given, and the
expulsion appears to have been the result of jealousy and squalid
academic intrigue.

[1] Quoted ibid., p. 209.
[2] ibid.

When we turn to public health, the picture is less depressing. Before the war there were some 300 hospitals, almost all government-run, about 1,700 doctors with registerable qualifications, of whom some 650 were in government employ, and 2,400 registered nurses and midwives. These hospitals provided 8,000 to 9,000 beds, say one to every 2,000 of the population. Other institutions included a medical school, the Pasteur Institute, the Bacteriological Laboratory, a vaccine depot, and two mental hospitals. In all of them scientific 'Western' medicine was practised. There were also an unknown number of *hse-sayas*, who practised traditional indigenous, entirely unscientific, medicine. For scientific medicine Burma leant very heavily upon the government medical services and in these there was an overwhelming predominance of non-Burmese doctors. In the upper grades these were mostly British, with some Indians, but only two or three Burmese. In the middle and lower grades Indians were predominant, but there were also Anglo-Indians and Anglo-Burmans. A slightly larger proportion of Burmese figured at this level, but still very few. The lack of Burmese doctors was not the result of discrimination – far from it. The long arduous training, however, deterred many candidates, and those who undertook it were apt to be outclassed in examinations by Indians, who were more industrious, more able, better examination subjects, and probably had the advantage of a more academic and scholarly background.

The Japanese war virtually destroyed this medical system, since the great majority of the upper and middle grades of medical officers fled to India. The British military administration achieved remarkable success in reviving it, but the civil war brought about a fresh collapse, insurgents senselessly destroying more than half the hospitals in the course of their attacks on government buildings. And with independence, the foreign doctors had nearly all gone. At the worst period there were only 400 doctors left in government service as against 650 before the war. Reconstruction began in 1951. By 1961–62 there were 184 hospitals, as against the pre-war figure of 300, forty-six dispensaries, and about as many beds as before the war. By 1965–66 there were 304 hospitals, sixty dispensaries, and 16,000 beds. Doctors numbered 2,100, nurses and midwives 3,250. Because of the increase in population there were still fewer hospitals, doctors, nurses, and midwives than there had been in proportion to pre-war population. But the growing scale of medical provision is overtaking the increase in population. And in the matter of hospital beds the proportion has been improved, with one bed to 1,500. Since the number of hospitals is virtually no more than before the war, this presumably means that the new hospitals are larger. But another way of achieving the increase in beds is suggested by the fact that the Rangoon General Hospital which before the war provided 750 beds now has 1,400. This has been done, not by adding to the buildings, but by putting beds into verandahs, passages, and basements.[1] The beds are there, but conditions are far from satisfactory and can operate to make efficient working impossible.

Every sort of pressure has been brought to bear on those responsible for medical education to shorten courses and lower standards; by the government, in order to hasten increase in provision of doctors; by others, for the reasons that have brought down standards over the rest of the educational field. But on the whole these pressures have been successfully resisted. Proposals by the U Nu régime to cut down the medical course from seven to five years were 'met with a blunt rejection'.[2] And the fact that the General Medical Council in London has agreed to recognize Burmese medical degrees is evidence that the medical profession has gained its point, and that medical education is an exception to the general decline of educational standards.

Another hopeful feature of the medical services is the plan for creating Rural Health Centres, introduced by the U Nu régime and energetically persevered with by the revolutionary government. The scheme involves the provision of one health centre to every fifteen village tracts, a total of some 700 to 800. By 1958–60 just over 400 had been brought into existence. It is not known what further progress has been made. Each centre is in the charge of a health assistant and is intended to have as well a lady health visitor, a vaccinator, and five midwives. Health assistants in no way approximate to doctors. But they receive a two-year training which at least inculcates the principles of hygiene and first-aid and teaches how the medical services are organized and work. They can do a good deal towards diffusing better knowledge of health rules, towards relieving the doctors of the more simple troubles for which home treatment is sufficient, and towards acting as a liaison between patient and doctor in more serious matters. These centres may be expected to play a valuable part in pushing the benefits of modern medicine off the motor-roads into the villages – which are still the real Burma.

In the struggle to maintain standards and to keep abreast of the rapid advances of present-day medicine the policy of sending doctors to the West, mostly to Britain, to gain further qualifications, undergo refresher courses, or undertake research plays an important

---

[1] Woodruff, *British Medical Journal*, 26 August 1967, p. 553.
[2] Tinker, op. cit., p. 215. For the present policy of the medical authorities see above p. 210.

part. There may be as many as ninety or so on courses in the United Kingdom at any one time.

The greatest handicap is probably that which afflicts other professions too: that the Revolutionary Council, through its army officers, seeks to control and direct in detail matters of which it has insufficient knowledge or understanding. Highly trained, dedicated doctors suffer endless frustration.

Chapter 15

Religion and the Arts

IT HAS BEEN SAID earlier[1] that, for the Burmese, religion is an integral part of their lives, not perhaps on an exalted philosophical or mystical plane, but at the everyday level of belief, of pagoda-attendance, of aspiration to observe the basic rules of Buddhism, and of respect for the monks.

Buddhism first came to Burma by sea, probably from Conjeevaram in south India, not from Ceylon. It reached the Mons in Thaton in Lower Burma, as opposed to the Burmese in Upper Burma, probably in the fifth century A.D. With it came considerable Indian influence, especially in pagoda architecture. It was Hinayana or Theravada Buddhism, a 'pure' form of the religion. Meanwhile corrupt forms and other less desirable religious influences seeped into Burma overland from northern India and Tibet, reaching the Burmese proper in Upper Burma. During the eleventh century the pure form of Buddhism came, or rather was brought, to Upper Burma when King Anawrahta of Pagan invaded Lower Burma and, it is said, carried away from Thaton the stones (but perhaps, after all, it was only palm leaves) upon which the scriptures had been engraved, on the backs of thirty-two white elephants. Meanwhile, in India, Hinduism ousted Buddhism, and the links between Burma and Conjeevaram died out. But Buddhism continued to flourish in Ceylon and has done so to the present day, with the result that strong links have grown up between that country and Burma.

Buddhism recognizes no god and no soul, but it does teach a belief in reincarnation. For the Buddhist, life is evil and it is a misfortune to have been born into the world at all. The motive power of his religion is to be found in the belief that it is possible to escape from the perpetual round of reincarnation in misery, into Nirvana where self-consciousness ceases, and misery therefore is no more. This escape is to be achieved by gaining merit through right living. Right living involves following the eightfold path of right views, right aims, right speech, right behaviour, right livelihood, right effort, right mindfulness, and right concentration, and in observing the five precepts: not to take any life at all, not to commit any sexual

[1] See above, p. 47.

crime, not to steal, not to lie, and not to drink any intoxicating liquor. In practice the preservation of life, the bestowal of alms, the offering of food to monks, the founding of a monastery, the building of a pagoda or of a resthouse for travellers, are all works which will gain merit and hasten liberation from endless reincarnation.

Since there is no god, and no godlike status attaches to the Buddha, there is no worship and no priesthood for the organized conduct of this. A pagoda is not intended as a place of worship or prayer, but rather as a place and focus for meditation, for self-examination, and for the renewal of aspiration towards right living. But since Buddhism, like most other religions, has a liberal admixture of earlier Animism, and has not been unaffected by the superstitious tendencies of the Burmese, many visitors to pagodas do in practice worship or pray, whether it be to the Buddha, or to the spirits, or merely to the relics of the Buddha over which so many pagodas are, or are believed to have been, built.

But if there is no priesthood there is a very large, important, and influential community of monks. Visually these constitute a striking and picturesque element in the Burmese scene, with their shaven heads, their orange-yellow robes, their palm-leaf fans, and their alms-bowls. They live in monasteries built by laymen fortunate enough to be able to gain merit on this scale. Life being evil they are required to cut themselves off from the world and to undertake no worldly tasks. They may not earn a living, and for their food are required to depend upon the oblations of laymen. They may have no property except their robes and what is needed for their mendicancy. They conduct no services. They are required only to observe the rules of their order and in so doing to furnish such a shining example of other-worldliness that men will be moved to charity towards the monks and to further attempts to lead the good life themselves. In this way monks will both gain merit on their own behalf, and also confer upon others the opportunity to gain merit through the support they give to the order. Monks sometimes preach, expounding the law, but this is in no way their main function. The only exception to the rule that they must not involve themselves in matters of daily life is in respect of education. Before the British period there were virtually none but monastery schools. Since then the monks have continued to play an important part, especially in the villages, in many of which there is no schooling other than that provided by them.

The order is held in great respect and veneration by all Buddhists throughout Burma. It has from time to time inevitably become the refuge of criminals on the run, or a safe haven for politicians whose views were unpalatable to those in authority. But the majority of its members are men of a gentle saintly character and of deep humility.

Buddhism is not a proselytizing religion. And the good Buddhist in Burma is tolerant as well as devout. Not unnaturally, however, he expects others to be tolerant also. Christian or other missions have made little or no impact upon Burmese Buddhists, though they have gained converts and brought comfort in the case of some of the non-Buddhist minority races. And the Buddhist can react swiftly and violently to the cry that his religion is in danger, as he did for example in 1938 when he turned upon the Muslim community, and murdered more than 150 Muslims and Hindus in riots throughout the country – though it should be added that religion was not the only cause of these disturbances.

Possibly the greatest difficulty in the context of Burma is to understand how Buddhism, this remote, austere, negative, pessimistic religion, is to be reconciled with the lighthearted gaiety, friendliness, enjoyment of life, and ever-present optimism of the Burmese character.

After independence the personal popularity of U Nu throughout Burma was in great measure due to the widespread and justified belief that he was a good Buddhist. And under his governments there was a considerable revival of interest in religion. The care of pagodas improved markedly. The Sixth Great Buddhist Council was held in Rangoon from 1954 to 1956. Burma was on the way to becoming the acknowledged centre of the Buddhist world.

The military *coup* brought a very different atmosphere. In the first place, the doctrinaire Marxism of the new government had no room for religion. It is remarkable that in *The Burmese Way to Socialism* there is no mention whatever of Buddhism, and a bare two lines referring to religion – 'The Revolutionary Council recognizes the right of everyone freely to profess and practise his religion'. In the constitution of the Burma Socialist Programme Party there is no mention at all of either Buddhism or religion. This, in Burma, is unprecedented.

In the second place, General Ne Win himself is not an U Nu. The army and its officers follow his less religious line in public, but many of the officers are in fact much more devout, much more typically Burmese, and observe the customs of Buddhism in their own homes. But the whole idea of an army, and the life of a soldier, are repugnant to Buddhism which in no circumstances allows the taking of life.

Shortly after the proscription of all political parties, other than the Burma Socialist Programme Party, on 1 April 1964 a law was enacted requiring all kinds of organizations to apply for registration, and religious organizations were specifically included. This measure evoked sharp resentment in the monastic order and among devout laymen. It seemed an attempt by the state – by laymen – to interfere with religious matters. Just a year later trouble broke out with the monks. First, some ninety were arrested, then a further thirty-four, on charges of anti-government activities. These arrests were due in part to genuine fears and resentment, but, as ever, opponents of the established régime tended to seek sanctuary in the monasteries, and much of the opposition was political. An attempt is being made to bring the monastic schools into the national education system and in September 1965 a six-day course was held in Rangoon for monastic school education officers. Moreover, in January 1966 the government continued the practice of awarding certificates to those monks or nuns who had passed the *Dhammacariya* examinations, or the *Pahtamagyi, Pahtamalat,* or *Pahtamange* examinations, tests of proficiency in the canons of their religion. In general, however, religion receives little official encouragement under the Revolutionary Council, though it undoubtedly remains an important part of the life of the great majority of the Burmese.

In her art and culture Burma shows traces of Hindu influence, of ancient rather than recent origin – for example, in her pagoda architecture. China exerted far less influence and Burma never acquired the standards of craftsmanship for which China is so justly famed. There were naturally certain similarities between the arts of the Burmese and of their closest neighbours, the Siamese. But in the main the culture of Burma was a home-made article, and that in two senses. First, it was distinctively Burmese, a product of the geographic isolation of the country. Second, although standards of fashion and taste were largely set by the king and court, it was home-made in the sense that it was a small-scale, traditional village activity with its roots firmly in the villages, rather than a more sophisticated outpouring of court or aristocracy – indeed there was no aristocracy.[1] It was essentially a Buddhist culture for the monasteries were the only schools, indeed the only centres of awareness of anything outside the daily round.

Of architecture as an art there are not, or at least until recently there were not, many examples outside the field of religious buildings. Chief of the latter are the pagodas – Burma is above all things the land of pagodas. The construction of these is conditioned by the purpose for which they are built. Pagodas are places for worship and prayer (though strictly the Buddhist religion does not recognize these), for meditation and spiritual refreshment. They are in no sense a church or assembly hall and there is no need for space to

[1] See above, p. 46.

accommodate a congregation or audience. Such preaching as there is takes place in the adjoining monastery. Pagodas are built perhaps to cover a relic of the Buddha, to attract attention to this, above all to provide a focus for contemplation and meditation. They can therefore be solid, or, if space is needed for shrines or statues of the Buddha, the interior hall or halls need not be of any great size. They are built of brick with moulded plaster or stucco facing (there is practically no building or carving in stone). In general style they display strong Hindu influence. Their decoration is similarly inspired, but has developed a genuine indigenous character. They are, broadly speaking, of two kinds: those which consist of a *stupa*, in shape not unlike an inverted handbell, standing on more or less numerous superimposed diminishing platforms, generally rectangular – these are solid except for a sealed chamber containing a relic of the Buddha or of a Buddhist saint; others are generally square or cruciform in ground plan, with a vaulted hollow or hollows containing a shrine or shrines, and with entrance porches projecting on one or more sides. These rise either by diminishing storeys, or solid terraces in a pyramidal shape, or by the superposition of a bell-shaped *stupa* of solid brickwork on the lower storeys or terraces, or by a combination of these methods, to a slender and often very graceful spire, crowned by a decorative metal finial, hung with bells that tinkle sweetly in the breeze. Many pagodas are of great age. Sometimes a new pagoda has been built over an existing one – there are cases in which several older buildings are buried under the visible exterior. New pagodas are generally built on traditional lines, so that there is a striking consistency in style. They are generally white or gilt, brilliant in the sunlight, and sited with unerring taste and judgement to cap a rise, a hill, or a rock, or to overlook a village or a river. Every village has its shrine. They convey, by their lines or by their positions, a great sense of permanence, aspiration, and repose. Many are buildings of elegance and delicacy, and even the humblest often possess great charm. The great museum of pagodas is where the vast city of Pagan once stood, in the eleventh, twelfth, and thirteenth centuries A.D. Here are many styles and here can be seen clearly the influence of northern India. In the country at large the only departures from the traditional style are a few modern tasteless aberrations, facile with concrete and corrugated iron sheeting.

Other religious buildings are monasteries; also buildings set apart for rites peculiar to the monastic order, such as ordinations of monks; and shelters for those visiting, or on pilgrimage to pagodas or monasteries. Monasteries, generally of timber, sometimes of brick (though the timber buildings, particularly the older ones, were aesthetically the more successful), consisted for the most part of one large hall, pillared with teak trunks, with many doors on three sides, which when open virtually removed the walls and threw open the interior to the outer world. Along the fourth side would be a raised dais and one or more shrines and images of the Buddha. Character was given to an otherwise somewhat barn-like structure by the arrangement of the superimposed roofs, several in number, the higher decreasing in size and rising to a point, so as to give the impression of a spire. There was also carved decoration of the eaves and sometimes of the balustrade of the platform surrounding the monastery. The flame-like ornamentation of much of this carving is in many ways typically Burmese and is felt to be so, but it seems in fact to be a form natural to the material used, for something very similar is to be found on the roofs and eaves of timber churches as far away as Norway.[1] Wood is a material that the Burmese handle with skill, judgement, and finesse, and in these timber-built monasteries is embodied, with great success, a genuine and distinctive Burmese art, which, although borrowing from elsewhere, remains essentially something of its own. Proportions are satisfying and the carved decorations are (or were, because carving now seems to be a dying if not a lost art) sometimes of great beauty. Many more recent buildings are of brick and plaster, or of concrete, and roofed with corrugated iron sheeting. In the handling of these, perhaps more difficult, materials, the Burmese are less sure; emancipation from the discipline of the old materials and exposure to foreign influences have combined to produce a less distinctively Burmese, and far less successful, architecture.

The only non-religious buildings of comparable significance were the royal palaces. Of these only one survived into living memory, the palace at Mandalay, and a disastrous fire and the Second World War destroyed what was left even of this.

Let two eye-witnesses describe Mindon's palace, a journalist and a young civil servant, who both saw it immediately after the Burmese surrender in 1885. The journalist writes:

'The Royal Palace occupies the centre of the city, and is enclosed by a strong teak stockade, twenty feet in height, and by two brick walls, the first a hundred feet inside the stockade, and the second two hundred feet, all three being like the city walls, in straight lines as if the purpose was to minimise the difficulties in the way of an assailant ... The eastern gate was reserved for the King, but is now thrown open. Looking towards the Pavilion of Audience from this gate, the royal throne, raised on a dais, is seen amidst the gilded pillars and under the canopied roof. This Hall

[1] Harvey, *History of Burma*, p. 330.

of Audience is the finest structure of all that go to make up the
totality of the palace. A beautiful pinnacle of wonderful lightness
and grace surmounts it. Corrugated iron has been turned to
ornamental use in filling in the light timber framework which
soars up to bear the resplendent golden umbrella that crowns the
whole. The fluting of the corrugated iron harmonises very successfully with the bold and aspiring lines of the structure. Iron
ropes of great tenuity run from the ground to the slender spire,
and give it a certain amount of support; they too harmonise with
the general flow of the lines upwards and seem to be a necessary
and artistic detail of the general design . . .

The Palace consists of a series of pavilions and other buildings
differing in size and detail, but all composed of teak, elaborately
carved, and painted red when not covered with gilding. The
application of gold is on so liberal a scale that the eye gets tired
of it, and the Indian red of the bases of the pillars is a welcome
relief. The ingenuity of the designer and the skill of the workmen
give variety and interest to every varying detail. There is no
monotony and no straining after the grandiose.'[1]

The young civil servant, as befits an administrator, was a little
less carried away by what he saw. He wrote:

'Barbarous Byzantine mirrors of colossal size still lined the walls; a
motley heap of modern toys, French clocks and fans, mechanical
singing birds, and the like, mingled with lovely specimens of
Burmese carving, gold and silver and lacquered trays and boxes,
forming a heterogeneous collection characteristic of degenerate
taste . . . The Palace it must be confessed, was a mass of somewhat
tawdry buildings, mostly of wood and of no great antiquity,
desecrated by corrugated iron roofs, yet of interest as a unique
specimen of Burmese domestic architecture. Perhaps the most
striking features were the great halls of audience, supported by
mighty pillars of teak, red and golden, the several Royal thrones
often described, and the Pyathat, the graceful terraced spire sur-
mounting the eastern throne-room, which travellers have been
taught to call the centre of the universe. The title was invented by
an enterprising journalist, but will, no doubt, always be cited as a
mark of Burmese arrogance.'[2]

The general flavour of the building was comparable to that of the
greater monasteries, except that it was more extensive, the teak
pillars were more magnificent and more numerous, the carving was
more elaborate. The whole was infused with that airy touch of
whimsy that is in all Burmese creations.

[1] Grattan Geary, op. cit., pp. 88–90.
[2] H. Thirkell White, *A Civil Servant in Burma*, London, 1913, pp. 117–18.

Domestic architecture is severely utilitarian. The materials used, and always used in the past, by the great majority of Burmans are timber posts, timber planking, bamboo posts, woven bamboo walling, and thatch. Since none of these are proof against fire or white ants, there are no domestic houses left from earlier times. At the site of the ancient city of Pagan, remains of thousands of pagodas are sprinkled over an area of about 16 square miles. Of the monasteries and multitude of houses that must have covered the now barren and deserted spaces around and between the pagodas there is left no trace. But it is unlikely that they were significantly different from the houses of the present day. For these are built of the same materials, in the simplest way that the materials or the skill of the builders – and many build their own houses – allow, on traditional lines. There is no conscious straining after architectural effect, but a house well built of solid timber posts and planks, oiled to a mellow darkness to protect against the white ants, or a bamboo house with matting walls patterned and textured by the weaving of split bamboos, has, in the proper setting, a spontaneous beauty that tends to elude the more self-conscious building of the present day. This, in the cities, and in the case of those who can afford it, is now of brick and other conventional materials, and of that cosmopolitan style to be observed around most airports. Fortunately the great majority of Burmans will, for as long as can be foreseen, continue to build and live in houses of the traditional Burmese kind.

The poorest and most rudimentary houses are built entirely of bamboo and thatch, the frame of bamboo poles, the floor of split bamboo, the walls of bamboo split more finely and woven into matting, and the roof of grass or leaf thatching. The ingenuity and skill displayed in the use of bamboo is quite remarkable. In better houses timber replaces bamboo for the framework and flooring. A step further up in the scale and the walls are of timber also, and the roof of wood shingles or, since this was introduced from the West, of corrugated iron sheeting. Not many houses are built of brick. All, save the brick houses, stand on posts, raised some feet above the ground, as protection from snakes and other animals and, in many parts, from floods. If such houses seem flimsy, and inadequate protection against the weather, it should be remembered that there is little or no cold to guard against, that protection against rain is adequate, and that an insubstantial house, although it may be hotter than others for the hours of midday heat, cools off far more quickly when the sun loses its strength. In such houses there is little or no conscious design. Tradition and the easiest way of using the available materials dictate their shape and character. But there is much to give pleasure in the materials chosen and the skill displayed in their handling.

There has scarcely been an independent indigenous art of painting in Burma. When it was indigenous it was largely subservient to architecture, its function being to decorate walls or other surfaces in pagodas or palaces. When it became independent of architecture it took the form of meeting the largely European demand for pretty sketches of the country, not unskilfully done in conventional Western style. A few painters penetrated to the reality of Western art, but most of these paintings were pastiches without originality and certainly without roots in the indigenous style. Of this style not many examples survive. The most notable are the twelfth- and thirteenth-century wall paintings in some of the pagodas at Pagan. These are executed with a delicacy and sophistication quite beyond the reach of the West at that time, or, it may be added, of Burma now. They display strong Hindu influence. Later, nineteenth-century, survivals of wall decoration in monasteries or the Mandalay palace, are rougher, less sophisticated, less finished works, though possibly more essentially Burmese in style and inspiration.

The art form which makes by far the widest and strongest popular appeal is that of the entertainment known as the *pwè*. Writing in 1882 Sir George Scott said:

'There is no nation on the face of the earth so fond of theatrical representations as the Burmese. Probably there is not a man, otherwise than a cripple, in the country who has not at some period of his life been himself an actor, either in the drama or in a marionette show; if not in either of these, certainly in a chorus dance. It would be wrong to say that there is no other amusement in the country, but it is indisputable that every other amusement ends up with a dramatic performance. When he is named there is a pwè; when a girl's ears are bored; when the youth enters the monastery; when he comes out again; when he marries; when he divorces; when he makes a lucky speculation; when he sets up a water-pot; builds a bridge; digs a tank; establishes a monastery; dedicates a pagoda, or accomplishes any other work of merit; when there is a boat or horse race; a buffalo or cock fight; a boxing match, or the letting loose of a fire-balloon; a great haul of fish, or the building of a new house; when the nurseries are sown down, or the rice garnered in; whenever in fact anything at all is done, there is a theatrical representation. Finally there is a pwè, as grand as his friends can make it, when the Burman dies.'[1]

[1] Shway Yoe (Sir J. G. Scott), *The Burman, His Life and Notions,* London, 1910, p. 286.

And what was true then is still largely true today.

It is possible to enumerate a number of kinds of *pwès* but for present purposes it is sufficient to distinguish three main types: *Zat pwès* are performances by live actors (*Anyein* and *Balasaing pwès* can for the present purpose be considered as simplified or economy forms of the *Zat pwè* – with apologies to the purists). Indeed there is a tendency for the *Zat pwè* and the *Anyein pwè* to assimilate, a tendency fostered by the government which does not want socialist workers to spend the hours, when they should be recovering their energies by sleep, enjoying themselves at full-length *Zats*.

The *Zat pwè* has sometimes been described as Burmese opera. But this misplaces the emphasis. In opera it is the music that imposes its tempo upon drama and dancing – opera in fact is a form of music. In a *pwè* it is dramatic action that dictates to the music – the *pwè* is more theatre than opera. But it is, at the same time, a great deal more than a dramatic performance. Onto the theme of a religious drama, or a romantically fantastic tale of kings, queens, princes, and princesses, are added scenes of the present day, or out of the contemporary cinema, clowning and buffoonery of a high order, wisecracks (often at the expense of authority), miming and mimicry (often of the hero and heroine or of persons in the audience), singing and dancing by those on the stage, and the music of the orchestra. Here is something essentially Burmese, romantic, humorous, irreverent, enormously vital. Performances take place on a stage in the open, and continue all night, perhaps several nights. Whole families attend, sitting on mats on the ground. Occasionally the children sleep. Carts are parked and bullocks tethered on the outskirts of the crowd. An appetizing smell of hot food is wafted from improvised food stalls. There is no paying for admission; someone is giving the party to give thanks or gain merit. Of course there is drink and occasional quarrelling. But it must be hard to find anywhere else in the world a crowd so happy, so friendly, so hospitable.

All that has been said of the *Zat pwès* applies also to the *Yok thé pwès*, the puppet shows, with the addition that the puppeteers display a very high degree of skill in their art, that puppet shows are almost more esteemed by the Burmese than live shows, and that the medium makes possible even greater flights of romantic fancy, even more outrageous quirks of humour.

Yein pwès consist of singing and dancing by a chorus or *corps de ballet*, without soloists. A high degree of concerted skill is achieved but movement is of the body, head, arms, hands, and even fingers, rather than of the legs; it is dancing of posture rather than of movement. Flexibility, grace, and expressiveness are combined in high

virtuosity, but the restricted leg and footwork make Burmese dancing monotonous to Western tastes.

There is no *pwè* without music; and music is an equally essential
ingredient to most ceremonies. To form a subordinate part of these,
is the main function of music, though there are also more intimate
chamber music, shanties or work songs, solo songs, and the piped
melodies floating across the paddy fields of an evening. In general,
however, music takes a subordinate, though important, part together
with acting or dancing. Perhaps only in the case of the cowherd's
bamboo pipe is music played for its own sake alone; and then it
is a slight, trivial affair – but charming. Rhythms are characteristic, vigorous, and interesting – never martial, or what strikes the
Western ear as martial. Melody is the frame for elaborate variation
and decoration, often improvised as in jazz, often ranging far from
the original, and for that reason often missed by Western ears.
There is no harmony – except such haphazard and meaningless
combinations as may result from the members of the orchestra
improvising differently on the same theme. There is nothing comparable to the key-system of the West with its endless variety,
though there are limited variations of mode. There is supposedly an
accepted scale, but scales claimed to be identical are found, in fact,
to vary considerably. With apologies once more to the purists, one
can for general purposes best say that whereas the Western major
scale consists of tone, tone, semitone, tone, tone, tone, semitone,
the Burmese scale consists of tone, tone, three-quarter tone, three-
quarter tone, tone, three-quarter tone, three-quarter tone. Orches-
tras for public occasions include some or all of the following: a
xylophone, a circle of drums, a circle of gongs, gong racks, an oboe,
and a flute – all these tuned to the scale (whatever it may be) and
treated as melody instruments. In addition there are rhythm instruments, mostly various kinds of drums, but also cymbals, bamboo
clappers and bell-like instruments. Singing is nasal and strident. For
private and more intimate occasions, for chamber music, there are
the harp, the xylophone, chamber equivalents of some of the drums,
and the human voice, less strident but still nasal. The general effect
to most Western ears is harsh, tinkly, repetitive, and somewhat
approximate. But there are those who have penetrated to a more
sympathetic understanding.

Literature, before the influence of the West made itself felt, mostly
took the form of verse, but there were religious works, royal bio-
graphies, and historical or quasi-historical chronicles in prose form.
There was a deep cleavage between the literary and the colloquial
languages, the former long-winded, extravagant, and involved,
seeking to pay tribute by its pomposity to the glory of the court, the

latter short, slangy, and deftly apt. By the middle of the eighteenth
century, under Siamese influence, plays began to be written. This
literary form was easily grafted on to the strong indigenous dramatic
traditions of the *pwè*. Printing was introduced to Burma in the
early nineteenth century, but it was not until 1870 that printing
presses became common. In 1886 the monarchy was abolished by
the British and with it went the patronage of the court. From this
time on the appeal of literature could be, and had to be, to ordinary
people, not to a comparatively sophisticated court. In view of the
vitality of the *pwè* form, it is not surprising that for some twenty
years writing took the form of drama. In 1904, however, under
Western influence, novels began to oust plays. After the First World
War there was further diversification, largely as the result of
advances in education and increasing exploration of the field of
English literature. Novels, novelettes, short stories, political writings
appeared. The cinema began to exert its meretricious influence.
There were translations of English works. Most important, however, was the emergence of the so-called *Khit-san* or, in somewhat
loose translation, New Age group of writers. These stood for the
development of a terser, more vigorous, style approximating to the
lively colloquial, rather than to the stilted, traditional, literary,
language. Since the Second World War and the achievement of
independence there has been a revival of interest and pride in
Burmese which has been reinstated as the official language. There
has been translation of both literary and technical works, and novels
and short stories have been written. Despite nationalist and utilitarian pressures that have sought to harness literature to politics,
and in so doing have discouraged spontaneity and originality, the
Khit-san movement has continued and there seems to be a real if
slow advance towards the emergence of a natural, vigorous, incisive,
and genuinely indigenous style.

Burma is, or was, a country of many crafts. There is weaving of
silk, of cotton, and now of artificial materials. There is weaving
also of mats of rush, or of split bamboo. There is pottery. Wood is
worked for many purposes, for buildings, for boats, and for carts.
The carving of wood was at one time a considerable art but is now
rare. There is metalwork and the making of jewellery, including
the casting of bells of incomparable tone (and sometimes of great
size) and the tempering of steel to make *dahs* – a word which in
various combinations includes the whole family of swords, daggers,
and knives of all kinds from diminutive penknives to great heavy
knives used as hatchets or axes. There are lacquer work, the carving
of ivory, and gaudy glass mosaics. And this does not exhaust the
list. Of these crafts it is probably weaving and woodwork that dis-

play the greatest technical skill and artistic excellence – but this is a subjective assessment by the author and others may well be found to contest it. Handwoven silks are of fine finish and show a great flair for the blending of colours. Some wood carving is of fine quality and there is beauty in every line of the country boats which the Burmese both build and handle with such artistry. Other crafts are interesting, and often not unattractive, but lack the finish and the artistic taste of Chinese and Indian work, from which nevertheless they have borrowed a great deal. All these crafts are being ousted, and there is an eroding of inherited natural taste, as a result of cheap imports and the introduction of machine techniques and mass production in Burma. As elsewhere, technical mastery outruns artistic understanding of new materials and techniques. And in Burma the technical mastery itself is often unimpressive.

To summarize, before the annexation of Burma by the British, the arts (as opposed to the crafts, upon which in fact much artistry was lavished, particularly in the making and decorating of articles of domestic use) were a response either to court patronage or to religion. If court patronage evinced a degenerate taste, as the young administrator quoted some pages earlier thought, and if the religious impulse was sometimes overlaid by the desire for self-glorification, nevertheless these two stimuli resulted in the creation of works of art that were indigenous, honest, and, if they did not display the sophistication and delicacy of the products of India and China, nevertheless attained considerable artistic excellence. Annexation by the British destroyed the monarchy and the court and their patronage. It destroyed also the sense of identity and pride of race, fertile soil for the arts, which do not often flourish in a subject people – at least, not until they are in revolt against their rulers. Religion remained, but the compulsion of this stimulus dwindled too. There had been interplay of Church and state, and perhaps the people were affected by the loss of their symbolic and ceremonial representative in dealings with the monastic order. And, although religion was in some ways a stimulus, it is quite possible that, taken all in all, its effect was to inhibit the development of the arts. For art works largely through material things; not all the arts carry a spiritual message; not all dedicated Buddhists recognize it when they do, and the quintessence of Buddhism is the rejection of material things in order to concentrate on the spiritual. Then, with the arrival of the British, began the disastrous influence of the West on both the arts and crafts of the Burmese. For included amongst their imports were new materials, new techniques, all the glossy, repetitive, ingenious miracles of mass machine production. Worst of all, perhaps, corrugated iron sheeting arrived, with all its convenience and tinny ugliness. It is possible to make the best of a disaster – the first description of Mandalay Palace quoted above reads that 'Corrugated iron has been turned to ornamental use ... The fluting of the corrugated iron harmonizes very successfully with the bold and aspiring lines of the structure.' But a disaster it remained, in texture and colour, and in the shoddiness it conveys, as was recognized in the second description quoted.

When the British left Burma, independence returned to the Burmese. But there was no revival of the monarchy or the court. Instead there was established a government on the lines of Western parliamentary democracy, with a President and a cabinet, headed by a Prime Minister. These men had attained their position because they had agitated and fought in the jungle, first against the British, then against the Japanese, and then again against the British. This was their background, and for some of them their education. U Nu was an author, but for most of them there had been no opportunity and no urge to develop any appreciation of the arts or any desire for their products. And if there had been, it would have made little difference for, as we have seen, the government was plunged immediately into a civil war in which the bare struggle to survive demanded all their thoughts, energies, and resources. And yet the stimulus of religion did revive. There was a great outpouring of effort to gild and whitewash pagodas, even to restore them. Perhaps it was just a symptom of regained independence and self-respect. Perhaps it was a search for escape from the dangers and chaos of the times. Perhaps it was the example and regained leadership of that devout Buddhist, U Nu, who politically cannot have been unaware of the advantages of identifying himself with the strong religious urge of the Burmese. It was largely through the initiative of U Nu that the World Peace Pagoda and the Great Cave (for use as an assembly hall) were built for the Sixth Buddhist Council. These buildings, inspiring as the fruits of piety, devotion, and combined religious effort, have, however, sadly little to recommend them architecturally.

In the early days of the revolutionary government its members came from much the same background as their predecessors. The victory of the extremists within the government in February 1963 led to changes that moved further out of sympathy with the arts. The present rulers of Burma are interested in them only as a medium for propaganda, for the inculcation of the principles of *The Burmese Way to Socialism*.

But, of course, it is not only Burma that is faced with the problem of coming to terms with new materials and new techniques, and with the facile transplantation of modern styles resulting from the vast improvement in transport and communications. The restraints formerly imposed by custom, tradition, and the limitations of the materials used, and by the lack of easy communication with the rest of the world, meant that taste and art were local, with roots in the past of the locality, and were a part of the culture of the people of the area. Now, with these restraints removed, the arts have been deprived of their local and racial idiosyncrasy and have tended to acquire instead an impersonal, metropolitan, uniformity and mediocrity. One can only hope that Burma's resolute isolationism, if it can be maintained, will one day lead to the revival of an art that does not merely absorb undigested the less attractive qualities of the Occident, but is genuine because it is Burmese.

Chapter 14

Burma and the Outside World

THERE ARE, NATURALLY, VARIATIONS in the attitudes of Burma to particular countries. But there is one ingredient that is common to her relations with all countries at the present time, and that is that she would much rather not have any such relations at all. This extreme isolationism has developed only since the military takeover in 1962, but even before that the government's policy of neutralism was tending that way. It is difficult to find any parallel in the present day to this extreme, almost fanatical, self-imprisonment. But it is exactly the attitude of Burma to the outer world before the British annexation. And this, clearly, is what she would like to hark back to. It is not easy, however, in the present shrinking world.

Fundamentally this is a matter of national temperament. It has been said earlier that the Burmese have a 'strong national and personal pride that can easily turn to conceit'. They do not always do so. Burma has her full share of finer spirits, sensitive, perceptive, balanced, humble. Many others, however, enjoy a brisk confidence that they have nothing to learn from other peoples – except, perhaps, technological know-how – an attitude that is not endearing and does not, in fact, facilitate the acquisition of knowledge. The Burmese word for man, *lu*, is normally applied only to the Burmese, possibly to other indigenous races of Burma. The Chinese are *tayok*, not *lu*. The rest of the world's peoples, or at least those originating west of Burma, are lumped together as *kala*, 'foreigners', perhaps even 'barbarians', for the word carries a slight connotation of inferiority. And this justly reflects the attitude of many Burmese. They are convinced of their own superiority and of that of their own way of life, and do not welcome foreigners who may criticize or seek to alter it. To the West, in the days of its confidence, this attitude was totally incomprehensible. Now that the old certitude has gone, that it is no longer self-evident to the West that its contributions are all blessings, it is probably less so.

If conceit is one reason for Burmese isolationism, fear is another. It is their experience that all foreigners who have come into their country, whether missionaries, traders, soldiers, or administrators,

have without exception established a hold on some sector of Burmese life, religious, economic, or political, and that this hold has
been exercised, not as the Burmese would have wished, but as
seemed proper to the foreigners, or as would suit them best. All
foreigners, in their opinion, have in some degree 'exploited' Burma.
They are resolved that this shall not happen again if they can help
it. They fear also that foreigners will criticize the régime, even that
they may seduce some Burmans from their allegiance to it. There is
a particular fear of China.[1]

Many Burmese realize now, if they did not when they first gained
their independence, that it is the foreigners who discovered and
made fruitful the wealth of the country, and that by excluding them
and their capital, and expertise, they will inevitably force down the
standards of living of their own country. But apart from the
westernized intelligentsia, and some of the city-dwellers, who have
grown to look upon the consumer goods imported from abroad as
necessaries of life, it is doubtful whether this prospect is particularly
distasteful. A British employee of an oil company, which had
operated in Burma in the British period, revisited the country after
independence. When he re-embarked to depart homewards he gazed
around at the deserted, lifeless port of Rangoon, and, thinking of the
bustle and activity of other days, said to the Burman who was seeing
him off, how sad and depressing he found this sight. 'But we like it
that way', replied his companion. This is probably true of many
Burmese – they would prefer it that way if by so doing they can
avoid being at the beck and call of the foreigner. And, indeed, who
would exchange life in the more agreeable Burmese villages for life
in an industrial location?

There is probably also a streak of puritanism in the Burmese
attitude to foreigners. Until the mid-1960s it was government
policy, and genuine if somewhat unsuccessful attempts were made,
to encourage a foreign tourist traffic. But the government's attitude
was always ambivalent – tourists were said to be wanted, but entry
was not made easy for them, and little was done to facilitate their
movement about the country. The attitude under the present
régime then hardened to a point at which it was against allowing
tourists to enter at all. At the time of writing there are suggestions
of a more relaxed policy, but it is not yet clear what this will amount
to. The Burmese look at neighbouring Thailand where the gates
have been thrown open to foreigners and foreign capital. There the
economy has boomed. But at the same time Bangkok has become a
garish city with night clubs and brothels, in its efforts to cater for
foreign visitors, particularly American servicemen. The Burmese,

[1] See below, pp. 233–6.

perhaps only subconsciously, have set their faces against any comparable debauchery of the life of their capital. It is a puritanism that often goes with the idealism of Marxists, and something that one can but respect.

These various factors have coloured the whole field of Burma's relations with the outer world and have led her to try to put the clock back to the isolationist days before the British annexation. Virtually all foreigners have been expelled from the country, or conditions have been made so unappetizing that they have preferred to go. Foreign correspondents are not ordinarily allowed to enter, though a slightly more liberal attitude seems to have developed in 1969. News into and out of Burma is channelled exclusively through the News Agency Burma, a tightly controlled government organization, so that nothing is allowed in or out unless it suits the Revolutionary Council. Government publications are unconcealed propaganda and it is a matter of great difficulty to obtain any factual information regarding the country. It is virtually impossible for foreigners to obtain visas for entry to Burma, unless their services are specifically needed, or they have influence with General Ne Win. It is quite as difficult for Burmese nationals to obtain permission to travel out of the country, unless they are sent by their government. If so sent, husband and wife are not allowed out together, one being kept in Burma as a hostage for the return of the other. Government employees are forbidden to correspond with foreigners.

Against this background of what can only be described as xenophobia, we can now turn to consider Burma's relations with particular countries. And here we have the choice of starting with China, because Burma fears her most, or with the United Kingdom because, despite all the hard words that have been spoken and all that has happened, Burma clearly still feels closer to the British than to any other people. Perhaps the realities of the situation will be best served by taking first the case of China.

However neutral and unaligned Burma may be formally, it is China that looms greatest in her calculations. China is the largest, the most powerful, and for practical purposes the nearest, of Burma's neighbours. She has, as we have seen earlier, traditional claims upon Burmese territory. The two countries have a 1,200-mile long common frontier. This frontier is totally indefensible by the Burmese with the resources they could deploy. Burma is obviously in no position to take any stand against China. On the other hand, as we have also seen earlier, throughout the time of the U Nu governments China was neighbourly and was cultivating the friendship of Burma. There was the 'friendship and non-aggression pact'

concluded between the two countries on the first occasion when
General Ne Win took over the government. There was the border
agreement signed soon after by the reinstated government of U Nu.
There was the grant by China to Burma of a £30 million interest-
free loan. There have been many cultural and other missions from
China seeking to woo the Burmese. China was Burma's biggest
customer for rice. In particular, the Chinese were extremely for-
bearing over the Kuomintang troubles in Kengtung when it would
have been easy to pick a quarrel, or for a quarrel to develop
without any picking. But China is ruthless, and the Burmese cannot
but be conscious that their independent existence continues on
sufferance.

For a time it appeared that the military *coup* must have moved
Burma closer to China. The Revolutionary Council, although it has
never discarded the conception of democratic socialism, has clearly
modified its ideology into something much nearer to doctrinaire
communism. The resultant ideological link brought about a much
closer alignment between the two countries. General Ne Win is
Sino-Burmese, as was Brigadier Aung Gyi. And when the latter
was ousted from power it was by the more extreme communist
elements in the Revolutionary Council, elements that were the
most favourably inclined towards the Chinese. It is also quite
possible that the final settlement of the Kuomintang difficulties in
Kengtung was procured at the cost of an infiltration of Chinese
communist troops. It appears that military aid from China may
have been accepted by Burma early in 1961 in order to eliminate
the Kuomintang forces left behind in Kengtung. It has been
reported that later in the same year, after the completion of this
task, groups of Chinese communist forces remained in Kengtung,
wearing Burmese army uniforms and working within the Burmese
army.[1] Until the end of 1965 it certainly looked as if the régime
must inevitably be drawing closer to China. But in 1966 there was
considerable exchange of missions between the two countries, and
this probably represented not an improvement in relations but
rather a certain anxiety on the part of the Chinese, caused perhaps
by the visit of General Ne Win to the U.S.A. As late as April 1967
the Burmese government went out of its way to placate the Chinese
by repatriating some 500 refugees who had fled to Burma to escape
the cultural revolution.

On the other hand there has for the best part of twenty years
been the irritant of the support given by the Chinese to Than Tun,
the leader of the White Flag communists, and the supply of arms
from China to this party. For twenty years Than Tun waged war

[1] Robin Saunders, *Observer*, 15 July 1962.

against the Burmese government, whether this was civil or military, and if he could not defeat the government, neither could it defeat him. More recently there has been the movement of arms and trained guerrillas from China to the Naga Hills. This support of the Nagas was directed not against the Burmese government but against the government of India. Nevertheless, the movement took place across Burmese territory and involved a total disregard of Burmese sovereignty, all the more threatening because it was through parts of the country to which the Chinese have long laid claim.

Then suddenly, in June 1967, as in other countries at about the same time, trouble flared up with the Chinese. Chinese students attending schools in Burma began displaying Maoist badges. When required by the school authorities to desist they refused. There can be little doubt that they were acting under instructions but with what object is not clear, though it was a part of the general Maoist attitude of the period. Tension developed and four days later anti-Chinese riots broke out in Rangoon. It has been suggested that these also were officially inspired, because it suited the Burmese government to distract attention from the economic situation. A member of the Chinese embassy staff was stabbed to death by two Burmese. Many other Chinese were attacked. It is said that some fifty lost their lives. There was much damage to houses, shops, and motor-cars owned by Chinese. Martial law was proclaimed and troops were brought in to restore order. This incident has completely antagonized the Burmese. Any *rapprochement* that took place in the early years of the régime has been nullified and relations between the two countries have deteriorated sharply. It is probable that Chinese aid to rebels in Burma has been stepped up, though it may be that this is now going not so much to the White Flag communists, split by internal dissensions and deprived of the leadership of Than Tun, who was killed by one of his own guerrillas in September 1968, as to the Kachins, Shans, and other hill peoples in the north-east of Burma, near the Chinese border. Whether there has been any compensating improvement in relations with other countries, specifically the United Kingdom, has not yet become clear, but there are slight indications that Burma is looking more towards the West.

But the ever-present, overriding fear in connection with China arises from the existence of the White Flag communists. They are a strong underground opposition to the Revolutionary Council and, apart from the racial minorities in revolt, are responsible for most of the armed insurgency in Burma. This opposition professes a communist ideology, of the Chinese, not the Russian, pattern. There are strong links between China and the White Flag communists. Than Tun spent much time in China, and there has been support and a flow of supplies from China for the Burmese communists. There is here ready to China's hand a pretext for intervention at any time. She has not made use of it yet. But it seems almost inevitable that at some time she should. And if she did, she could count on the support of this opposition. It is this danger above all others that the Burmese must keep in mind, both externally in their relations with China, and internally in their relations with the White Flag communists.

Much has been said earlier in this book about the relations between Britain and Burma in the past. Writing in 1956 Dr Tinker said: '... in Burma perhaps more than in most countries it is accepted that Britain's days as a world leader are over.'[1] Since then Burmese realism has been vindicated by events and by Britain's decision to withdraw a military presence from east of Suez. In terms of power and politics, Britain counts for little in Burma. Economic links have been almost entirely severed. Very shortly after seizing power the Revolutionary Council suspended acceptance by Burmese nationals of scholarships offered by the British Council. This was followed in due course by the withdrawal of permission for any British Council activities in Burma and the demand that its representatives be withdrawn. The refusal to grant visas for entry into Burma and the exclusion of newspaper correspondents are part of a more general hostility to foreigners, but have probably hit the United Kingdom hardest because she had more contacts before. Then in October 1966, when the pound showed signs of collapsing, Burma left the sterling area. The reasons given were 'to secure freedom of action to take necessary protective measures such as purchase of gold and investment in hard currencies, in the public interest, for the conservation of the country's exchange reserves obtained from export of goods and services ...'. There is no reason to doubt these, but it also seems that relations with the members of the sterling group had deteriorated and that the latter were not sorry to see Burma go. So long as there was a *rapprochement* with China, particularly on ideological grounds, it was inevitable that Burma should move away from Britain and from the ideal of her parliamentary democratic institutions. Running through all these events is an underlying suspicion of British intentions – though perhaps no longer of any plot to raise the minorities against the Burmese. This suspicion is largely a legacy of the economic hold once exercised by the big British firms. Of these it is reported that 'Nationalized British firms in Burma were still scheduled to receive

[1] op. cit., p. 352.

compensation' – a delicate way of recording the facts.[1] All this must
be held to amount to a deterioration in relations or certainly to an
absence of improvement in relations with Britain as compared with
those in the time of the U Nu régime.

On the other hand, Britons and Burmans have, in English, a
common language. It is therefore easier to do business of all kinds
with the United Kingdom and the United States than with other
countries. It is easier to establish real personal contact. And there
are cases, not many, perhaps, but some, in which a bond is created
by the ability to share the cultural heritage of the English language.
How long this will continue to be so is more doubtful since
although, as we have seen, English is more widely taught now than
ever before, it is probably at no point taught with sufficient fullness
and understanding to convey much feeling for its finer points.
There is also shared experience of the past, which despite the tensions, temporary one may hope, of emergent nationalism, serves to
draw Britain and Burma closer together – though here again, the
respect felt for British parliamentary institutions, which was once a
strong bond between the two countries, has become less as Burma
has moved towards totalitarianism. There is even a shared enthusiasm for football and golf. Technical co-operation continues, especially in the medical field. Finally, there are still warm friendships
between Britons and Burmans – though these must now with the
passage of time grow fewer. And in any case these tend to be not
with the present ruling class, but rather with the more widely
educated and experienced members of society, many of whom
suffered imprisonment at the hands of the present régime. For many
Britons who are true friends of the Burmese the incarceration of
these persons, many of them the best of Burma's sons, has made
the continuance of friendship between Britain and Burma difficult.
The release of all political detainees in February 1968 has done
much to improve relations.

But all in all, the Burmese probably feel closer and more at ease
with the British than with any other people, a friendship that is all
the firmer and more genuine for the fact that Britain is no longer
influential as a world power. In their heart of hearts the Burmese
know, despite the continuing propaganda about 'imperialists',
'colonialists', and 'expansionists', that Britain treated Burma not
ungenerously. In *Burma's Fight for Freedom*, a commemorative
record issued by the new government at the time of independence,
it is said that:

'The title of this publication "Burma's Fight for Freedom" is
perhaps a little misleading. Freedom has been won without a

[1] *Far Eastern Economic Review*, 1967.

fight, a fact which testifies to Britain's wisdom and Burma's
unity.'

Relations with the government of the U.S.A. have existed only
since the Second World War. But contacts with the American
people reach much further back. It is not true that Americans
reached Burma before the British, but it is true that the American
Baptist Mission operated in the country before the British government did, from 1813 in fact, when Judson, the founder of the
mission, landed in Rangoon. The mission gave Burma schools,
hospitals, and later a college and a printing press, all of which
brought much benefit to the country. It established a particularly
successful agricultural school in Pyinmana under the Reverend
B. C. Case. To some of the inhabitants of Burma it brought the
Baptist religion. Where this sought to supplant Buddhism it often
did more harm than good. Baptist Christianity tended to be narrow
and restrictive. But above all it created a community within the
community that was apt to consider itself specially chosen and
meriting special recognition. Where it brought religion to those who
worshipped spirits and regulated their lives by omens, it gave
strength and a new-found freedom from fear. The other, the highly
coloured, end of the American social spectrum was for many years
represented by a community of some 400 oil-well drillers working
for British companies on the oilfields.

With the spread of the Second World War to South-East Asia, a
more general American interest in Burma developed, and in due
course American staff officers, and even some American units, saw
the country themselves. Permeating all their thoughts about Burma
were dislike of colonialism, particularly British colonialism, and
sympathy for a country seeking to throw this off. There was great
goodwill towards Burma but often little understanding of the problems involved. Burma, on her side, admired the power, wealth, and
technical brilliance of America. She was flattered and encouraged
by the anti-colonialist sympathy extended to her and after independence it was natural for her to turn to the U.S.A. for aid and moral
support. It was not long, however, before a strong revulsion set
in. Economic aid was given to Burma but disenchantment soon
followed. It was a condition of the grant of aid that the United
States exercised far-reaching control over the purposes to which
aid was applied. Such control by the British would have been
considered an infringement of sovereignty and quite unacceptable;
exercised by the United States it was initially acceptable, but
only just. For its exercise, missions were sent to Burma which
by any standards, but particularly by Burmese standards, were
extravagantly manned, and which demanded conditions of living

normal to their members but grossly luxurious to the Burmese. And the cost of these missions was paid for out of aid funds – indeed, under 'counterpart fund' arrangements, the expenses of the missions in Burma were actually to be paid by the Burmese government. But what made the missions unpopular, even more perhaps than their financial extravagance, was that their standards of living set them apart and created a barrier between them and the Burmese. (It is a question whether any country as wealthy as the U.S.A. can hope to understand a people whose normal standards of living are so far removed from its own. It was difficult enough for the British, but for the Americans it is far harder.) Worst of all was the fact that the missions did not really deliver the goods. There were failings on the Burmese side, as we have seen in an earlier chapter,[1] but there were failings on the side of the missions too. In particular, they had no experience or knowledge in depth of either the country or its people. Then, just as confidence in the missions was waning, came the discovery in 1953 that the Americans were supporting the Kuomintang forces which the Burmese had been at such pains to try to eject from the Shan State. The attitude swung right round and Burma refused to receive any further aid from the United States.

The present régime has not been responsible for any marked change in policy towards the U.S.A. To the extent that it was initially somewhat more pro-Chinese it became more anti-American. But in 1966 General Ne Win visited the U.S.A. Since the breach with China in mid-1967 Burma has moved back nearer to the United States and towards the end of that year arms and ammunition were supplied by the Americans to assist the Ne Win government against its supposedly communist enemies. Most of these are probably receiving aid from China, but they are all far more nationalist than communist. The most important factor in relations with America is probably the war in Vietnam. A few Burmese may feel that the United States is fighting communism and in so doing is defending Burma against ultimate absorption into communist China. These will view with apprehension the prospect of the withdrawal of American forces. The reaction of the majority of Burmans is merely to resent the attempts of the U.S.A. to interfere with a South-East Asian people, and to fear greatly lest Burma should ever become an American theatre of war against China, another Vietnam.

India, like China, was a buyer of rice from Burma and, to the extent that there is any surplus available for export, she still is. The chief irritant to relations between the two countries has been the policy of nationalization pursued by the Revolutionary Council.

[1] See above, pp. 152–4.

An element in this, as already observed, has clearly been xenophobia. Of the formally constituted businesses that were nationalized, some 60 per cent were Indian. Their owners and employees (for these were mostly Indians) lost their means of livelihood and, since there was little or no prospect of employment in other spheres, many were compelled to leave Burma for India. More seriously, the nationalization of the internal wholesale and retail trade meant that all petty traders and their employees, of whom the great majority were Indians, were thrown out of business. No compensation was paid. And Indians leaving the country were allowed to take only K.75 for each adult, K.15 for each child, and K.250-worth of gold. Women were not permitted to take jewellery in excess of this total amount. This was harsh treatment, and inevitably there were many attempts to smuggle out gold in contravention of the rules. There is a story told of an attempt that was detected, an attempt to smuggle out gold in the body of a dead child, clasped to its mother's bosom.

The flow of Indians returning to India as a result of these policies began in 1964. Some 150,000 had probably gone by the end of 1968.[1] Some 200,000, accounting for most of the remaining Indian population in Burma, are reported to be hoping for ships to repatriate them in the future. At the end of 1965 Lal Bahadur Shastri, Prime Minister of India, visited Burma in connection with the treatment of these unfortunates. The negotiations appear to have done something to improve relations between the two countries. But the Revolutionary Council has in fact done little to improve the lot of these people. In the last resort there is little that India can do to bring pressure to bear on Burma. She is too hungry to afford to boycott such rice supplies as Burma can spare her. Any attempts at more forcible retaliation would create the danger that China might be provoked into interference. And China has amply demonstrated how much more powerful she is than India. It is probably true that relations with India have deteriorated since the *coup*.

Russia, although physically much nearer to Burma than Britain or the United States, somehow feels far more remote. A part of the reason for this is presumably that she has had no communication in the past. On the other hand, the military and the political leaders of Burma since independence, both alike nurtured in the A.F.P.F.L., all turned originally to Russia as the shrine of their political thinking. Closer contacts, however, have brought a certain disillusionment. Russia has been concerned in a number of so-called gift-schemes, including that for a hospital in Taunggyi in the Shan

[1] *Daily Telegraph*, 8 November 1968, Harold Sieve, 'Burma's Nationalized Nightmare'.

State. But the scheme was that the 'gift' of the hospital by Russia would be balanced by a 'gift' of rice by Burma. And some of the schemes have proved less than satisfactory. At no time has there been any improvement in relations. Yet in 1966, of the students sent abroad on state or other scholarships, the great majority went to the U.S.S.R., forty-five as against thirty-two to all Colombo Plan countries, thirteen to Britain, thirteen to East Germany, eleven to Australia,[1] and about fifty more distributed to various countries in much smaller numbers. And towards the end of 1967, as a part of her reaction to the Chinese troubles in the middle of the year, Burma accepted aid from Russia in the form of arms. Burma's relations with Russia are probably fairly typical of her desire to steer an unaligned, uncommitted, middle course in her relations with the outer world.

Contact with Japan arises mainly out of reparations. Just before being ousted from the Revolutionary Council, Brigadier Aung Gyi negotiated a reparations settlement under which Japan agreed to pay an additional £50 million in goods and services and to grant Burma a loan of over £10 million in return for the prospect of technical assistance contracts and possibly of participation in joint ventures. This settlement was not popular with the doctrinaire Marxists in the Revolutionary Council who opposed all foreign investment in Burma, particularly by private enterprise, and probably contributed to his downfall.

Of other countries, Indonesia is, with China, the largest buyer of Burmese rice. Friendly relations subsist with Thailand, though a source of minor irritation must be the presence on Thai soil of Shan rebels and conspirators in contact with the underground Shan rebel organization in the Shan State of Burma. There is little contact with Malaysia and Singapore, which until recently were felt to be somewhat artificial creations of the British for their own ends. Burma's relations with Israel and Yugoslavia are cordial. West Germany has offered Burma a loan and guarantees of private credit in Germany, and trade between the two countries has developed to a level at which it is greater than that with any other European country.

Much of Burma's contact with the outer world is made in the context of the Colombo Plan for Co-operative Economic Development in South and South-East Asia, generally more briefly known as the Colombo Plan. This was drawn up in 1950 by the Commonwealth Consultative Committee on South and South-East Asia and was primarily designed by and for Commonwealth countries, though it was hoped that other countries would also participate,

1 In addition to Colombo Plan scholarships.

both as recipients and as donors of aid. The U.S.A. associated herself with the plan as a donor from the beginning. Burma and most countries of the region joined. Japan became a full member in 1954. The plan established an organization to co-ordinate and channel grants, loans, and technical assistance to, and within, South and South-East Asia. Technical assistance includes the training of persons from and in the region, the sending of experts, and the provision of equipment, especially for research. Arrangements are made for liaison with the appropriate United Nations agencies. There are few countries in South and South-East Asia that have not received aid of one kind or another through the plan. Predominantly recipient countries make such contribution as they can by offering training facilities. Of the donor countries the U.S.A. is by far the most important, contributing 80 per cent or more of aid distributed under the plan.

Since complete isolation is not in fact possible, Burma from the time of independence has sought to follow a policy of neutralism that demands circumspection and impartiality in the making of friends. In 1949 U Nu said:

'Our circumstances demand that we follow an independent course and not ally ourselves with any power bloc . . . Be friendly with all foreign countries. Our tiny nation cannot have the effrontery to quarrel with any power.'[1]

For U Nu this policy was almost a matter of religious conviction, of gaining, as it were, international merit by leading a good life. The military régime adopted and followed this policy with even greater dedication, seeking always to keep a balance in the matter of contacts and the acceptance of aid as between countries, but particularly as between the three main power blocs, of China, of Russia, and of the West (in which, of course, the U.S.A. is included).

Through all this period, however, Burma has been most in fear of China. For the first few years of independence she may have thought, out of force of habit, that it was European influence that she must guard against at all costs. But she has now grown out of this and China has clearly emerged as the greatest menace. In the light of this, there is probably some truth in the contention so often put forward by the Burmese that many of the restrictions they impose on foreigners are primarily intended against the Chinese only, but that they cannot, without giving offence to China, impose them except as part of a policy of restriction or prohibition, applicable, not exclusively to the Chinese, but to all aliens. This is just one aspect of the policy of neutralism.

---

[1] Quoted Tinker, op. cit., p. 343, out of U Nu, *From Peace to Stability*, pp. 51–2.

Chapter 15

Conclusion

BEFORE ATTEMPTING ANY SUMMARY of present conditions it is perhaps of interest to ask what, if anything, survives from the British period in Burma.

From 1917 onwards, until their departure from Burma in 1948, the British were committed to a policy of '... the gradual development of self-governing institutions, with a view to the progressive realization of responsible government ... as an integral part of the British Empire'.[1] To Britons this could mean but one thing, the gradual introduction of parliamentary democracy as practised at Westminster. This was a process that had gone a long way by 1941 when the Japanese invaded Burma and then drove the British out in 1942. When the Japanese in their turn were expelled, and independence came to Burma in 1948, the constitution which the constituent assembly for the Union of Burma drew up incorporated elements drawn from many countries. But basically it was a parliamentary democracy of the Western form, as practised at Westminster. This constitution lasted just over ten years until the military *coup* of 1962. The present régime never formally abrogated the constitution. It happened that at the time of the *coup* parliament was in recess. It has never been reassembled. There have been no elections. The army at the time probably saw itself as taking emergency action in order to safeguard, not indeed the constitution itself, but the essential principles and policies which it believed to have been enshrined in the constitution. It acted in order to keep in being the state which the constitution had brought to birth. But the constitution itself was totally ignored and parliamentary democracy was quietly discarded. These contributions of the British to the form of government in Burma have completely disappeared. They need not be overmuch lamented for they did not thrive in Burmese soil. And it is probably better that the Burmese should create and develop something of their own.

As to the administrative machine which the British built up, this was the most competent and effective that Burma has yet known and was able to confer an unprecedented degree of protection to

[1] See above, p. 105.

persons and property. All this has been lost. But again this is a loss that need not be too much lamented. It would be a far greater hardship to Britons than to Burmans, whose way of life is less organized and regular, and whose background is less settled. And there is the consolation that if the present government could exercise its power more effectively, it would probably do so to interfere more drastically with the liberty of individuals. The hard fact remains, however, that life and property are extremely insecure. One of Burma's most devoted friends has described life in the villages as 'murderous'.

The British sought to establish in Burma the fact and the concept of the rule of law. The difficulties they encountered have been described earlier.[1] If the idea of the rule of law ever took root in Burma at all it was but a tender plant and has now totally died out, except perhaps in the inner recesses of the minds of a few of Burma's distinguished lawyers trained in the West.

It is fashionable for the Burmese now to make the accusation that the educational system established by the British was designed only to produce clerks for government and the European firms. There may have been truth in such a criticism about the period before the First World War. But experienced and educated clerks were indispensable members of the administration: there were opportunities for promotion; and if the government wanted good clerks it was equally true that it was government service that most literate Burmans aspired to, at their respective levels. But whatever may have been the case earlier, from 1920 onwards, when the University of Rangoon was established, the British made a genuine and sustained attempt to raise academic standards and to create a university in the image of the best as this was understood in Britain at that time. It was the politically conscious Burmese who rejected this and fought to lower standards, and in great measure succeeded in doing so, on the grounds that Burma needed more, not fewer, graduates. They would not, or could not, realize that no number of graduates would be worth anything if the degrees they had gained were worthless. At bottom, however, it was not education they were concerned with, but the winning of political support and power. Since independence the process of devaluation for political ends has continued. Little now survives from the British period except the introduction of the English language, and the imperfectly digested concepts of Western political thought and theory: and although these may still survive, any distinctively British contribution to them has largely disappeared. The devaluation of standards originally undertaken for political reasons has been worsened by the

[1] See above, pp. 83–5.

attempt to spread education too widely without sufficient teachers.

But the greatest change brought about by the British, for better or worse, was in the economy. What had been a static, quasi-feudal, subsistence economy was transformed by the operation of *laissez-faire* principles, and by capitalist enterprise, into an expanding, booming, 'colonial' economy, dependent upon exports of a single crop. This brought much prosperity, though too little of it reached the Burmese. *Laissez-faire* is now universally out of fashion; in Burma, capitalism has been swept away. The foreign firms, who were the capitalists, have been expropriated. In their place have come state ownership, state direction, and a closely controlled economy. Profits are no longer sucked out of the country. The only trouble is that the profits have shrunk almost to vanishing point. There is no longer any boom. The standard of living of the people has fallen. And the economy of Burma is still dependent on a single crop. There must be many people in Burma who are beginning to wonder whether the complete expulsion of the foreigners was worth the cost.

Of the British contributions, it is probable that the only one that survives in vigour and is of unmixed benefit to the people of Burma is the introduction of Western medicine and the creation of the medical services. Indeed the present régime has in many respects improved upon the services provided by the British. Partly this is due to the general advances in medical knowledge. Partly it is the result of the interplay, on the one hand, of the present government's determination to spread medical benefits more widely at all costs, at the cost even of maintaining standards, and on the other hand of the medical profession's equal determination to maintain standards, if not for all, at least for an élite of those displaying potential ability.

It is difficult to see that much else survives from the contact with the British between 1826 and 1948 – except, of course, the Marxist socialism that found its way in with the entry of English books and now has taken such a hold on Burmese thinking.

The present régime is a military dictatorship. Real power is very largely centralized in the Chairman of the Revolutionary Council, General Ne Win himself. He enjoys a good reputation for honesty. Indeed, there was much idealism in the initial seizure of power by the soldiers. There was impatience with the politicians who were venal and infirm of purpose. There was fear that they would allow the disintegration of the Union of Burma. There was distrust of civil servants who were often obstructive and corrupt. When the soldiers first seized power a clean, clear wind blew through the stuffy corridors of the administration. Over the years, however, this has died down, and the present régime is probably no better ventilated than its predecessor. Indeed, it is probably even more corruptible, if only because the growth of nationalization and the increasing interference in the daily lives of the people have so greatly extended the opportunities for bribery. But if the General is a man of integrity, the advisers who surround him, and upon whom he must inevitably lean, do not enjoy the same reputation. Few of them have been trained to their responsibilities or have any particular knowledge of the matters concerning which they advise. The advice they give is naturally not always good or consistent. It is probably often what they think their master wants to hear rather than what he ought to know. The General's decisions are accordingly liable to be arbitrary and unpredictable. He is an oriental potentate surrounded by his court. If the spying and tale-bearing, the pettifogging control, the interference in the affairs of the ordinary citizen were more efficient, their existence might suggest that Burma had become a police state, and in some ways she has. But a much closer parallel to the present absolutism is the Burma of the Burmese kings, before the annexation by the British. Burma is now back to government by the personal whim of a monarch. In the official commemoration of independence issued by the Burmese government it is said that 'The history of nations is always a history of the popular will struggling to assert itself and the few in power trying to keep the will down.'[1] Although aimed at the colonialists, this seems as true now as it ever was.

There are other respects in which the present régime recalls pre-annexation Burma. There is the insecurity to life and property. There is the isolationism, the desire to withdraw behind its frontiers, to exclude foreigners. Partly this is the result of a sensible policy of neutralism, of non-alignment, and a desire not to estrange the major power blocs, or to give to any of them a pretext for demanding admission. Partly it is rooted in the Burmese character and past. Despite recent hints of a more liberal attitude, it is probably as difficult to get in or out of Burma now as it was before the annexation. There is the drift back to a subsistence economy and the resultant fall in standards of living. Even the present system of state monopolies is not without certain parallels in the past, when the right to trade in teak, oil, and precious stones of all kinds was restricted to the king. But this parallel must not be pressed too far. The monopolies of the present day are imposed in keeping with Marxist ideology and in part at least for the benefit of the people. There is no parallel in the past to the allocation of one-quarter of the government's spending to education and public health.

When the army seized power in 1962 it was with the avowed

[1] *Burma's Fight for Freedom*, p. 42.

object of preventing the disintegration of the Union of Burma. It seems fair to ask how far they have succeeded. At the time of the *coup* it was believed that U Nu, the Prime Minister, was preparing to allow the Shans to secede from the Union, as, subject to certain requirements of the constitution, they had a right to do. The other minorities were not far behind in pressing for a measure of independence. Formally the soldiers succeeded in preserving the Union. By tough measures, by imprisoning many of the leaders of opposition, they have ensured that the Union of Burma still exists in name. Whether in fact unity is any more real than it would have been under the politicians, is not so clear. For despite efforts to win over the minorities, it is doubtful whether relations between them and the Burmese have significantly improved. And the measures taken to preserve the Union inevitably created and increased hostility. Insurgency continues both in the minority areas and in the Burmese homeland. Some 30 to 40 per cent of the country is admittedly not under the effective control of the government. One may wonder whether the government now exercises any wider territorial control than it would have done if the minorities had been allowed to go their own way and the army's efforts had been concentrated on putting down the communist revolt in Burma proper. In that case, however, it is necessary to reckon with the possibility that the minority areas would by now have been swallowed up into China's sphere of influence. If the soldiers have not preserved the real unity of Burma any better than their predecessors would have done, they may nevertheless have kept the effective Chinese border the other side of a no-man's land consisting of the hill areas inhabited by the minority races of Burma. Recent events, however, make even this seem doubtful.

It can be claimed for the government that it has so far managed to feed its people, and that this is more than some of its neighbours have been able to do. But in Burma, which at least until 1966–67 had a safe surplus of rice, this is no great achievement, or it has not been so far. In fact the Burmese people seem to have fed themselves notwithstanding the difficulties put in the way of production by the government's attempts to socialize agriculture. But there is nothing to show that the government have yet found any way to increase food production so as to keep pace with growth of population. The gradual overtaking of food supplies by population and the resultant fall in exports of rice have indeed brought about a fall in the standard of living. If this affects more the townsman, and the minority that has come to expect imports from the West (necessities to them now, luxuries in the view of the government), it has also made itself felt in the villages.

The one objective to which all parties in Burma subscribe is the complete elimination of foreign capital from the economy, and the retention within the country of the profits that used to be remitted abroad. The process was begun by the politicians but has been pushed by the army to virtual completion, with results that have been mentioned earlier. On purely economic balance the Burmese are clearly losers for their standard of living has fallen. Whether in the broader terms of human happiness they are also losers is another matter. But the present régime has clearly achieved its objective.

The government has so far kept out of serious trouble with its neighbours. This is probably the result of circumstances rather than of any positive action by the government. But the policy of neutrality, inherited from the civil government, and followed by the Revolutionary Council, has doubtless contributed. It is probable that the danger of invasion has grown, and will grow, less. China is the potential enemy. To the Chinese, the Burma surplus of rice must have been eminently covetable. But if, as seems probable, there is to be no surplus in future, Burma may well look a liability rather than an asset to China and be delivered from this danger. And in any case China has run into her own troubles.

It is one of the clear demerits of the present government that it has built up a régime of spying and fear which affects not only the people in general but the government's own employees. With the latter it is a major reason for the all-pervading unwillingness to make decisions or take responsibility.

In the policy declaration of the Revolutionary Council, *The Burmese Way to Socialism*, issued in April 1962, the Council stated that 'the vanguard and custodian of a socialist democratic state are primarily peasants and workers' and it is the improvement of the lot of these people that the government is professedly seeking. If they were achieving this, much could be forgiven them. For a while they did, while enthusiasm and integrity lasted, and while these attributes were by themselves sufficient to work an improvement in the state of the country. Administration was cleaned up, the process of expropriating and evicting the capitalist scapegoats was completed, the people of Burma regained their self-respect, the young were fired with enthusiasm and patriotism. But as the initial momentum was lost, corruption returned, and as qualities beyond mere enthusiasm and integrity began to be required, things no longer went so well. The standard of living fell, the security of property and person deteriorated, increasingly the government interfered with the liberty of the people. In 1966–67 there was scarcely enough rice to feed the country.

This indeed is the basic problem that Burma and her government have to face. It is a new problem because ever since the annexation of Lower Burma by the British there has until now been a surplus of rice available for export. And before the annexation a balance of food and population had been established within the framework of the subsistence economy. Now, the great increase in rice production over the last hundred years, the vast improvement in the effectiveness of medical and public health measures, and, at least until the last twenty or thirty years, the improvement in security, have allowed the population to increase from 4 million in 1824 to an estimated 25 million in 1966. Over most of this period the production of rice has increased and kept well ahead of the growth of population. But rice production no longer increases and population has just about overtaken food supplies.

There have been important events in the course of 1968 and 1969 the significance of which cannot yet be assessed, but which may hold promise of liberalization in the future. In the first place there was the release, in February 1968, of political prisoners. It is claimed, and there is no reason to doubt, that all persons detained without trial on political grounds were then set free. Most of these persons were originally imprisoned because they were leaders, or potential leaders, or perhaps merely potential centres, of opposition to the government. That they should have been released might suggest that the régime was feeling more safely established – it has always seemed that this would be a necessary prerequisite to any releases. But in fact there is little to indicate that the régime is any more secure now than it has ever been, and a good deal to suggest that the deteriorating economic situation has weakened its position. Perhaps, indeed, it is the economic deterioration that has made the government feel that the time has come to forget old enmities and make common cause for the good of the country. Perhaps alternatively or additionally the government judges that six years in prison is enough to destroy any man's will and ability to oppose. But it may be that the releases should be looked upon merely as a necessary preparation of the ground for the next important event.

This was the setting-up in December 1968 of the Internal Unity Advisory Body whose terms of reference were to advise the government on the best way to achieve national unity with a view to drafting a new constitution. More than thirty of the old political leaders were on the Body. Many of them and their followers had been imprisoned. It may be that the releases were necessary to enable them to serve, and to create an atmosphere in which they would be willing to do so. These leaders have not been permitted to reactivate their old parties and party organizations, though inevitably they must do some sounding among their old supporters in order to gauge and make some presentation of public opinion. They naturally contend that they would be of much more use if they were allowed to revive their party organizations. The chairman of the Body is Mahn Win Maung, a Karen. It is natural to hope that the setting-up of this board denotes some liberalization in the attitude of the government. Such a hope is supported by the facts that there has been some relaxation of the ban on foreign journalists, that it has been made easier for foreigners to enter Burma and for Burmans to come out of the country, and that a number of senior officials have been prepared to talk unexpectedly freely. On the other hand, while the Body was deliberating, the government issued orders nationalizing the cinema industry, which included over a hundred picture theatres and accessory businesses, and nationalized a further 168 miscellaneous concerns together with forty-nine saw-mills. These were very unpopular measures, and their adoption does not suggest any liberalization or any eclipse of the dogmatic Marxist left wing of the government.

It is possible that the economic deterioration forced the appointment of the Body. The collapse of exports has meant that the government can no longer acquire foreign exchange to pay for the arms it needs if it is to continue in existence. Burma needs aid from the countries of the West and it seems that aid may not be forthcoming unless the government affords evidence, or makes some gesture to show, that she is liberalizing her régime. Time alone will show whether any genuine liberalization is in the air. It is possible that General Ne Win hoped to associate the political leaders with his government, so that they should bear some responsibility and some of the unpopularity resulting from the failure of the General's policies. It is just possible that the General would like to escape from his difficulties and leave the political leaders to face the problems that are shortly going to beset Burma.

The Internal Unity Advisory Body completed its report at the end of May 1969 and, particularly, recommended a return to constitutional government. It suggested that the old constitution should be taken as a starting-point and should be modified as required. It also recommended that steps should be taken to improve relations with foreign countries, particularly China and Thailand. At an early stage of this Body's deliberations, ex-Prime Minister U Nu suggested a procedure for a return to constitutionalism. The main features of U Nu's proposals were that he should himself be reinstated as Prime Minister, with the task of forming an interim government, that parliament should be convened and invited to elect General Ne Win as President of the Union, that the interim government should then resign, and that an early general election should be held. Further steps back to normality should be governed by the provisions of the constitution. To consider and recommend what changes are required in this a National Convention should be set up. The report of the 'Thirty-three Wise Men' was published by the ·government (together with U Nu's proposals for a return to constitutionality). Some two months later the recommendations were rejected by General Ne Win.

It is difficult to understand this rejection, for it must have been foreseen that the recommendations of a body composed of political leaders would inevitably take some such shape. It is difficult to reconcile it with any of the possible reasons put forward earlier for the setting-up of the Internal Unity Advisory Body. It will not encourage foreign opinion to believe that any genuine liberalization of policies is intended. It will not draw in the politicians and make available their expertise or make them share responsibility and unpopularity. It will not enable General Ne Win to effect a graceful retirement from public life. There would seem to have been a change of policy. There may have been a shift of power within the government. It may be nothing more than another manifestation of the General's unpredictability.

The rejection may have polarized opposition within Burma to the present régime though it is impossible yet to make any assessment of the extent and strength of such opposition. U Nu was in India when the rejection became known. Early in August 1969 he went to Bangkok where many of the leading opponents of the present régime, both Burmans and members of the minority communities, had gathered. On 11 August U Nu publicly denounced the régime and then set out for the United Kingdom and the United States to arouse interest and mobilize international support for his cause. In London on 29 August he gave a press conference and repeated his denunciation. After reviewing the unsatisfactory conditions in Burma, political and economic, he called upon General Ne Win 'to relinquish the power which he has illegally usurped' so that democratic government might be re-established. He concluded with a pledge to the people of Burma that he would:

'... not rest until parliamentary democracy is restored to Burma and all the guarantees under the Declaration of Human Rights are honoured. Buddhism shall flourish, while every encouragement shall be given also for the practice and propagation of other faiths; the Burmese press shall again be free; the dignity of labour will be re-established; the plight of government employees will be improved immediately; the tragic brain-drain of its ablest sons and daughters will be ended; and opportunities will be afforded to farmers, workers, businessmen, artisans, in fact to all citizens to contribute – in a manner worthy of free people – towards the rapid re-building of Burma's shattered economy. Most important, he pledges that the people shall freely choose that system, and those leaders, under which they wish to be governed.'

It is impossible to say yet whether this constitutes a serious threat to the régime. Much has gone wrong in Burma and quite certainly there is extensive and serious discontent with the government and its performance. There is almost certainly strong public support for U Nu. But can U Nu mobilize this and make it effective? If General Ne Win decides to stay, and if he can count upon the support of the army it is difficult to see how a change of government can be brought about.

As to the army, it has never been a highly professional force. Its officer corps has not the flavour and tradition of a Sandhurst or West Point training. Its morale is reported to be low. It is probably far from apolitical. And yet it is difficult to conceive of it, or any portion of it, preferring to throw in its lot with the old political leaders.

As to General Ne Win himself, it is quite impossible to forecast what he will do. On the one hand he is certainly out of his depth and cannot fail to realize that his government is unpopular, and into what straits the economy is drifting. He is not a fit man. Beyond this rumour has it that an aircraft is permanently standing by to fly him to Switzerland where it is further rumoured that he has established bank balances. And, even if these rumours are totally unfounded, why has U Nu, with his long experience of Burmese politics, felt it worthwhile to make this challenge?

On the other hand, if General Ne Win is seeking an escape from his difficulties, why did he reject U Nu's offer?

And what does it mean that General Ne Win has given full publicity to the declaration of U Nu? Does he feel so sure of his position that he can afford to do this? Or is he seeking to build a bridge between himself and U Nu?

Time alone will tell – and may, of course, have told before these pages are in print.

Bibliography

A SELECT BIBLIOGRAPHY follows for the general reader. The student in search of full bibliographies is referred to J. F. Cady, *History of Modern Burma*, New York, 1958; D. G. E. Hall, *History of South-East Asia*, London, 1955; G. E. Harvey, *History of Burma*, London, 1925; Dorothy Woodman, *The Making of Burma*, London, 1962; and to the two bibliographies prepared by Frank N. Trager, *Burma Bibliography* (Human Relations Area Files), and *Japanese and Chinese language sources on Burma. An annotated Bibliography* (Japanese sources, Hyman Kublin; Chinese sources, Lu-Yu Kiang; Human Relations Area Files, New Haven, 1956–57).

Andrus, J. R., *Burmese Economic Life*, Stanford, Calif., 1947.

Ba Maw, Dr, *Breakthrough in Burma*, London, 1968.

Cady, J. F., *History of Modern Burma*, New York, 1958.

Collis, Maurice, *Siamese White*, London, 1936.

—— *Last and First in Burma*, London, 1956.

Crosthwaite, C. H. T., *The Pacification of Burma*, London, 1912.

Donnison, F. S. V., *Public Administration in Burma*, London, 1953.

—— *British Military Administration in the Far East, 1943–46*, London, 1956.

Fielding, H., *The Soul of a People*, London, 1898.

Fielding Hall, H., *A People at School*, London, 1906.

Furnivall, J. S., *An Introduction to the Political Economy of Burma*, Rangoon, 1931.

—— *Colonial Policy and Practice*, Cambridge, 1948.

Geary, Grattan, *Burma after the Conquest*, London, 1888.

Gouger, H., *Personal Narrative of Two Years' Imprisonment in Burmah*, London, 1860.

Hall, D. G. E., *Burma*, London, 1950.

Harvey, G. E., *History of Burma*, London, 1925.

—— *British Rule in Burma 1824–1942*, London, 1946.

Htin Aung, Maung, *A History of Burma*, New York, 1967.

Khaing, Mi Mi, *Burmese Family*, London, 1946.

Lewis, Norman, *Golden Earth*, London, 1952.

Maung, Maung, *Aung San of Burma*, The Hague, 1962.

Morrison, Ian, *Grandfather Longlegs, The Life and Gallant Death of Major H.P. Seagrim, G.C., D.S.O., M.B.E.*, London, 1947.
Mya Sein, *The Administration of Burma*, Rangoon, 1938.
Nu, Thakin, *Burma under the Japanese*, London and New York, 1954.
Phayre, A. P., *History of Burma*, London, 1883.
Saimöng Mangrai, Sao, *The Shan States and the British Annexation*, New York, 1965.
Shein, Maung, *Burma's Transport and Foreign Trade*, Rangoon, 1964.
Shway Yoe (Sir J. G. Scott), *The Burman, His Life and Notions*, London, 1910.
Talbot Kelly, R., *Burma*, London, 1912.
Thirkell White, H., *A Civil Servant in Burma*, London, 1913.
Tinker, Hugh, *The Foundations of Local Self-Government in India, Pakistan, and Burma*, London, 1954.
—— *The Union of Burma*, London and New York, 1961.
Trager, Frank N., *Burma – From Kingdom to Republic*, New York and London, 1966.
Tun Wai, *Burma's Currency and Credit*, Calcutta, 1953.
Woodman, Dorothy, *The Making of Burma*, London, 1962.

Cambridge History of India, Cambridge, 1932, volumes V and VI.
Report of Indian Statutory Commission, 1930, volume XI.
Burma's Fight for Freedom
Is Trust Vindicated? — Published by
Annual Reports to the People by the Union of Burma Revolutionary Council on the Revolutionary Government's Budget Estimates. — the Burmese Government

Index

255

Sayedawgyis, 66
scheduled areas, 115, 135; *see also*
frontier areas; hill areas
Searle, H. F., 97
Second Burmese War, 41, 60, 75, 76
Second World War, 121
secondary education, 207
secretariat, 78, 79, 81
Secretary of State for India, 83, 105, 116
Security and Administration
Committees (S.A.C.s), 173, 178, 179, 180, 181
Sein Win, Brigadier, 163
self-government, 115
senate, 115
separation, 106, 113, 114
Seventh Day Adventist Hospital, 201
Shan chiefs, 82, 159; *see also* Shan *Sawbwas*
Shan Hills, 21
Shan language, 35
Shan plateau, 23
Shan *Sawbwas*, 164–5; *see also* Shan chiefs
Shan State, 146
Shan States, 24, 25, 50, 54, 55, 81, 82, 154
Shans, 33, 34, 51, 52, 73, 110, 136, 142, 161, 162, 165, 167, 177, 235, 247
Shinsawbu, Queen, 52
shipyard, in Syriam, 58
shoe question, 104
Shwe pyi daw, 1
Shwe Thaik, Sao, 136, 163
Shwebo, 30, 33, 49
Shwenyaung, 26
Siam, 53, 54, 56; *see also* Thailand
silver-lead mines, 168
Simla, 124
Singapore, 124, 241
single-party state, 177
Sinyètha Party, 117, 122, 125
Sittang river, 21, 22, 25
Sittang valley, 124
Sixth Great Buddhist Council, 218, 229
Slim, General Sir William, 123
social bar, 95
social contact, 93
Social and Economic Advisory Council, 152
Social Planning Commission, 152
social services, 204
socialism, 140, 141, 245
Socialist democracy, 171, 172, 173
Socialist Economy Planning Committee, 174
Socialist Party, 140, 156
socialists, 144, 156, 160
Sooratee Burra Bazaar, 154

South-East Asia Co-Prosperity Sphere, 125
squatters, in Rangoon, 159
standard of living, 203
State Agricultural Marketing Board, 155, 184, 198
State Jute Factory, 203
state monopoly, 184
State Timber Board, 152
Statute of Westminster, 137
statutory commission, 110
sterling area, Burma leaves, 236
Stewart, J. A., 97
Stilwell, General Joseph W., 123
strikes, 107, 118, 144, 211; of the police, 133; of other government employees, 133
struggle for power, 117, 155
student politics, 210
students, 107, 118, 211
Students' Union, 118
Students' Union building, 211
subdivisional officers, 80
subdivisions, 80
subordinate civil service, 81
subsistence economy, 246
Suez Canal, 61, 86, 88
Supayalat, Queen, 65
superstition, 43, 46, 120
Supreme Allied Commander, 132
Swithinbank, B. W., 97
Symes, Capt. Michael, 58
Syriam, 55, 57, 58
System of Correlation of Man and his Environment, The, 176

Tabinshweti, 53
Tai, 49
Tai–Chinese peoples, 34
Taikkyi, 144
taiks, 67
Taikthugyi, 67
Tan Yu Saing, Col., 163
Tarabya, 51
Tartars, 51, 52
Taungdwingyi, 49
Taunggyi, 26, 145, 150, 240, 242; college at, 210
Taungup Pass, 24
tax on income, 85
Tayayon, 66
Teachers' Training College, 209
teak, 30
Tenasserim, 21, 59, 65, 75, 167
Tet-pongyi Thein Pe, 126
Thailand, 20, 241; *see also* Siam
Thakin group, 140
Thakin or 'Master' Party, 118, 122, 125, 166, 211; *see also Do-Bama* Party
Thakins, 127, 140, 197; *see also* under name, e.g. Aung San

*Printed in Great Britain by
Western Printing Services Ltd, Bristol*

72
74
76
79
88